BROADCAST WRITING

BROADCAST WRITING

DANIEL E. GARVEY

California State University, Long Beach

WILLIAM L. RIVERS

Stanford University

Longman

New York & London

BROADCAST WRITING

Longman Inc., 19 West 44th Street, New York, N.Y. 10036
Associated companies, branches, and representatives
throughout the world.

Copyright © 1982 by Longman Inc.

Developmental Editor: Gordon T. R. Anderson
Editorial and Design Supervisor: Frances Althaus
Interior Design: Pencils Portfolio, Inc.
Manufacturing and Production Supervisor: Anne Musso

Excerpts from the following have been reprinted with permission
as noted.

Dying, by Michele Gallery — "Lou Grant." © 1978 Lorimar
Productions. Used with permission.
Prisoner, by Seth Freeman — "Lou Grant." © 1978 Lorimar
Productions. Used with permission.
My Kingdom for a Horse — "Sanford and Son." © 1974 Tandem
Productions. Used with permission.
Operation Mercy, by Michael Morris — "The New Temperatures
Rising Show." © 1973 Columbia Pictures Television. Used with
permission.
The $5.20 an Hour Dream, by Robert Thompson. © 1979
Thompson/Sagal Productions, Finnegan Associates.
Helen's Job, by Paul Wayne and George Burdett — "Three's
Company." © 1977 N.R.W., T.T.C. Productions.
Mary Jane's Boyfriend, by Fred S. Fox and Seaman Jacobs —
"Here's Lucy." © 1973 Lucille Ball Productions, Inc.

Library of Congress Cataloging in Publication Data
Garvey, Daniel E.
    Broadcast writing.
    Bibliography: p.
    Includes index.
    1. Broadcasting—Authorship.   I. Rivers,
William L.   II. Title.
PN1990.9.A88G3   808'.066791021   81-13745
ISBN 0-582-28173-3   AACR2

Manufactured in the United States of America

9 8 7 6 5 4 3 2

Preface vii
1. Broadcast Writing 1
2. Script Formats 21
3. Television Drama 53
4. Television Comedy 88
5. Television Commercials and Public
   Service Announcements 110
6. Radio Drama and Comedy 147
7. Radio Commercials and Public Service
   Announcements 163
8. Radio News Writing 179
9. Television News Writing 206
10. Semiscripted Programs: Music, Talk, and
    Interview Shows 217
11. Special-Interest Programming 228
12. The Job 243
    Glossary of Special Terms 256
    Bibliography 275
    Index 277

PREFACE

This book is designed to teach the basic skills of broadcast writing. It covers the major kinds of writing found in American broadcasting today. A companion volume, *The Broadcast Writing Workbook,* is designed to be used with this book, but we have prepared the volumes so that each can be used separately.

Writing is a skill that grows with practice and with helpful criticism from others. You can learn the rules for broadcast writing from this book, but you can learn to be a writer only by writing and having those who know the field read and criticize your work.

Chapters 1 and 2 are particularly important because they establish the basic rules by which all your copy will be written. Read them carefully, and refer to them frequently. The other chapters deal with the more specific problems of individual kinds of writing such as radio drama or television commercials.

Don't expect to find everything in this book—or to learn all there is to know about broadcast writing in one semester. This book is meant only to provide a beginning for you. Once you have mastered its basics you will be ready to move on to more demanding and more specialized broadcast writing. If you have already decided what kind of broadcast writing you want to do, don't ignore the other kinds of broadcast writing described in this book. You might be surprised at your skills in areas other than the one you originally chose. More important, every new writing skill you acquire makes you a better all-around writer.

Daniel E. Garvey
William L. Rivers

THE WORLD OF BROADCASTING

In the New York studio of a television network, the director calls, "Stand by." The hubbub in the studio and the control room halts. The anchorwoman of the network newscast adjusts her microphone, smooths the lapel of her jacket, and looks at the camera. "Ready to come up from black on 'One,' " says the director. "Ready, audio. Ready to key first slide." The red hand on the clock touches 12. The director punches the start button of his stopwatch. "Bring up the theme. Fade in on One. Key Slide One. Cue announcer. Take out Slide One. Key Slide Two. Dump the music. Take out the slide. Cue talent."

"Good evening," says the anchorwoman. "In the news tonight . . . " As she calmly and authoritatively tells 60 million viewers the news of the day, the words she is speaking—the script—glide silently by on the one-way mirror of the Teleprompter in front of the camera lens. To the millions of viewers it appears she is speaking to them, but in reality she is reading a script prepared for her by a staff of well-trained writers.

In the surprisingly cramped space of a Hollywood sound stage, a team of actors gets ready to videotape a segment of a television comedy series. The several hundred people who waited patiently in line outside for a chance to see the show are now in their bleacherlike seats. They have been introduced to the cast and principal members of the production staff and been "warmed up" with a few jokes by a staff member. Now the cameras are in place. The lights are set. Final checks are made on the microphones. From a control room somewhere, hidden from the sound stage, the director calls for silence and begins a countdown. A production assistant steps forward, holding a slate before a camera, and reads off the identifying material for the scene to be shot. As the scene about to be shot is being "slated," an actor takes a final glance at the script and hands it to another production assistant. Without the script, none of them would be there.

In a radio studio in Elgin, Illinois, a recording ends, and the disc jockey twists the knobs on the control board. Glancing at the combination of typed pages and scribbled notes that he uses as a script, the DJ tosses out a few comments he has prepared about the record, then turns to the carefully scripted copy for a commercial and begins to read the words that pay for the show.

In Washington, D. C., at a studio for National Public Radio, a reporter sits in a studio with a U.S. senator. The engineer asks for a microphone check for the reporter and her guest. "We'll start in 'ten,' " says the engineer over the intercom. For a few seconds, there is silence, almost as if time were standing still. The red "On the Air" light flashes on, and the engineer's finger points through the glass window of the control booth to the reporter. She begins to read the scripted introduction she has prepared for the senator's interview.

In the studios of a university-operated radio station in Albuquerque, New Mexico, a group of drama students stands around the microphones in a studio, scripts in hand, turning the words on the pages into a radio drama.

The world of broadcasting is a vast one, with enormous diversity. There are networks, network affiliates, and independent stations. Television has UHF and VHF stations. Radio has AM and FM stations. Within the world of radio and television, there are big stations and little ones, commercial stations and noncommercial ones. Some stations broadcast only news, some produce only instructional material for schools, some provide programming for ethnic minorities, some specialize in business reports. Cable systems carry not only the radio and television programming of local stations but can also bring in distant stations and produce their own programming. Pay television systems bring you more programs, paid for either on a monthly basis or on a per-program basis. In the future, satellites will beam shows directly into your home, adding more programming. For every program, whatever its source, there will be some sort of script.

Currently there are about 10,000 radio and television stations and around 4,300 cable systems in the United States. Most of the material that goes out over those many sources of programming begins as a script. The people who prepare those scripts are as varied as the programs for which they prepare them. There are staff writers for shows, there are newswriters, there are freelance writers, and there are advertising copywriters. They are all part of the sometimes bewildering world of broadcasting. A writer for a 10-watt college station may feel satisfied if her or his words are heard by a hundred listeners. The writer for a network program may reach an audience of 60,000,000 or more people with a single program—more than the number of people who have seen Shakespeare's plays on the stage since he wrote them. A writer may write the words spoken by some of the most famous people of our age—or may turn out the copy for a local cooking show or a commercial for headache pills.

Whatever form of writing you choose, you won't be bored. It's an exciting, demanding, and sometimes exasperating field. Whatever else it may be, it is never dull. Wherever you work, there is always that satisfying moment when the words come over the speaker and you say to yourself: "Those are my words—on the air!"

KINDS OF BROADCAST WRITING

There are many different kinds of writing. You probably practice two or three of them every day. You use one style of writing to make notes for yourself, another to write term papers, and still another to write letters. A journalist learns a different style of writing than does a fiction writer. The person who writes magazine articles must write differently from the one who writes for a wire service. Yet all these people are *writers,* and they all share a certain common core of skills. As you learn to write broadcast copy, you will have to learn different skills from those you may have learned for other kinds of writing. As you learn more about broadcast writing, you will find that you must write differently for radio than for television, for commercials than for news. But a certain basic writing skill is common to all these forms.

Part of our efforts in this book are directed to improving your basic writing skills—the skills that every writer needs to practice the craft of writing. The rest, of course, is devoted to those specific skills that are unique to broadcast writing. We'll begin by spelling out for you a list of rules for broadcast writing. Most of them are little different from the rules for all other forms of writing, and you may be surprised to find that some rules you might have thought could be skipped for broadcast writing are just as much needed as they would be for print.

RULES FOR BROADCAST WRITING

Let's start by immediately getting one idea out of the way. *Yes,* you must spell correctly. If your copy is full of errors, it will be difficult for performers to read. It may cause them to make foolish mistakes. Even more important, people who read your copy will probably put it down after the first couple of errors and write you off as someone who lacks professional polish. You can lose a job or have a script rejected simply because your spelling marks you as an incompetent.

Writing for the Eye

Every broadcast writer is writing for both the eye and the ear. You may think that the radio writer only has to be concerned with the way copy sounds—but that is wrong. Before your copy gets on the air, someone has to *read* it. Therefore, everything you write must be not only easy to *say* but also easy to read with the *eyes*. Visually scan whatever you write for broadcasting. Is there anything that makes you stop? Is there anything you might read incorrectly? If so, go back and change it. Use every trick you can think of to make it easier for your reader. For example, many words are easier to read if you separate the stem word from a prefix by inserting a hyphen. "Co-operate" is easier to read than "cooperate." "Re-confirm" is easier to read than "reconfirm."

Be careful about using the same or similar phrases several times in the same passage. Repetition is not necessarily poor writing in broadcasting. Repetition has many uses in broadcast writing. But in using repetition, pay attention to the way your copy *looks* on the page. Are you creating a visual trap for your performers? Could the reader accidentally skip over material and begin reading the second appearance of the phrase instead of the first? This danger is usually greatest if you begin two lines of copy on a page with the same words. This, for example, can cause trouble for a performer—particularly a television performer who has to operate off a teleprompter:

```
What are you holding back, Sylvia?  What is it?

There is a certain . . . I don't know what . . .

There is a certain . . . . I guess it's smugness.

There is a certain way you look when we talk.

There is a certain nastiness in your voice tonight.
```

Be sure to call tricky material like this to the attention of performers. You or the performers might use underlining for some phrases and put wavy lines under others to distinguish them. The best course, however, is to avoid such problems when you write the script. Remember to write for the *eyes* first.

Writing for the Speaker

Next, make copy readable for the lips. Not every well-turned phrase can be spoken with ease. Don't prepare a commercial that urges people to buy a "quartz crystal wristwatch." Not until you've tried to say "quartz crystal wristwatch" aloud. Some lines may be pronounceable but may still not be good writing for the air because the microphone tends to distort certain sounds.

Microphones can be oversensitive to the sounds of *s, p,* and *b.* Obviously you cannot write English without using these sounds, but you should be careful not to overuse them. Poe's famous line "And the silken, sad, uncertain rustling of each purple curtain" is good poetry, but it's bad broadcast writing. In general, avoid alliteration.

Writing for the Listener

Finally, of course, your writing must be understood by the listener and the viewer. Here you must read as carefully with the ear as with the eye. For example, a radio news program recently mentioned a rally to be held to protest "a tax on homosexuals"—at least, that was what it *seemed* to say. Only after some time did it become clear that what the newscaster had said was "attacks on homosexuals." As far as the eye is concerned, there is no reason to confuse "a tax" with "attacks." They don't look at all alike. But to the ear, the two sound identical. The newscaster could have distinguished between the two phrases by speaking carefully, but the writer should have foreseen the problem in the first place. It is also best to avoid deliberate word play such as puns, although there is some role for this in writing comedy.

Other word combinations can cause confusion because of the natural tendency to let words run together in spoken English. Such combinations may cause problems if a word ending in a consonant is followed by one beginning with a vowel. In French and other Romance languages, liaison—the joining together of two words—is an essential characteristic of the language. In English we tend to pretend it does not exist. "If the performer had read that line *carefully,*" the writer insists, "it would have made perfectly good sense." But that is wishful thinking. If you write, "his solution was costly and effective," you should realize that *some* of the audience will think you said "costly and defective."

Clarity

The first requirement of almost all forms of writing is clarity. The means by which clarity is achieved may be different in different forms of writing. For example, in writing for print, it is not good style to repeat the same words over and over, but in writing for the ear, a certain amount of repetition is helpful. It guarantees that we hear the important words. It is a general rule in commercials that you try to mention the product name at least three times. In writing dialog, your characters will sound stilted and odd if they come up with a fresh new term in every speech because everyday speech abounds in repetitions.

Broadcast writing must also be *economical.* People can and do sit about for hours, chatting aimlessly, but a broadcast writer must get the message across quickly because every second has a price tag on it.

Writers in other media sometimes have a vested interest in being wordy. Some magazines still pay by the word. Nineteenth-century writers like Dickens published stories in serial form, padding and drawing out stories from issue to issue of the magazines that carried them. There are broadcast forms—the soap opera, for instance—in which the writers have a similar task of dragging the plot on from day to day, but even the soap opera must fit into its time slot. The cardinal rule for broadcast writing is to make every word count.

When you write broadcast copy, every word must have a purpose. That does not mean that you cannot repeat words or use a bit of dialog occasionally that does not advance the plot—but you have to do these things deliberately. You should do them because you know there is time for them and because they add to your story. You do not just throw them in because you like the sound of them. Remember: Everything that is in your script should be there for a purpose.

Simplicity

In broadcasting (and in most other kinds of writing) the best writing is *simple* writing. How do you keep your copy simple? Here are some things to look out for.

Long Sentences. Ideally, a sentence should contain only one idea. When you begin to add to that single idea, your listener has to stop listening to sort out the thoughts. Once you've lost the listener, you may never get her or him back.

One cause of excessively long sentences is careless use of subordinate clauses. William Faulkner probably holds the Olympic Gold Medal for use of subordinate clauses in American writing. That was, of course, his style, for which he was justly famous. But imagine a radio or television audience trying to follow this sentence from *Light in August:* "He made the journey in his truck, carrying with him, since the truck (it had a housedin body with a door at the rear) was new and he did not intend to drive it faster than fifteen miles an hour, camping equipment to save hotels." You must wait 30 words to find out *what* the man was carrying with him.

Faulkner, of course, won a Nobel Prize, and no one would argue that he was not a great writer. But Faulkner was striving for a specific *style* to carry his message—and he made few concessions to his readers in achieving that style. Faulkner is *not* easy to read. Much of his writing is impossible to follow by ear.[1] What makes it difficult to follow is Faulkner's refusal to use simple sentences. He loads every sentence with subordinate clauses.

Long Words. Not every long word is a poor choice, but if you find many sprinkled through your copy, it is time to start checking. Did you say someone was "recalcitrant" when you could have said he was balking at doing something he was supposed to do? Did you call something "antediluvian" when you could have said it was old-fashioned? Words are fun, of course. It is a rare writer who does not love words. But the broadcast writer is writing for an extremely varied audience. Its members are young and old, bright and

---

[1]Faulkner's movie scripts and the dialog in his books make it clear Faulkner could write beautifully for the ear when that was his purpose.

stupid, educated and illiterate. True, with radio, you can get a somewhat more homogeneous audience, as you can with public television, but you still have to assume a great variety in the vocabularies of those you write for. (For example, you'd be well advised to avoid a word like "homogeneous.")

Simple does not have to mean childish. Very great ideas can be expressed with simple words. Look at some of the masterful prose of Winston Churchill. It would be hard to find plainer English than "I have nothing to offer but blood, toil, tears and sweat."

One of the greatest masters of simple writing in this century was a broadcaster, Edward R. Murrow. Here is an excerpt from his description of the Buchenwald concentration camp as he saw it just after it was liberated:

> As I walked down to the end of the barracks, there was applause from the men too weak to get out of bed. It sounded like the hand-clapping of babies. As we walked out into the courtyard, a man fell dead. Two others—they must have been over sixty—were crawling towards the latrine. I saw it, but will not describe it.[2]

Read that over any time you think that simple, unadorned writing cannot be powerful and moving.

Difficult Words. Not all short words are easy, nor are all long words hard. "Interrelationship" is a long word, but not very hard to figure out. On the other hand, "yclept" is a short word that few people know the meaning of (despite its too-frequent appearance in *Time*). Long words are a tip-off that you are probably not writing good broadcast copy, but be sure you check your short words as well.

Jargon, Clichés, and Buzz Words. All these categories are closely related. Perhaps the major distinction is that you usually don't want to hear clichés or buzz words *again,* while you don't even want to finish listening to jargon the first time.

Buzz words are fad words and phrases. They are popular for a while, then drop out of sight. No one is sorry to see them go. While they are popular, they are so overused that everyone gets sick of hearing them. Buzz words that have dropped out of use, to no one's sorrow, are once-popular phrases like "military posture" or "keeping a low profile." Back in the 1960s the Cosmos Club of Washington, D.C., published a "Buzz Word Projector," prepared by Phillip Broughton. It contained three numbered lists of certified buzz words. It was Broughton's contention that, by picking from the three lists words corresponding to any three-digit number, you could come up with a guaranteed meaningless but important-sounding phrase made of buzz words to meet any need.

0. integrated	0. management	0. options
1. total	1. organizational	1. flexibility
2. systematized	2. monitored	2. capability
3. parallel	3. reciprocal	3. mobility

[2]Rebroadcast on the "CBS 50th Birthday Special," November 18, 1977.

4. functional
5. responsive
6. optional
7. synchronized
8. compatible
9. balanced

4. digital
5. logistical
6. transitional
7. incremental
8. third-generation
9. policy

4. programming
5. concept
6. time-phase
7. projection
8. hardware
9. contingency

Suppose this has been a particularly bad term in school for your grades. Pick a three-digit number. Suppose you picked 266. You could explain that you are going through a "systematized transitional time-phase," but next term (912) you expect to develop "balanced organizational capability."

As you can see, buzz words are more than just overused expressions; they are ways of saying *nothing* and making it sound important. In 1977 the *New Yorker* magazine published a tongue-in-cheek exercise in buzz words that included the following:

> We have failed to identify enormous problems, apparently intractable problems, chronic problems, and major problems. We denied that there are problems. We were unable to cope with problems that should have been anticipated. We were reluctant to adopt known solutions. . . .
>
> But we were not completely at fault. We had to deal with snags, slumps, impasses, summary uprootings, slights, dilution. There were erosions, reversals, slouchings toward and fallings behind, inescapable aftermaths.
>
> There were various outbreaks.[3]

The distinction between the buzz word and the cliché is often no more than age. Buzz words come and go. The cliché we have with us always.

The durability of clichés is surprising. Look at the first *recorded* use of these phrases, and keep in mind that they must have been in use *before* they were written down:

> "The proof of the pudding is in the eating." Joseph Addison, 1714.
> "Don't look a gift horse in the mouth." St. Jerome, 400.
> "One foot in the grave." Plutarch, 95.
> "One man's food is another man's poison." Lucretius, 45 B.C.
> "A chip off the old block." Theocritus, 270 B.C.

If clichés were gold, they would have to store sportswriters in Fort Knox. Writer Frank Sullivan created the character of Mr. Arbuthnot, the cliché expert, for a series of articles in the *New Yorker.* Here is a short excerpt from Mr. Arbuthnot's explanation of baseball:

> **Q:** Mr. Arbuthnot, how do you, as a cliché expert, refer to first base?
> **A:** First base is the initial sack.
> **Q:** And second base?
> **A:** The keystone sack.
> **Q:** What's third base called?

[3]"Notes and Comment," *New Yorker,* October 31, 1977, p. 31.

A: The hot corner. The first inning is the initial frame, and an inning without runs is a scoreless stanza.

Q: What is one run known as?

A: A lone run, but four runs are known as a quartet of tallies.

Q: What is a baseball?

A: The pill, the horsehide, the old apple, or the sphere.[4]

What's wrong with those phrases? some would ask. They still do the job. But they have been used, and used, and used. Whatever vitality they might have had is gone. You don't think they're that old and tired? Look when Sullivan first singled those terms out as clichés—in 1949—before most of the people reading this book were born.

Put simply, using clichés is verbal junk-shopping. Of course, there will be times when it is appropriate for a character to use clichés in dialog. Some people *do* speak in clichés. But think for a moment what it means when you let clichés slip into dialog unintentionally. We've just pointed out that using clichés says something about a character—just as the use of poor grammar or bad pronunciation says something about a character. You cannot *afford* to let most characters prattle on in clichés because that will create the wrong image of those characters with the audience. Using clichés in dialog helps define a character just as much as giving the character a stammer or a French accent. It is a tool for the dialog writer, but one that is not appropriate for most characters. Like any tool, it works best when used for the right job.

How can you avoid using a cliché? To make use of one ourselves—the woods are full of them. No one can write or think without using a few clichés. And how do you identify one? "It's two o'clock" has certainly been said millions of times by millions of people over hundreds of years. Why isn't it a cliché? Because it does not call attention to itself. It is a group of words that goes about its job of conveying meaning efficiently and unobtrusively. Clichés give you the feeling of seeing a television rerun for the fiftieth time. "Oh, no. Not *that* again!" Like the television program, it was written to be used once or twice, then forgotten. Like fruit, most phrases are good only when they are fresh.

Most clichés are similes or metaphors describing something. Through overuse, they have lost their effectiveness as meaningful descriptions. "Heavy as lead" is a simile that no longer says much to us; it's been overused. What do you think of when you hear a character in a broadcast script use a metaphor like this: "That Harry! He's a real pistol!" "Cornball" might be one thought that comes to mind. Now if you intended the character to *be* a cornball, fine. Otherwise, get rid of that cliché.

The best time to get rid of clichés is while you are rewriting your copy. Clichés are certain to creep into your writing on the first draft. Don't waste time trying to come up with a substitute for each one while you are writing. Finish the material, then go back and look for better terms than the clichés you find.

Here are a few you should watch out for:

[4]Frank Sullivan, "The Cliché Expert Testifies on Baseball," *New Yorker,* August 27, 1949, p. 22.

aching void	like a bolt from the blue
babe in the woods	nipped in the bud
crystal clear	reigns supreme
food for thought	shattering effect
imagination run riot	wrapped in mystery

Jargon might be described as a language of clichés and buzz words spoken by a specific group. Any group of people who communicate regularly about a specific topic will begin to develop a specialized vocabulary. There are at least three reasons for this. One is the need for special words. Most of us can survive without knowing for certain what that funny gizmo on the engine is, but a mechanic had better know whether it's a distributor or a carburetor.

A second reason is simplicity. If I am only going to say it once in my life, I could say, "I need one of those things that go over the lens of my camera so I can use indoor-type color film when I shoot out-of-doors and it won't look all blue and washed out." If I do much photography, I'd better learn to say, "I need an 85B filter, please."

The third reason is the sense of "belonging" that goes with speaking a language "outsiders" do not understand. Even little children love codes and secret languages. Nevertheless, it is this last aspect of jargon that makes it particularly exasperating to outsiders.

There is obviously a fourth reason in some cases. Like buzz words, jargon is a wonderful way of saying nothing and having it sound important. "Optimum conformity to contractual agreements may be operationally nullified and specified times of making materials available will be re-scheduled as a result of grade one difficulties with word-processing equipment" is one way I can tell the producer my script is late because my typewriter broke. By the time his legal department figures it out, I may have the script finished.

Whatever the *reasons* for jargon, the effect is always the same. The audience doesn't understand it. Or the audience does understand it, and has tuned out.

Public organizations are always fountains of jargon, and the writer must be cautious not to drown in one. Policemen, in accordance with regulations, are not allowed to say somebody was hit over the head, knocked out, and left black and blue. No. "The victim suffered multiple blows on or about the head from a blunt instrument wielded by a person or persons unknown which rendered said victim unconscious and caused multiple bruises and contusions on the head, neck, shoulders and adjacent parts of the victim's body."

You *think* you would never use such words in your writing, but they are as contagious as a cold. News programs now regularly report that firemen are fighting "a greater alarm fire." Do you know what a "greater alarm fire" is? Does the audience? And we no longer say the "whole building was on fire"; we now report that "the building was fully involved in flames when the firemen arrived." *Involved in flames*? It sounds as if the next step will be "the building was fully 'into' flames before the firemen arrived."

But I'm not going to be a newswriter, you say. Shouldn't I make use of some of these things to make my dialog sound natural? *Only* if you are certain your audience understands them. Dialog should sound natural, but that does not mean that it *is* natural. Later we'll discuss dialog in greater detail. Here we'll simply point out that dialog must be economical and understandable. You will, of course, use some intentional errors of grammar and pronunciation to portray certain characters. But don't overdo it. Some dialog can be confusing not only to the listener but also to the performer. Take this example from one of Finley Peter Dunne's turn-of-the-century stories about Mr. Dooley:

> "You know Dorsey, iv coorse, th' cross-eyed May-o man that come to this country about wan day in advance iv a warrant f'r sheep-stealin'? Ye know what he done to me, tellin' people I was caught in me cellar poorin' wather into a bar'l"[5]

Can you imagine an actor trying to read 30 pages written like that?

Too Many Adjectives. Mark Twain wrote: "As to the adjective, when in doubt, strike it out." He would have made a good broadcast writer. Adjectives, like clichés, get thrown into our writing from force of habit. If you keep adjectives at a minimum, the ones you do use will carry the force they deserve to have. Again, some writers "get away with it" because it is part of their style. Indeed, Thomas Wolfe got away with it beautifully:

> The threat, they knew, was preposterous, but the white judicial face, the thoughtful pursing of the lips, and the right hand, which she held loosely clenched, like a man's, with the forefinger extended, emphasizing her proclamation with a calm, but somehow powerful gesture, froze them with a terror no amount of fierce excoriation could have produced.[6]

This writing is simply too rich for radio, and infinitely too rich for television, in which the words must compete with the pictures. It takes Wolfe 22 words here to get from subject to verb—too long for a listener to keep in mind what the subject was. Each adjective tends to conjure up a new image in the mind. The reader can take time to savor them in a book, but the words come on relentlessly in broadcasting, and the listener cannot cope with all these images at once. Instead of adding to enjoyment, they detract both from enjoyment and comprehension.

Compare Wolfe's excerpt with the simplicity of this description broadcast by Eric Sevareid. During World War II, Sevareid, American Diplomat John Davies, and the other passengers of a military plane were forced to bail out over the jungles of Burma. Certainly there was plenty of opportunity for adjectives in describing an event like that, but note how few were used:

> There was no organization at all, and everything was confusion. There was a jam at the doorway. Everyone hesitated. Then John Davies with a curious grin on his

---

[5]Finley Peter Dunne, "On New Year's Resolutions," *Mr. Dooley in Peace and in War* (Boston: Small, Maynard & Company, 1899), p. 96.
[6]Thomas Wolfe, *Look Homeward Angel* (New York: Modern Library, 1929), p. 23.

face hopped out and was whisked away. I said to myself, "Good-bye John." I never expected to see him again. And he was a man I liked. John had broken the ice. A few more went over. Then I jumped, like the others for the first time in my life.[7]

In dialog, there is even less room for adjectives. Take, for example, this short excerpt from an episode in the television series "Sanford and Son:"

```
                         FRED

He's mine, Grady.  You're looking at one million

dollars worth of horse there.



                         GRADY

Yeah???  Where is it???  Behind this one?



                         FRED

Not BEHIND this one.  This one, Grady.



                         GRADY

This horse don't look like he's worth anything.



                         FRED

That's 'cause you don't know anything about

horses.  That horse isn't just a junkwagon horse

. . . he's a race horse.



                         GRADY

That's a race horse?
```

[7]Quoted in Paul W. White, *News on the Air* (New York: Harcourt, Brace, 1947), p. 271.

                        FRED

That's right.

                        GRADY

Well, bring over the turtle he's racin' and I'll

bet two dollars on the turtle.[8]

When broadcast writers do lay on a heavy dose of adjectives, it is usually to poke fun at a character or a situation. Here is how radio comedians Bob and Ray parodied the style of old-time soap operas:

ANNCR: Can it be that Edna's newfound sense of
            hearing will at last become the turning point
            in her struggle against misfortune? · · ·

ANNCR: Will her realization that the cat has been
            outside all day with its earmuffs off while
            she's been inside with hers on only lead to
            further heartbreak? Join us for the next
            exciting episode, when Edna finds herself
            face to face with a frostbitten kitten in
            "The Gathering Dusk."[9]

Note that even in this parody, adjectives are used judiciously. There are enough of them to make a point, but no more. In the essay written in buzz words on page 8 note that it is primarily adjectives that turn perfectly good nouns into buzz words. Look at the adjectives paired with "problems": "enormous," "intractable," "chronic," "major." In each case, the adjective weakens rather than strengthens the noun.

Of course, the right adjective in the right place is good writing for broadcasting or any other medium. In radio writing in particular, the adjective can be used to give more detail to the mental picture of the event. Take, for example, this line from the BBC's "Goon Show": "By the way, Moriarity—did you notice the brass name-plate on our host's door?"

The addition of the adjective "brass" gives us a better picture than if he simply said "name-plate." The single adjective "brass" is about as far as one can usually go in dialog. In radio narrative you might write "polished brass nameplate." On the other hand, there is no purpose in describing the nameplate in television dialog because you can show it. Actually, you can apply the same rule for the use of adjectives in both radio and television writing: Use

---

[8]"My Kingdom for a Horse," September 6, 1974; author not specified.
[9]Whitney Balliett, "Their Own Gravity," *New Yorker,* September 24, 1973, p. 62.

them to describe things the audience cannot see but that you want it to know about.

One final note before leaving the topic of adjectives. Be sure you place them correctly. Sometimes a misplaced adjective can cause ambiguity. Suppose you write in a television drama, "Did a tall man and woman run by?" Is your meaning that *both* the man and woman were tall? If not, you need to rephrase the question: "Did a tall man and a blonde woman run by?" Or: "Did a woman and a tall man run by?"

Often writers simply are careless in placement of adjectives. This phrase from a news story *almost* sounds right. "Later, he would recall the advice of a close professor and friend . . . ." What *should* it read?

Passive Verbs. In all forms of writing, overuse of the passive voice makes for dull, overlong sentences. In broadcasting, there simply isn't time for it. The active voice is always quicker than the passive voice.

Wonderful, you say. I'll avoid the passive voice. By the way, what is it?

Few students today have any training in formal grammar, which makes it difficult to discuss some writing problems. Let's review a few basics. Verbs are words that show action. *Run, sing, dribble* and *fall* are all verbs. The subject of a verb is the part of the sentence the verb says something about. If the subject *acts,* then the verb is an active verb. If the subject does not act and the action of the verb is done *to* the subject, then the verb is passive. For example:

> *Active:* John *hit* the ball.
> *Passive:* The ball *was hit* by John.
> *Active:* I *laugh* at the world.
> *Passive:* The world is laughed at by me.
> *Active:* It *has rained* on the road.
> *Passive:* The road *has been rained* upon.

Note that the passive voice is almost always longer and less interesting to listen to. There will be times, of course, when you will need to use passives. It makes far more plausible dialog for someone to yell, "I've been robbed," which is passive, than to yell, "Someone has robbed me," which is active. But in general, you'll find your scripts move faster and sound better if you make maximum use of the active voice.

Misused Adverbs. Broadcaster Edwin Newman has devoted much of the past ten years to fighting the misuse of English in the mass media—particularly in broadcasting. High on his list of sins is the misuse of the adverb *hopefully.* As Newman points out, most people do not seem to know what the word means. The correct meaning is to do something in a way that is full of hope. "They waited hopefully for the men to come home." Instead, people use *hopefully* as if it meant "I hope that," as in, "Hopefully the men will be home by dawn." The word has become a buzz word, and probably should be avoided for that reason alone.

The misuse of most other adverbs is of a different nature. The problem is usually placement. Misplacement of adverbs leads to ambiguity or misunderstanding. Compare these two lines of dialog: "He also is a liar!" "He is also a liar!" There is no doubt about the meaning of the second one. It means that, among other things, the man is a liar. But the first version is less clear. It may mean the same thing as the second version, or it may mean, "He too is a liar!" Note, oddly enough, that the situation is exactly reversed if you use "too." There is no ambiguity about "He too is a liar!" but "He is a liar too!" is ambiguous.

Of course, you say, the meaning will be clear in context, and if it is not, I can solve the problem simply by underlining the right words, making it, *"He* is a liar too!" or "He is a *liar* too!" True, but the point is that *first* you must be aware of the problem.

Using the Wrong Word. In French there is the expression *le mot juste*—freely translated, "exactly the right word." That is what every good writer is constantly striving for. There are two kinds of sins a writer may commit here. The first is merely a venial sin—one that can be forgiven—not choosing the *best* word. You should always strive to find a better word than the first one you put on the page. You type in your script, "All that night, I read the report." Later you go back and change it to "I pored over the report." You keep looking for a word that says *exactly* what you mean.

The other sin is a mortal sin—one that condemns you forever. It is using the *wrong* word. Sometimes it is carelessness, sometimes it is misunderstanding. It works out to the same thing. The word does not say what you meant it to say. Here are a few from student scripts and assignments: "His words were mushed together." "It distracted from the story's significance." "The film seemed fairly non-active." "The audience became disinterested."

Suppose you prepare a commercial urging people to take Fizzo when they feel "headachy and nauseous." Fizzo might help a headache, but it probably won't help a person who is "nauseous." Dictionaries now accept *nauseous* as one definition of *nauseated,* but the first listed meaning remains "disgusting." "Nauseous" doesn't mean *you* are sick at your stomach; it means anyone who looks at you wants to vomit.

It isn't clear either if former Vice President Spiro Agnew meant "effete" when he talked about "effete snobs." "Effete" is not a synonym for "elite." It means worn out from overproduction. When a farmer finds a cow has borne so many calves that she can produce no more, Old Bossy is effete, and she's sent off to the packing house. That's not much to be snobbish about.

The lesson is simple: Be certain you know the meaning of every word you write.

However, if you do know the meaning of a tricky word, does the audience? There are two levels on which to work here. First, many words will be unfamiliar to *any* audience. Second, some words may be unfamiliar to the audience of the program for which you are writing. A writer must always know the audience. In most cases, if you have a specialized audience, you will be able to use a broader vocabulary than for a program targeted for a mass audience. A specialized audience will know everything the mass audience knows plus some terms used primarily by the group for which you are writing. You might use terms like "tessitura" or "leitmotiv" in a program for opera lovers, but you would be out of your mind to use them on a more general audience. It may also be the case that a specialized audience may have a more limited vocabulary than the general audience. Children's programs are an obvious example. Know your audience, and use terms you are sure that audience can understand.

At the risk of belaboring the point, the average writer, or even the average person studying writing, is *not* an average person. The writer is certain to have a better vocabulary than the average citizen because the writer will be better educated and more widely experienced than the average citizen. Don't use yourself and your friends as models when you write for the *average* viewer or listener.

Excessive Detail. The broadcast audience cannot absorb the kind of detail that is common in print. The audience cannot reread the material if something is missed or misunderstood. It cannot slow down the pace at which the information is delivered. Take this passage from Cornelius Ryan's *The Longest Day:*

> Leading the thirty-eight British and Canadian convoys bound for Sword, Juno and Gold beaches was the cruiser H.M.S. *Scylla,* the flagship of Rear Admiral Sir Philip Vian, the man who tracked the German battleship *Bismark.* And close by was H.M.S. *Ajax,* one of the trio that fought the *Graf Spee.* There were other famous cruisers—the U.S.S. *Tuscaloosa,* and *Quincy,* H.M.S. *Enterprise* and *Black Prince,* France's *Georges Leygues*—twenty-two in all.[10]

Or this sentence from the same book:

> They came, rank after relentless rank, ten lanes wide, twenty miles across, 5,000 ships of every description.[11]

Let's see, thinks the listener, did he say "ten lanes, twenty miles across," or did he say "twenty lanes, ten miles across?" And was each lane ten—or twenty—miles across, or was the whole shebang twenty—or ten—miles across?

Clearly the kind of detail that Ryan could supply in a book simply doesn't work for broadcasting. Try to minimize numbers, names, and similar details in your broadcast writing. Where they must be used, try to spread them out—one to a sentence—and use repetition to make sure the audience gets the point. In the case of the Ryan quotation above, if you were preparing a broadcast adaptation, it might go something like this:

---

[10]Cornelius Ryan, *The Longest Day, June 6, 1944* (New York: Simon and Schuster, 1959), pp. 90–91.
[11]Ibid., p. 89.

```
They came . . . rank after relentless rank . . .

There were ten lanes of them . . . ten seemingly

endless columns of ships . . . a procession that

stretched 20 miles wide.  And in it were five

thousand ships of every description.
```

Here the writer has modified Ryan's tight prose to let the facts reach the listeners one fact at a time. It is longer than Ryan's description, but this does not violate the rule of making broadcast writing economical because anything shorter might have sacrificed clarity for the audience.

Redundancy. Unneeded words easily slip into your writing because every-day speech is full of repetition and redundancy. You may expect to put some of this into your dialog, but you must never let repetition and redundancy use up time needed for more important material in your script. The time to seek out excess words is after you have completed your first draft. If you need to cut—and usually you will—*that* is the time to go after those unneeded words.

Redundancy is more likely to be a sin than repetition. Repetition is simply using the same word or phrase more than once in a short space of time which is perfectly normal for spoken English. Repetition is useful for making sure that the audience gets certain information, such as the name of the sponsor's product. Redundancy, on the other hand, is using more words than you need to when you say something. Let's take some examples.

```
                    GEORGE

I saw Paula on Easter Sunday.  Since the year of

1980, she's been living in the city of New Orleans

with her canary bird and her collie dog.
```

The repetition of the name looks bad in print, but the dialog follows normal speech patterns. The audience would not find anything odd in hearing the name Paula repeated three times—and would also be certain who was being talked about if that were important. But compare that with this:

```
                    GEORGE

I saw Paula today.

                    ALICE

(COLDLY)  How was Paula?
```

GEORGE

```
Paula was fine.
```

Even if the dialog could be defended as being true to natural speech —and some of it isn't—it is full of redundancies. *That* is where you should make your first cuts when you begin tightening your script.

GEORGE

```
I saw Paula on Easter.  Since 1980, she's been

living in New Orleans . . . with her collie and

her canary.
```

By removing the redundancies, you have made the dialog more interesting to listen to and have cut out about two seconds of unneeded dialog. Two seconds may not seem like much, but if you do a similar tightening up throughout your script, you will be surprised to find how much you can shorten the running time.

To recapitulate, repetition is not necessarily bad, redundancy usually is. When cutting, hit the redundancies first. Here is a list of redundancies to watch out for. The words on the left mean the same as the words on the right.

the city of Jacksonville	Jacksonville
the sum of 25 dollars	25 dollars
past history	history
an oblong shape	oblong
completely decapitated	decapitated
canary bird	canary
collie dog	collie
start off	start
invited guests	guests
the year of 1967	1967
old adage	adage
entirely unique	unique
old traditions of the past	traditions
lift up	lift
in a dying condition	dying
future plans	plans
the hour of noon	noon
Easter Sunday	Easter
first of all	first
consensus of opinion	consensus
none at all	none

"Orphan" Pronouns. Like many of us in this country, pronouns can lose track of their antecedents. Pronouns pop up in writing, and we do not know what noun they stand for. In broadcasting, this is primarily a problem for news writers, but it can crop up in dialog as well.

> Sandra gave the ring to Nora. Paul told her to
> get rid of it.

Probably the meaning of that last sentence would be clear in context, but it contains the kind of potential ambiguity a writer should watch out for. Did Paul tell Sandra to get rid of the ring, or did Paul tell Nora to get rid of the ring? "Her" is ambiguous. The solution to the problem proves easier for the broadcast writer than for the print writer because repetition is not usually bad writing in broadcasting. Simply make the sentence, "Paul told Nora to get rid of it." Substitute the noun for the pronoun whenever the pronoun is ambiguous. Always read your script over carefully to make sure this kind of ambiguity has not slipped into your writing.

Keeping Style Informal

The structure of the broadcast sentence is slightly different from that of sentences used for other forms of writing. An informal style means that broadcast sentences sometimes depart slightly from the rules of formal grammar. In dialog in particular, there may be incomplete thoughts, or words that would be out of place in print. However, if you examine broadcast scripts, you will be surprised at how modest these deviations usually are. The reason is simply that the quickest, clearest way to get a point across is almost always a simple declarative sentence.

For example, broadcast sentences often begin with conjunctions. Remarks like: *"And* how did you get in here?" or *"But* I thought you took the train!" *Keep* the conjunctions there. Literary style sometimes calls for burying conjunctions in a sentence: "I thought, *however*, it made no difference." For broadcast writing, get the conjunction first: *However*, I thought it made no difference." This is more typical of spoken English and easier to follow.

The same rule applies to qualifying statements, but somewhat less strongly. It really depends upon what idea the writer wants to stress. "If you don't go, I'll scream" is usually better dialog than "I'll scream if you don't go," but the second version will work if the writer is trying to make the statement anticlimactic, the "if you don't go" more or less nullifying the threat of the "I'll scream."

Sources

Sources too are usually best at the start of a sentence. Again, the writer's intent must be taken into consideration. "The Duke says he will be beheaded tonight" reads better than "He will be beheaded tonight, the Duke says." However, if the writer's intent is to cast doubt on the statement, then the second form is better. (For news writing, there are very strict rules about the placement of sources. These are discussed in detail in the chapters on news.)

The best form for a broadcast sentence is usually the first-grade-reader style of "See Spot run!" Of course, too many short simple sentences can become boring, but in most forms of broadcast writing, speeches by one individual are not likely to last very long. The audience will not usually be listening to one source long enough to be bored by the sentence structure.

Perhaps the best advice that a broadcast writer can follow came from a novelist. Ernest Hemingway said it: "Strip language clean . . . lay it bare down to the bones."

SUMMARY

To sum up, here are some simple rules for broadcast writing:

1. Write simply. Use nothing without a reason.
2. Write conversationally, but with *economy*.
3. Use active verbs.
4. Put qualifying statements at the start of a sentence.
5. Put transitional words at the beginnings of sentences.
6. Minimize use of difficult words and sounds.
7. Avoid alliteration and tongue twisters. Use puns with caution.
8. Avoid excessive detail.
9. Avoid unneeded adjectives.
10. Avoid clichés, buzz words, and jargon.
11. Know the words you use.
12. Know the audience for which you write.

SCRIPT FORMATS 2

The beginning of most broadcast productions is the script. Sometimes a producer has an idea for a show and hires a writer to prepare a script. At other times, the writer's agent sells a script or an idea for one to the producer. Either way, before production can begin, there must be something on paper for everyone to work from. There must be a script.

Scripts are prepared in a great many forms. Each program uses a script format that fits its specific needs. Sometimes there is no good reason for using one format over another except "that's the way we do it here."

Each broadcast script should be prepared according to a specific format designed for its particular kind of production. In this chapter you will find a discussion of the major formats used. Instead of simply setting out a set of rules for you to follow, we have tried to explain *why* the differences in the formats exist. As you come to understand why a specific format is used, you will also come to understand the advantages and limitations of the kind of production for which it is used.

There is no way in which we could describe here *all* the variations in format you will find when you become a broadcast writer. We have tried to show you some of the most commonly found variations and have set out rules to follow for each of the five major formats when you are writing for this course.

Anyone who has ever taught a broadcast writing course knows the feeling of encountering a former student who announces: "What you taught us was all wrong. They don't do it that way where I work at all." We hope, by exposing you to some of the many variations of format, you will come to understand there is no one "right" format. You will have to adapt to the format being used where you work. We think the rules we have set out in this chapter will require *fewer* changes than most.

In a few instances we have suggested rules that we think work better than the ones most commonly used in the industry. In each instance we have also set out what the usual rule is in the industry and the reason we feel our recommended change will do a better job than the old rule.

So don't be overly concerned about these differences in script format. When you begin writing for a program, you can usually obtain sample copies of scripts that have been used on that program. You can copy the correct script format from these. Any important differences between the format of the script you prepare and the one used by the program will usually be caught and corrected by the secretarial staff of the show. Almost no scripts (except news scripts) go on the air as originally written. All must be retyped on stencils or some other duplicating device so that enough copies for the cast and staff can be prepared. Both before and after duplicating and binding the script, there are certain to be revisions. Any variations from preferred format not caught and changed by that time are likely to be of no consequence. It is doubtful that anyone ever rejected a script because it was typed in the wrong format, and it is certain that no one ever bought one just because it was.

Five basic script formats are used in broadcast writing: television film format, live television format, radio drama format, television news format, and radio news format. You'll learn that the name given to each of these formats does not always define its purpose. (For example, many programs that use television film format are not produced on film.) If you understand the differences in the basic formats, you can adapt easily to the specific script format used by any show. In this chapter we discuss some of the most common variations in these five formats and suggest one form for each format that you can use for preparing scripts for this course. Before we get to the specific formats, however, let's go over a few general rules for scripts.

GENERAL RULES

Some rules can be applied to the preparation of all kinds of copy for broadcast use.

1. Never staple a script. Stapling makes it noisy to turn the pages. Use a paper clip or put the script in a folder.
2. Scripts that are to be used near microphones should be on relatively soft paper that doesn't rattle much.
3. White paper is best for any script except one that may be seen on camera in television. In the latter case, use a pastel shade.

4. Type on one side of the page only.
5. Use only pica or elite type unless instructed otherwise.
6. Use one of the standard typewriter typefaces. Do not use script, italic, or other typefaces that are hard to read.
7. Use only black typewriter ribbon.
8. All copy must be clean, neatly typed, and free of errors in punctuation, grammar, and spelling. Pencil corrections may be made on news copy as long as the copy remains easy to read.
9. Always make a carbon copy. (For television news, multiple carbon copies are made on different colored sheets of paper so they can be sorted into the many scripts needed.)

TELEVISION FILM FORMAT

Television film format was developed to meet the special needs of the motion picture industry, but it is used today for many television programs, both those produced on film and those produced on videotape. It is less commonly used for the production of live television shows, but it is sometimes used for this purpose too, especially if the program is a drama.

The television film format script looks something like the script used for stage dramas—which is not surprising because that is what it was derived from. But motion pictures are not made like stage plays. Every film is a sequence of hundreds of individual "takes," each shot separately. They are rarely shot in the order in which they are ultimately seen on the screen. Instead, the various shots are made in the sequence that is the most economical to produce. To take an obvious example, if a film opens in Transylvania, moves to London, and winds up in Transylvania again, it makes no sense to shoot first in Transylvania, second in London, and third in Transylvania. You would shoot everything in Transylvania that you needed—start and ending—then go on to London (or vice versa). In film production, the shooting sequence is reduced to a much finer science. All scenes requiring wide shots of the set will be shot first because it may be necessary to dismantle parts of the set for close-ups and medium shots. All shots on a given set requiring the same lighting setup may be shot before time is spent moving the lights into location for a different setup of the shot. Contractual obligations may require that all scenes with a particular actor or actress be shot at a certain time. All these considerations require that a very careful schedule for shooting be laid out so that the film can be shot with the most reasonable expenditure of time and money.

For motion picture production, it is essential that the script be designed so that the director can keep careful track of what sequences have been shot and so that the film editor can take the disorganized sequence of shots he receives and put them back together into proper order. For these reasons, every camera shot in the script is numbered. Sets, costumes, action, and the characters themselves are all described in great detail in the scripts. Major camera transitions used are indicated in the script; virtually every camera angle and all camera movements are carefully described. In short, the writer paints a very precise picture of what the finished product will look like on the screen. The director is not bound to follow every instruction given, but every change is duly noted in a revision of the script.

Because scripts are in a constant process of revision, every page of the shooting script is dated when typed. Every revision also has a date on it, so it is always possible to tell what is the latest change. Different-colored pages are often used to indicate various revisions. If more than one revision is made on the same day, various techniques are used to indicate it. For example, in the days when MGM was a major producer, the rule in the MGM script department was to put no period after the page number on the first version of a given day. The first revision that day got one period after the page number. The second revision got two periods, and so on.

When television arrived, those accustomed to writing for the movies began turning in television scripts in their accustomed style. When live television began to be replaced with filmed programs shot in movie studios, the script form used for motion pictures became the standard script format for these productions, which were essentially "little movies." But the techniques developed to turn out a 75-minute film in six months of shooting and editing were too cumbersome for a medium that wanted a 23-minute film every week. So changes were made in production techniques, and these led to modification of the script form. Thus was born the television film script format.

Basically, the extent to which a television film format script conforms to the traditional film format today depends upon the type of show for which it is written and, to some extent, the preferences of the producer, director, and writer. In general, if a script is intended for a made-for-television motion picture, the traditional script format is used. If the script is intended for a television series done on film, the old style is modified. Only key elements of visual transition or camera angle and movement are described. Continuing characters and regularly used sets need no description unless something unusual is called for. Camera shots are often not numbered. When they are numbered, there are fewer numbers than on the traditional script because longer sequences are used to cut down on the time consumed in setting up for new shots. Some shows use more than one camera in filming scenes. Film producers traditionally shot all scenes with one camera. When, for example, two characters were speaking, all speeches by one character would be shot from one camera angle, then the camera would move to the "reverse" angle, and all speeches by the other character were shot. The speeches were intercut later, as called for in the script, by the film editor. Today, one camera may focus on one character while a second camera focuses on the other, completing the shooting of the sequence in far less time. There is no particular point in asking the writer to number and describe each cut with this kind of shooting.

When the script is intended for a program to be recorded on videotape, there is even less reason to provide all the information given in the traditional motion picture script. Live television, by its nature, had to be shot with more than one camera. When videotape arrived, some directors did experiment with motion picture style shooting, but the big, bulky television cameras, tethered by coaxial cable, were simply not designed to be used the way film cameras were. Multicamera shooting has always been the preferred technique. Instead of making individual shots, long sequences of action were shot at one time. The director used his cameras and electronic switching to achieve the effects achieved on film by the intercutting of shots.

For such programs, it makes no particular sense for the writer to spell out each individual shot. That is left to the director to work out on the set. Only when a special shot is required is it indicated. The writer is left with a highly simplified form of the old motion picture style script.

Format Rules

1. Each act of the script begins with a FADE IN, which means the screen is black and then the picture slowly becomes visible. An "act" is usually simply a designation for a portion of a script between two commercials. However, programs sometimes begin with a *teaser*, which is a brief scene between the opening credits and the first commercial. Some shows also make use of a *tag*, a short scene between the last commercial and the closing credits. (Parts of the credits may be shown over the teaser and the tag.) Tags and teasers also begin with a FADE IN. FADE IN is almost always typed (in full capitals) on the left side of the page, about one inch from the edge. (A fairly standard list of margin and tabulator settings for script preparation can be found in Nash and Oakey's *The Television Writer's Handbook.*[1]) Each act normally ends with a FADE OUT, which is typed (in full capitals) starting about two inches from the *right* edge of the page. "FADE OUT" means that the picture slowly fades to black.

2. Whenever there is a change of physical location of the action within an act or whenever there is a passage of time, a new "scene" begins. Between each scene in an act, some sort of transition must be specified. The most widely used transition is the DISSOLVE, in which one picture fades out while a second picture fades in in its place. During a SLOW DISSOLVE, the transition takes several seconds and at midpoint, the effect is the same as that of a SUPER ("superimposition"), that is, all elements of both pictures are visible at the same time. How slow a dissolve is depends upon the instructions of the director if the program is live or on videotape, or of the film editor if the program is on film.

It is increasingly common to see CUT TO used as a transition. In a CUT, one scene ends abruptly and the next begins instantaneously. The usual transition between shots in a scene is the CUT, but these are not usually specified in a television film format script. (Each shot *may* be specified if the production is a "made-for-television film" rather than a regular weekly series.) Using CUT TO as a transition between scenes can confuse your audience unless they are able to grasp immediately that the action is in a new locale or

[1]Constance Nash and Virginia Oakey, *The Television Writer's Handbook* (New York: Barnes & Noble Books), 1978.

at a different time. Often when such a transition is used between scenes, it is emphasized through use of a musical bridge or some similar sound-track device to alert the audience to the change.

On occasion, a transition between scenes may be made by use of a FADE OUT followed by a FADE IN. This slows the action of the program considerably, and gives a sense of a very complete break in the action between the two scenes. Consequently it is rarely used in today's fast-moving shows.

There are a number of other transitions that can be used between two scenes. There are HORIZONTAL, VERTICAL, and DIAGONAL WIPES. There are RIPPLE DISSOLVES. There are FLIPS. There are SWISH PANS. As the electronic wizardry of television increases, each year sees new transitional devices added. We will discuss some of the better-known ones later in this book. Unless you know that a program makes regular use of some special transitional device, you are best advised to stick to CUTs and DISSOLVEs unless there is a very special need for another type.

Most writers write all transitions in capital letters. In nearly all formats, they are underlined and followed by a colon. They are almost always typed at the right side of the page, starting about two inches from the edge—except for FADE IN, which traditionally goes on the left side of the page. (We've qualified all the statements in this paragraph with "almost" or "nearly" because some of the actual scripts of various programs that appear in this book differ slightly in one way or another from the rules we have stated.)

If a script consisted of nothing but transitions, it might look something like this:

FADE IN:

CUT TO:

DISSOLVE:

FADE OUT:

3. Start each scene with a one-line statement telling whether the scene takes place inside (interior, or *Int.*) or outside (exterior, or *Ext.*), the time of day, and the locale. The first line is usually written all in capital letters and underlined. It goes two lines below FADE IN or the last transition, about one inch from the left edge of the page. Typically, such a statement might read:

INT. HOUSEBOAT -- NIGHT

4. If shots are numbered, we recommend that you follow the most common technique, which is to number on the right side of the page (although you will encounter scripts numbered on the left and some numbered on both edges of the page). Put the numbers about one inch from the right edge of the page, and begin your transitions about two and one-half inches from the right edge instead of two. We recommend that you number the first line of each new shot like this:

```
1.   INT. HOUSEBOAT -- NIGHT
```

However, many writers place the number on a line with the first detailed description of the scene.

```
1.   INT. HOUSEBOAT -- NIGHT

     (THE CABIN IS CLUTTERED WITH...
```

Shots are numbered consecutively. If a shot continues on to a second or third page, there is a confusing difference among writers about the best way to handle the situation. All agree that the shot number is repeated at the top of each page onto which it continues and that the number should be followed by CONTINUED or CONT'D. We recommend that you put "(2)" after CONT'D on the first page on which the shot continues and "(3)" on the second page. Many writers insist that the first page of the continued shot should only be marked CONT'D, and the next page marked "(2)." Obviously, you must settle on one system or the other and stick with it. This is how we recommend you do it:

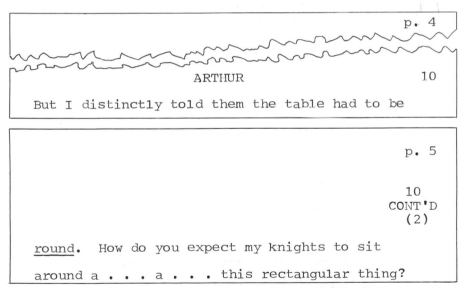

5. Next, two lines below the brief statement of the scene, comes a detailed description of the scene. The amount of detail you supply in this section depends upon whether the set and characters in the scene are ones that have been used before and what action you have planned for the characters. In a continuing television series, you would normally need to say little about a regular character or regularly used set. You would want to describe any new character and any new set needed. You might also describe in detail changes in a regular set or in the appearance of a continuing character that were related to the plot. This material is typed in many ways. We recommend using the same left margin as the brief statement of the scene. Set the right margin about one inch from the right edge of the page—or one and one-half inches if you are numbering in the right margin. Single-space the material. Write it all in capital letters, and put the entire description in parentheses.

6. Music cues and sound effects may be handled in a number of ways too. We recommend making them separate lines of capital letters, underlined, starting about one inch from the left edge of the page.

7. Dialog, too, is typed in many ways. Our suggestion is to type all dialog double-spaced, with the left margin about two inches from the left edge of the page and the right margin about two inches from the right edge.

Your script, then, should look something like this:

FADE IN:

INT. CASTLE -- DAY

(CAMELOT, NOT AS PAINTED IN THE LEGEND, BUT A RATHER SEEDY, DOWN-AT-THE-HEELS CASTLE. THE THRONE ROOM HAS CRACKS IN THE WALLS. THE UPHOLSTERY ON THE THRONE IS PATCHED, AND MUCH OF THE FURNITURE IS BROKEN. KING ARTHUR LOOKS UNKEMPT, AND HIS CLOTHES ARE SHABBY, AS ARE THOSE OF HIS KNIGHTS. ARTHUR IS STANDING IN FRONT OF THE THRONE, LOOKING AT A LONG, RECTANGULAR TABLE. WITH HIM ARE SIR LANCELOT AND SIR GAWAIN.)

ARTHUR

(PETULANTLY) I did. I know I did.

I distinctly told him round! Did I

not, Gawain?

GAWAIN

You did sire.

ARTHUR

(COMMANDING) Summon me the royal

carpenter!

GAWAIN

(TURNING AND SHOUTING) Summon the

royal carpenter!

MUSIC: BLAST OF TRUMPETS

VOICES

(OFF CAMERA, ECHOING AND GROWING

SOFTER) The royal carpenter . . .

The royal carpenter . . . The royal

. . . .

SFX: HOOFBEATS GALLOPING OFF INTO THE DISTANCE

DISSOLVE

Reexamine the script format, and you'll see that the rules are really simple. Dialog is the only material that is not written in capital letters. It uses normal lower- and upper-case letters—what is called *down style*. Underlining is used for transitions, the short opening description of the setting, music cues, sound effects (SFX) cues, and names of characters appearing in stage directions. Names of characters are centered above their speeches. All stage directions go in parentheses. Long stage directions are single spaced and set off from the rest of the material. Short stage directions are inserted into the dialog. The left margin in set about one inch from the left edge of the page for everything except dialog, which starts two inches from the left edge of the page. When no numbering is used, the right margin is set about one inch from the right edge of the page except for dialog, which has a right margin two inches from the right edge of the page. Transitions, other than FADE IN, are begun about two inches from the right edge of the page.

Because you are certain to encounter many variants of this format, we have prepared some short segments of scenes in several other commonly used styles of television film format.

INT. LAUNDROMAT -- NIGHT

The laundromat is one of those huge ones,   1
with rows and rows of machines. NORA opens
one, pulls out a pair of men's shorts. She
shrugs and tosses them back in. She opens
another machine. TELEPHONE ON WALL RINGS.
She runs to it.

NORA

Hello . . .

INT. LAUNDROMAT -- NIGHT   1

The laundromat is one
of those huge ones,

> with rows and rows of
> machines. NORA opens
> one, pulls out a pair
> of men's shorts. She
> shrugs and tosses them
> back in. She opens
> another machine.
> TELEPHONE ON WALL
> RINGS. She runs to
> it.

                    NORA

          Hello . . .

INT. LAUNDROMAT -- NIGHT

(THE LAUNDROMAT IS ONE OF THOSE HUGE ONES, WITH ROWS

AND ROWS OF MACHINES. NORA OPENS ONE, PULLS OUT A PAIR

OF MEN'S SHORTS. SHE SHRUGS AND TOSSES THEM BACK IN.

SHE OPENS ANOTHER MACHINE.)

SFX: TELEPHONE ON WALL RINGS

                    NORA

          Hello . . .

   Here are some different ways the same dialog might be typed. In these
examples, the dialog is interrupted to provide stage directions.

                    MACY

          I'm not sick. (CHECKING HIS OWN

          PULSE AND MAKING A FACE) I'm dead!

                    MACY

             I'm not sick.

          He checks his pulse and makes a face.

                    MACY (Cont'd)

             I'm dead!

We present you with these other ways of handling this format, not to confuse you, but to help you avoid confusion. If you are looking for the one right format for television, there is no such thing. There is only the right format for a particular show. Learn the simple basic format we have outlined, and you should be able to switch to the right one for your show with ease.

To give you an idea how scripts are prepared for some shows, here are some excerpts from actual scripts used on the air. The first is a script written for "Three's Company," which is shot on videotape. The writers are Paul Wayne and George Burdett.

<pre>
                    "Helen's Job"

        ACT ONE

        FADE IN:

        INT. ROPERS' APARTMENT - DAY

        (THE ROPERS ARE AT BREAKFAST. MRS. ROPER IS

        DRINKING COFFEE, WATCHING, FASCINATED, THE

        WAY STANLEY EATS HIS SCRAMBLED EGGS,...
</pre>

The descriptive material continues for another seven lines. Note that there is *no* description of the Ropers' apartment. This is a set used regularly in the series, so it does not have to be described. What the writers *do* describe in detail are Stanley Roper's actions, the way he eats his eggs, because this stage business is the basis of some of the gags that follow. It must be described clearly. Note also that the format follows the general rules we have outlined, but the stage directions here have been double-spaced and the right margin is set about two inches from the right edge of the page. As will become evident, the same right margin is being used for both stage directions and dialog. The dash typed between the words "apartment" and "day" raises a minor point that may cause you some confusion. We have presented the script here exactly as it was typed. The dash used does not conform to the style we specify later in this book. We recommend that you make a dash as two hyphens preceded and followed by a space, like this: APARTMENT -- DAY. However, many script typists make dashes with a single hyphen as was done in the script we are examining, like this: APARTMENT - DAY. And some even leave out the spaces around the dash, like this: APARTMENT-DAY. Do not be concerned by minor variations like this. Use the style we have recommended unless you are told to do otherwise.

<pre>
                    MRS. ROPER

        (AS HE STARTS THE SAME THING WITH ANOTHER PORTION)
</pre>

```
            Stanley, why don't you ever put the

            salt, pepper and ketchup on all at

            once, instead of piece by piece?

                         ROPER

            Because if I did it all at once,...
```

The writers continue the dialog, describing the action and tone of voice to be used by the performers. At the end of the scene, the writers indicate that the transition is to be a simple cut.

```
                    MRS. ROPER

            I'd love it!

        (ROPER REACTS)

        CUT TO:

        INT. TRIO'S KITCHEN -- SAME DAY

        (CHRISSY, JANET AND JACK ARE JUST FINISHING

        BREAKFAST: EGGS BENEDICT)

                      CHRISSY

            Boy, what a great breakfast!...
```

Instead of the more conventional DISSOLVE, the writers here have made the transition from the Ropers' kitchen to Janet, Chrissy, and Jack's kitchen with a straight CUT. This follows the usual style of the program, and makes any subsequent editing a bit easier to handle. No confusion is caused because the second scene is clearly in a different location with different characters. Note again, there is no need to describe the set, but the action is described. The CUT TO has been set at the left margin instead of the right. This is easier for the typists to handle, and by keeping all material on the left side of the page, room is left on the right for notes and camera directions the director might wish to scribble in. As you might guess, the show is a multicamera show, recorded on videotape. As the scene continues, the writers call for sound effects (SFX).

                    CHRISSY

        There was a chef named "Eggs Benedict?"

(JANET AND JACK REACT)

SFX: DOORBELL

                    JANET

        I'll get it.

(SHE EXITS)

After some additional dialog, the writers call for a shift of the action to the living room of Jack, Chrissy, and Janet's apartment. In this case, the living-room set is contiguous to the kitchen set, part of the permanent set for the apartment. Actors can move freely from the kitchen to the living-room areas of the set. Consequently, the writers do not call for a transition. Presumably the director simply cuts from one area to the other. However, the shift of locale is noted in a one-line statement.

                    CHRISSY

        No, thanks, I don't want to be that

        wide awake for work.

INT. TRIO'S LIVING ROOM

(JANET OPENS DOOR TO MRS. ROPER)

(All the rest of the action in Act One takes place on the living room set. The authors end Act One with the traditional FADE OUT. Like all the other transitions, it has been placed at the left margin.)

                    MRS. ROPER

        You just made me an offer I can't

        refuse!

SHE TAKES ADDRESS FROM JANET, AND STORMS OUT

THE DOOR, LEAVING A STUNNED ROPER)

FADE OUT:

END OF ACT ONE

The script format used for "Three's Company" represents an extreme simplification of the traditional television film format. The typist uses one right margin setting for all copy. One left margin setting is used for everything except dialog, which is indented about one inch. Everything typed is double-spaced. Dialog is typed in down style, and everything else in capitals. Underlining is used for transitions, sound effects, act designations, and the one-line statement at the start of each scene. Everything in capital letters that is not underlined is in parentheses. Shots are not numbered. Scenes are not designated as such. The script format has come a long way from its film beginnings.

Compare that stripped-down, multicamera script with this more traditional script, written for a television series that was shot on film. The script, by Michael Morris, was written for the short-lived "New Temperatures Rising Show." The script is titled "Operation Mercy."

<u>ACT ONE</u>

<u>FADE IN:</u>

<u>INT. HOSPITAL CORRIDOR - DAY</u>

1.   Sick City is jumping. Doctors are in   1
               consultation, a MALE NURSE is walking a
               MALE PATIENT, an INHALATION THERAPIST is
               steering his equipment through the oncoming
               traffic. Head Nurse AMANDA KELLY comes out
               of a room. This is one stunning creature
               even in her starched whites. Imagine what
               she looks like in her lacy blacks. The MEN
               in the corridor are imagining it. As she
               passes them, heads snap in her direction.
               It's whiplash time. As she arrives at the
               Nurses' Station, she calls to MARGE, a nurse
               manning a filing cabinet.

                        KELLY
               Marge, get Mr. Dawson's
               discharge ready, please.

                        MARGE
               Dawson? No kidding? His
               doctor just came by and said
               he still had numbness in his
               right hand.

                        KELLY
               Don't you believe it. If he
               had any more feeling in it,
               I'd have him up on morals
               charges.

```
They both laugh.  As NOLAND, coming from
surgery, enters shot, MARGE goes to phone.

              NOLAND
             (Cheerily)
       Good morning, Kelly.
```

Here there are only minor departures from the traditional motion picture script format. Long takes, instead of individual shots, are numbered. Nearly all the material is single-spaced and written in down style. Dialog is kept separate from other material by the use of different margins. All performers, even extras, are identified in capital letters. The format is harder to read, but the presumption is that with the material shot in short takes, there is time to go over each sequence carefully before shooting. Note that the writer has not merely described the scene in detail. He has given the cast and director indications of how to play certain scenes. "Imagine what she looks like in her lacy blacks" is neither a line to be read in the dialog nor a stage direction in the strict sense. It is an indication of the attitude he wants the performers to convey to the audience. Later in the script, the writer gives some very specific instructions about the camera angles and transitions he wants. This segment of the story begins at night in the children's ward of the hospital:

```
         CLOSE ON PAUL'S BED

21       Paul closes his eyes.  He feels a        21
         tugging on his covers.  He opens his
         eyes.

         ANGLE - LITTLE GIRL

22       Standing at the foot of his bed holding  22
         his bunny.

                    GIRL
             You dropped your bunny.

                    PAUL
                  (taking it)
             Thanks a lot.

                    GIRL
             I'm not scared any more.

                    PAUL
             Good.

                    GIRL
             Well, maybe just a little

                    PAUL
             Me too.
```

```
                                        DISSOLVE TO:

          CLOSE ON PAUL'S SLEEPING FACE

    23    PULL BACK to reveal that Paul is lying      23
          on his bed.  Noland's HAND is shaking
          him awake.

                        NOLAND'S VOICE
                It's up, up and away!

          PULL BACK TO reveal we are in:

    INT. CHILDREN'S WARD - DAY

    24    There is a screen around Paul's bed.        24
          TWO ORDERLIES are standing next to
          Paul's bed.  Paul's eyes snap open.
```

The techniques used here are typical of the traditional motion picture script. The shots are numbered and described in some detail. The writer has used a standard transitional device to show passage of time—the DISSOLVE. The writer has told us how he visualizes all the important shots, but left it to the director to decide what shots to use for most of the dialog between Paul and the little girl.

If you compare the excerpts from the "Three's Company" script and the "New Temperatures Rising Show" script, you can see that the variations in the format used are functions of the needs of the particular show and the way it is produced. In subsequent chapters you will learn that different production techniques do place limitations on what you write. The script format a program uses can often be a clue to a writer as to what some of those limitations may be.

However, we repeat, you do not have to learn every variation of format to be a television writer. Learn each of the five basic formats set out in this book, and you will have no trouble adapting to the minor changes any specific show may require.

LIVE TELEVISION FORMAT

Live television format was developed to meet the unique needs of live television. In the early days of television, that meant practically all production. Much television production soon switched to film and later to videotape, but the live format continues to prove useful both for those live television programs still on the air and for many videotaped programs as well. Because motion pictures are filmed one shot at a time, the script places no pressure on the technical crew to function on cue—except for occasional special effects. With the advent of live television, the technical aspects of production had to "perform on cue" just as the performers did. The director was faced with the problem of really directing two "casts"—one before the cameras and the other in back of them. This necessitated a script form that included all the "action" and "cues" for the technical staff—one that the technical staff could study in advance just as the performers learn their lines in advance—and one that the director could refer to easily for *both* "casts."

The solution was a sort of *double* script. The television script is split down the middle or sometimes slightly to one side of center, giving a bit more space for the dialog than for the technical matter. One side, usually the left, is marked VIDEO, the other is marked AUDIO. The terms are slightly misleading. It might make more sense if the left-hand column were labeled CREW and the right hand CAST.

Not all material that goes in the audio column deals with sounds; stage directions for the actors, for example, are included in this column. It is true that such stage movements are important to the audio crew because microphones must be in the right spots at the right times—but the same argument could be made for putting stage directions in the video column because the camera crews and lighting crews need the same information. To find a general rule, it would probably be best to say that the audio column contains all cues and information relating to audio, including dialogue, plus stage directions. The video column contains all sources of video (slide, film, etc.), all visual transitions (dissolves, etc.), and the various camera shots to be used.

The video column looks relatively blank when it emerges from the typewriter. It will not look so when the director and other members of the technical crew have finished making notes and marking in additional information needed for their jobs. In commercial writing, the video column is frequently more detailed because of the need for special effects and the need to crowd a lot of information into a brief time.

You will find as much variety in specific formats for live television as you did for television film. The major differences between live television scripts and TV film scripts are those of terminology. For example, the fairly standard FADE IN of the television film script may appear in live television scripts as FADE IN, FADE UP, FADE UP FROM BLACK, or COME UP FROM BLACK. FADE OUT can be FADE TO BLACK or GO TO BLACK. Terminology is discussed in another chapter, and a list of suggested terms for your use is provided.

Live TV Rules

1. Leave about one-third of the page for the video column and two-thirds for the audio column. Many stations use paper that has a line printed down its length to divide it into two columns, and the words *Video* and *Audio* printed at the top. While a few stations still put audio on the left, we recommend putting the audio column on the right, which conforms to the practice of most stations today.

2. For dialog, double space and use caps and lower case type (down style). Use capitals and single spacing for everything else in the audio column. Underline cues for sound effects and music. Underline act and scene designations. Put all stage directions in parentheses. As you can see, these rules conform fairly closely to those we spelled out for the television film format. The major difference is that all this material is confined to the right two-thirds of the page, and there is no indenting of dialog.

3. In the video column list all your transitions, special visual effects, and all camera directions. The directions themselves go in capital letters. Further details usually go in down style. For example: ZOOM BACK TO MS: Nora looking at picture. The camera direction in capitals says for the camera operator to zoom back to a medium shot. In lower case, we are told that the shot is of Nora and a picture. The descriptive material becomes very important when you are using several visuals of the same type. If, for example, you were preparing a public service announcement to be read over a series of slides, you would be certain to identify each slide by the number of the slide and also the material on the slide. That provides a double check against getting the slides on in the wrong order. Usually there is no underlining used with material in the video column.

Here's what a brief live television format script might look like:

AMBER ROSE PROMO   10 Sec.

VIDEO	AUDIO
	ANNCR (OVER SLIDES)
FADE IN ON SLIDE: A17 "Rose & Dylan"	When big names are in town, who do they talk to? . . .
SLIDE: A31 "Rose & Reagan"	There's only one . . .
SLIDE: B108 "Amber Rose"	Amber Rose! . . . Ten every morning. Here on KDEG.
FADE TO BLACK	END

RADIO DRAMA FORMAT

The simplest format to use is that developed for radio drama. As noted, it is used for all forms of radio writing except news. Type the name of each speaker about one inch from the left edge of the page. Use capital letters and follow the name with a colon. Indent all dialog about two inches from the left edge of the page, and set the right margin about one inch from the right edge of the page. Music and sound-effect cues go one inch from the left edge of the page in underlined capitals. Type dialog with regular upper- and lower-case letters. Type all directions in capital letters. Put short directions in parentheses inside the dialog. Start longer directions one inch from the left edge of the page, running to one inch from the right edge, and do not use parentheses.

Variations

There are only a few variations from the style we have described here that you are likely to encounter. Some writers do not put directions and sound effects in upper case. Some put sound effects into the dialog in parentheses. The most important difference you are likely to encounter is that some scripts are prepared with each speech numbered, and a few (usually news scripts) may have each line numbered.

There are some obvious advantages to numbering in a long script. It makes it easy to identify specific lines for deletion or change—or for extra rehearsal by a performer. They can also be of some help in editing a tape recording of your script. However, numbering is an added complication. Moreover, most radio scripts today are likely to be short. For every half-hour radio drama script written today, there are no doubt at least a thousand 30-second commercial scripts. Consequently, numbering scripts has gone out of style. We do not recommend it unless you are specifically asked to do so. If you do number, set the numbers about one inch from the left edge of the page and begin names of speakers and other material about one and one-half inches from the left edge.

For radio and all other broadcast writing formats, we recommend against indenting for paragraphs. Simply double space to indicate a new paragraph. Indenting paragraphs simply gives you one more tabulator setting on your typewriter to worry about.

Copy for radio scripts is traditionally single-spaced. We have adhered to that rule in our recommendations for format. However, a strong argument can be made for double spacing anything meant to be read aloud. It certainly is easier to read, and is much easier to edit if any last-minute changes are required in your script. It is worth checking to see if the producers of the program you are writing for might prefer double spacing. If there are no specific instructions, stick with the traditional single spacing.

Speeches sometimes must be continued from one page to the next in broadcast writing. The rule in that case is to break the speech about an inch from the bottom of the page, double space and type "(MORE)" centered under the dialog. On the next page, repeat the name of the speaker and type "(CONT'D)" under it. Then continue the speech. You can help your performers in such continued speeches if you borrow a trick from newswriting for a continued speech. Try to break the speech on the first page at the end of a paragraph, or if not a paragraph, at least at the end of a sentence. Making the switch to the next page will be easier for the reader if the change comes at a natural break in the speech.

Here is a brief example of radio drama script format:

"LONESOME GUN"

MUSIC: THEME UP AND UNDER

ANNCR: Fidelio Products presents "Sagebrush Theater"
    . . . stories of America's western frontier
and the men and women who tamed it. . . .
brought to you by FIDELIO WAX . . . the only
wax that contains floristan. . . . Tonight's
adventure . . . "The Lonesome Gun."

MUSIC BRIDGE

NARR: In the 1880's, the mining town of Tiger,
Arizona, was known as the roughest place this
side of perdition. There was only one law,
the six gun. . . . And then one day, a
stranger rode into town.

MUSIC BRIDGE

SOUND OF HOOF BEATS

LONESOME: Whoa, Chula, whoa. Hey, you . . . old timer,
. . . you know a man around here called
Morgan?

OLD T: Not no more I don't. What you askin' fer?

LONESOME: He kinda offered me a job. Ain't he here?

OLD T: Oh, he's here all right . . . if you count
being in the cemetery as "bein' here."

LONESOME: He's dead?

OLD T: Last I heard, that was his condition. It all
happened Tuesday week. I was over at the
saloon, kinda mindin' my own business, when
I looked out, and there was Charlie Morgan
sayin' some mighty mean things to One-Eyed
Krebs.

SEGUE

```
MORGAN:     Krebs.  You're a liar and a cheat.  You know
            that mining claim of yours is forged.

KREBS:      (SINISTER)  I wouldn't go 'round sayin'
            things like that, Charlie.  You might get
            hurt.

MORGAN:     Don't try to bluff me, Krebs.

KREBS:      I ain't bluffin', Charlie.  I'm just sayin'
            you better be ready to draw . . . right now!
```

GUNSHOTS

SEGUE

```
OLD T:      Well, sir, they both drew, and One-Eye put
            a bullet square between Morgan's eyes.  He
            never knew what hit him.  If he offered you
            a job, mister, I think you just lost it.
```

LONESONE: You're wrong, old timer. I just found one.

MUSIC: THEME UP AND OUT

COMMERCIAL

RADIO NEWS FORMAT

News scripts, either for radio or television, use a very different format from other broadcast writing. The scripts are designed to be easy to change, since news stories can change at any time, and they are designed to be read as typed. There is little time to retype material for news. So news scripts must use a format that makes them easy to edit while still remaining legible for the newscaster to read. Legibility itself is a key element because the newscaster has little time to read over and rehearse his material.

News scripts are usually triple-spaced. Double spacing is usually used only if the typewriter cannot be set to triple spacing. Single spacing should never be used. It makes copy harder to read and almost impossible to edit.

Capitals Versus Down Style

There is a common misconception that news copy should be typed all in capitals. It is not a trivial issue. A great many professional newspersons insist on copy being written all in capital letters. The reason given is always that it is "easier to read." For those individuals, that may be true. Yet, over the years dozens of studies on "readability" have been conducted, and it is generally agreed that plain everyday use of capitals and lower-case letters—down style—is easier to read.

The myth about the readability of capital letters may have come from the constant contact news writers have with wire copy. Teletype machines have no lower-case letters. They can only type copy in capitals. (The wire services do now offer some of their copy in down style—but not on the radio wires.) The reasons for putting wire copy in capitals are strictly electronic and mechanical, but over the years, newspeople have come to equate capital letters with readability. Some typewriters, too, can type only in upper-case letters, but these are usually found in television newsrooms, not radio newsrooms, so we'll skip over them here.

Margins

Margin settings are very important in news formats. In discussing other formats, we have simply suggested setting margins so many inches from the edge of the page. What precise *number* on the typewriter represents that distance will vary with the typewriter. For example, if you have elite type on your typewriter, one inch is equal to 12 characters. If you have pica type, one inch is equal to 10 characters. Do not carry this concept over into news writing. It is the number of characters per *line*—not per inch—that determines how long it takes to read a line of copy. When you set your margins at 10 and 80, you will use those settings whether your typewriter has pica or elite type. It is very important that there be a standard line length so that quick estimates can be made of reading time. A 70-character line takes approximately four seconds to read.

Of course, no system is perfect. Some things will throw your estimates of reading time off. For example, "1984" takes up no more space on a line than the word "this," but it takes much longer to read aloud. But these errors tend to even out. A more important point to keep in mind is that the four second per line estimate is based on a reading speed of 150 words per minute. The *average* person reads aloud at that speed. The person reading copy on a university station or in a small radio station probably reads at about this average speed. *But* skilled broadcast professionals usually read at speeds of 170 words per minute or faster. You may have to make adjustments in your margin settings or your time estimates. For the time being, stick with our "average" setting: margins at 10 and 80.

Pages and Paragraphs

Write only one story to a page. Even very brief stories are better handled this way. The point is that stories can be added to or removed from the script and the sequence in which they are arranged can be changed right up to the very last minute—even while the newscaster is on the air, if necessary.

Don't indent for paragraphs. Most radio news stories are one-paragraph stories by nature. If you must go to a second paragraph, skip an extra line or two, or simply use a string of dots . . . like this . . . to indicate a break in the copy. The major argument against indenting and writing in paragraph form is that it gives you too many lines of differing lengths. The estimate of reading time for broadcast news copy is made from the number of *full* lines in the story. If the last line of a paragraph ends in the middle of the page and then you indent the next line the length of one or two words, you have probably lost three or four seconds of reading time. Keeping track of all these short lines in your time estimates can be a problem.

Despite the arguments against it, quite a few stations do indent copy. Style books often recommend indenting five spaces. (Wire services indent four.) It may really make little difference, but it is worth noting that each five-space indentation shortens the reading time of a story by one-third of a second.

When a story continues on to a second page (which should not be a common event in radio news), type "MORE" at the bottom of the page. On the next page, repeat the slug at the top of the page, and add the words "FIRST ADD" like this:

```
TORNADO -- NOON NEWS -- 8/16/83 -- JONES -- FIRST ADD
```

or like this:

```
Tornado -- First Add
Noon News
8/16/83
Jones
```

In the exceptionally rare event that a story should continue to *another* page, the next slug would read "SECOND ADD."

Slugs

The traditional radio news slug—that is, title and relevant information about the story—goes in a block in the upper-left-hand corner of the page, about an inch down from the top. It looks like this:

```
Tornado
Noon News
8/16/83
Jones
```

Your copy begins about an inch below that. The slug contains four items: a brief name for the story (usually the one used by the wire services if the story has been on the wires), the program for which the story was written, the date, and the last name of the writer.

Again, we are breaking with tradition in our news format. We recommend that the writer use the television news format slug instead of the usual radio one. It contains exactly the same information, in the same order, but it is typed in a single line across the top of the page, about an inch and one-half from the top. It looks like this:

```
TORNADO -- NOON NEWS -- 8/16/83 -- JONES
```

Our argument for this slug is that it takes up less space, requires no shifting from triple spacing to single spacing, and gives students one less thing to worry about in learning formats. Unless you are instructed to do otherwise, we recommend you use this same one-line slug for both radio and television news.

Breaking Words and Sentences

An important rule of broadcast news format is that words never be split between lines by use of hyphens. The purpose is simply to make the copy easier for the newscaster to read. What do you do when the typewriter bell rings at the end of a line and you haven't room to finish the word you are typing? Back up. Use capital Xs to cross out the word. Begin it fresh on the next line. Broadcast news copy is one of the few formats that permit you to make corrections on the air copy—as long as the copy remains easy to read.

Sentences should always be finished on the page on which they were begun. In the rare case that you haven't room on the page to finish the entire sentence, cross out the whole sentence and begin fresh on the next page.

As a general rule, paragraphs should not be split between two pages either. For radio news, however, not many stories run more than one paragraph.

Try to avoid beginning two lines in a row with the same words. This can cause the newscaster to lose her or his place.

If the script contains tricky words, put a wavy line under them. If you notice a difficult word while typing the story, type a phonetic spelling guide of it in parentheses after the word. If you notice a difficult word later while reading over the copy, neatly print a pronunciation guide above the word. You can also make it easier for the reader if you either underline the word "not" or set it off with ellipses like this: "The senator says he has . . . not . . . decided if he will run again."

Cart Stories

A good newscast provides a balance of written material and recorded material. Recorded material in most newscasts is put onto cartridges or "carts." Here is how we recommend putting the information about material on an audio cart into your news script.

To begin with, each cart itself is labeled with identifying information, usually including a number. When you reach the point in your script at which the cart is to be played, drop down about an inch from the last line of copy and indent about three inches from the left edge of the page. On one line, type the number of the cart, the person whose voice is on the cart, the type of audio it is, and the topic of the material on the cart. All this material is usually also on the cart label. You may number the carts sequentially in the program, or you may have another system. We recommend that each cart be given an identification that is permanently marked on the cart for its lifetime. However, this is not practical for all stations. Whatever system is used to assign numbers to carts, be certain that no two carts are given the same number, or confusion could arise. As for the kind of material on the cart, news audio carts are normally of two types—voicers and actualities. A voicer is a report by a station reporter. An actuality is a recorded interview. Usually these are shortened to VCR and ACC.

On the line below this information goes the running time of the material on the cart and the out cue—the last three or four words heard on the cart. If the material on the cart is a voicer, the out cue is nearly always the Standard Out Cue (SOC) for that station—that is, the established sign-off that all reporters are supposed to use. It might be something such as, "For KDEG News, this is Marla Gelb." If a standard out cue is used, it can be indicated simply with the abbreviation SOC, instead of writing out the entire cue.

Some stations also put an IN CUE on the cart label and in the script. This is the first three or four words heard on the cart. It can be helpful to the engineer in identifying and cueing up carts. It is particularly useful if there is more than one audio cut on the same cart. If an IN CUE is used, it is typed after the running time, and the out cue goes on the line below it.

Skip a line below the cart information. Indent another five spaces, and type in a brief summary of the material on the cart. If something goes wrong with the cart, the newscaster can read the "fill" you have provided to fill in the audience on what they missed on the audio cart. The whole thing should look like this:

```
CART 3B -- BARNES -- ACC -- Pollution
:48  OC:  ". . . once dead river."

     FILL:  Congressman Barnes says
     that the new, 3 (M) million
     dollar sewage treatment plant
```

```
       will leave the Quincy River
       cleaner than it has been since
       1950, and that will bring fish
       and plant life back to that
       once dead river.
```

Winding Up the Story

When each story is completed, the mark "#" is put a few lines below the last line of the story to indicate the end. The writer then rereads the story and makes corrections where needed with a soft pencil. The writer uses the pencil to circle *everything* on the page that is not intended to be read on the air. For example, all the copy we have just described for use with an audio cart would be circled because it is not intended to be read aloud. Careful writers even circle the slug and the "#" mark.

Then the number of lines of copy are counted. We recommend that you simply write the number of lines in a story in the upper-right-hand corner. At some stations, the line count is converted to seconds or minutes, and this is written in the upper-right-hand corner. On balance, it is usually easier and quicker to work with line count. The line count is for the entire story, so if the story runs more than one page, the line count for its entirety is recorded on the first page.

Whether you use seconds or line count, the number in the upper-right-hand corner must include the running time of any audio cart. For example, suppose you had written six lines of copy for the story with the 48-second audio cart. If you were counting lines, you would know that the 48-second cart is the equivalent of 12 four-second lines, so you would add that to the six lines you had written for the story and write "18 lines" in the corner. If you were using seconds rather than lines, you would know that your six lines of copy, at four seconds a line, would equal 24 seconds, which added to the running time of the cart would equal 1:12, which you would write in the corner. Circle the material in the corner.

Pages of news scripts are often not numbered. If they are, the numbers are penciled in the upper *left* corner and circled. This cannot be done until the final sequence of stories in the show has been decided upon, which usually is just before air time.

TELEVISION NEWS FORMAT

Like the radio news script, the television news script is designed to be easily edited and changed. One important difference is that the radio news script is usually meant to be read by one or two people. Television news scripts must be read by all on-camera personnel and dozens of people behind the scenes who help get the show on the air.

Television news is customarily written on carbon "books," packets of paper with carbon paper interleaved. Each book produces the number of copies needed by a station for its news production—often eight or ten copies. Usually each sheet of paper in the book is of a different color so that the pages can easily be separated into scripts of those colors—each color designated for a different person or use. Pink might go to the newscaster, yellow to the director, green to the audio engineer, and so on. Any script that might be seen on camera is usually of a pastel color, since pure white is a difficult color for television cameras. The script pages usually have a blank in the upper-left-hand corner for a number. The numbers are penciled in at the last minute when the final form of the program has been decided upon. Scripts are almost never numbered page by page. At some stations, each story is numbered. At others, only segments of the program are numbered, and each story within that segment gets the same number, perhaps distinguished by a letter after the number, ("2-a," "2-b," and so on).

The segments so numbered usually designate a change in the source of the video picture. For example, all the opening material read on camera by the newscaster might be designated "I." The commercial might be "2." More on-camera material might be "3," and the first story using videotape might be "4." Regrettably, there is a wide variation in the numbering systems used by stations. Even different producers at the same station may favor somewhat different numbering systems. We recommend that you number each story, using "a" after the number for the second page, "b" for the third, and so on.

For pica or elite typewriters, set your margins at 35 and 70. This will give you a line that takes about two seconds to read. Write cues on the left, about one inch from the left edge of the page. Cues are written in capital letters. Copy to be read on the air is written in regular down style. Don't indent for paragraphs, skip an extra line. Triple-space copy. (Double-space if your typewriter has no triple-space setting.)

We gave margin settings for pica or elite type—but elite is rarely used because it is difficult to read. Quite often, television news is typed on typewriters with oversized typefaces. These usually type in upper case only. Most are "six pitch" machines, which type six characters to an inch. If you set margins on one of these machines at 24 and 42, each line should take about one second to read. Type cues as usual, about one inch from the left edge of the page, which, in this case, would be a setting of "six" on the typewriter. Just as the margin settings for radio, these margins are based on an estimated reading speed of 150 words per minute. Longer lines usually have to be written for skilled newscasters, who read considerably faster than 150 words per minute.

It is essential that the estimated reading time of a line of copy be standardized in a newsroom so that reading times for stories and scripts can be estimated quickly. Whatever line length is chosen, the left-hand one-third of the page should be left free for cues and notes.

The slug used for television in most cases is the one we also recommended for radio use: a single line, written all in capital letters, running across the top of the sheet about two inches from the top. It contains the name of the story, the program it was written for, the date, and the name of the writer.

> JONES TRIAL -- 10/15/81 -- NOON UPDATE -- JOHNSON

Like all copy not to be read on the air, it is circled. As mentioned before, a blank space is left to the left of the story for a number to be filled in later. The number of lines or the running time of the story is penciled in in the upper-right-hand corner and circled.

Cues for Visuals

Just as the radio writer must integrate audio material into her or his script, the television news writer must use visual material. Visual materials may go into a script as slides, visuals on a stand in the studio, motion pictures, videotape, or via specialized visual equipment such as opaque projectors. Film, videotape, and slides are the most common. The material may either be shown "full screen" or it may be shown as part of a picture including the newscaster. All visual media can be rear projected onto studio screens with a system called Vizmo. All media can be shown on large screen television monitors in the news set. And all media can be matted into specific areas of the picture through Chromakey, a system by which pictures from one television camera appear in areas of the picture from another camera when those areas are a particular color, usually blue. Only slides or other nonmoving visuals can be presented through regular rear projection. Lettering can be added to pictures through use of a character generator.

An extensive system of cues is used to achieve these effects. Those cues are discussed in later chapters. Do not concern yourself with them here. Instead, concentrate on the format used to include these materials in the script.

Mayor Gloria Mundi laid the

cornerstone for the new city

hospital today. Mayor Mundi had

some problems wielding her shovel.

The ground was....

When there is sound on the videotape or film used, in most circumstances there will be no need for copy. In that case, you provide the out cue for the audio material and fill to be used in case of a loss of audio much as you did with radio format:

<table>
<tr><td>(JOHN OC)</td><td>Governor Ernest Doolittle again

promised voters today that, if

elected to another term, he <u>won't</u>

run for President.</td></tr>
<tr><td>(SI VTR/VO)</td><td>Speaking at a health food store in

Los Diablos, the Governor explained

why he would . . . not . . . want

to live in the White House.</td></tr>
<tr><td>(SOVTR (:42))</td><td>OC: ". . . find wheat germ."

FILL: The Governor said
it is too difficult to
find organic foods and
wheat germ in Washington,
D-C.</td></tr>
</table>

As with radio news writing, all copy not to be read aloud is circled. If a cue is to be tied to a specific word in your copy (not really a good idea, it's too hard for the director and his crew), you can link it with a line while you are circling things like this:

JOHN OC   There's a major brush fire raging

in the Sabino (sah-BEE-no) Canyon

SI VTR/VO   area tonight. Helicopters are

being used to drop....

In making your line count or time estimate, be sure that you include the running time of any sound-on-film or sound-on-videotape segments. Suppose a story has eight lines of copy plus a 42-second sound-on-videotape segment. Since television lines are supposed to take two seconds each to read, the story runs 29 lines or 58 seconds.

Television News Format Example

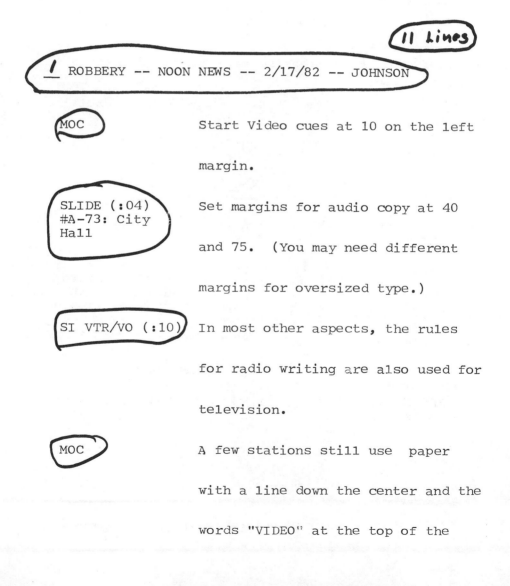

11 Lines

ROBBERY -- NOON NEWS -- 2/17/82 -- JOHNSON

MOC   Start Video cues at 10 on the left

margin.

SLIDE (:04)   Set margins for audio copy at 40
#A-73: City
Hall   and 75. (You may need different

margins for oversized type.)

SI VTR/VO (:10)   In most other aspects, the rules

for radio writing are also used for

television.

MOC   A few stations still use paper

with a line down the center and the

words "VIDEO" at the top of the

```
left column and "AUDIO" at the top

of the right column.
```

Reminders

Generally, the same rules apply to television format as to radio format. Do not split words between lines. Do not split sentences or paragraphs between pages. Put pronunciation guides in parentheses after difficult words or pencil them in later above the word. Set off "not" with dots. Underline words to be emphasized. Put wavy lines under tricky words. Type only one story to a page. Put "MORE" at the bottom of the page and "FIRST ADD" after the slug on the next page when a story runs more than one page. Use "#" to indicate the end of the story.

If your script is to be used on a teleprompter, the format may be different. It depends upon the teleprompter used. For some, the pages of the script must be taped together in one continuous strip. If your studio uses that type of teleprompter, ignore the rules about splitting sentences and paragraphs between pages.

SUMMARY

A great many script formats are used in broadcasting. Certain rules are applicable to all broadcast writing. For example, it is not good policy to split words between lines or sentences between pages for any material that is to be read aloud (as opposed to memorized).

The five basic formats are television film format, live television format, radio drama format, television news format, and radio news format.

Television film format breaks the script into acts, scenes, and shots, which are sometimes numbered. It provides a description of the key camera shots to be used. Transitions are specified. The setting is briefly described. Music and sound-effect cues are indicated. Dialog and stage directions are typed in several different styles.

Live television format splits the script page into an audio column and a video column. All dialog, sound-effect cues, and stage directions go in the audio column; transitions and camera directions go in the video column.

For radio drama format, names of characters delivering lines and music and sound-effect cues usually go at the left margin, with dialog indented.

Broadcast news scripts are designed to permit easy modification and a rapid way to estimate reading time. Margin settings are specified according to reading speeds and size of type on the typewriter. Stories are written one to a page. Each story has a slug at the top of each page to identify it. Fill copy is provided for recorded material in scripts. Material not to be read on the air is usually circled. For radio news format, cues and data about audio inserts must be included in stories. Television news format uses a split page with cues on the left and news copy on the right side of the page.

Despite the lack of uniformity in script formats, you should find that you can adapt easily to the form you need if you spend a little time learning these basic formats.

TELEVISION DRAMA 3

Television drama comes in many forms. Some television dramas are made-for-television motion pictures. Some are parts of continuing dramatic series. Most adventure and mystery series are dramas, although an occasional comedy may slip into such a series.

As with any form of broadcast writing, your first job is to study those programs you may want to write for and learn their formats. For example, is this a half-hour, hour, 90-minute, or longer program? How is it structured? Is there a regular "teaser" at the opening? How much time is there between station identifications and commercial breaks? Is there usually a brief segment at the end in which loose ends are tied up, or does the denouement come almost at the last minute of the program? Is there time at the end of the program used to preview upcoming programs? Your best beginning is to sit down with a stopwatch and time several programs so that you get a good feeling for their time structures.

THEMES

Make a careful study of program themes. Some programs function essentially as anthologies, with little relationship among the programs used. However, most series have a fairly small list of the kinds of scripts they like to use. "Little House on the Prairie" is not "Lou Grant," and "The Waltons" is not "Family." Each series has particular themes it likes to deal with. Of course, any series may select an atypical theme from time to time. But the best bet for a writer who wants to sell a script is to stick with the kind of story a program usually uses.

Make yourself a list of the themes you know are regularly dealt with on a show. See if you can't find a pattern to them—this show likes stories that validate customary moral standards, that show likes stories that involve social activism. Try to decide which themes would *not* be welcome on the shows you are studying. A script that suggested sexual experimentation was a good thing for young people would probably not turn up on "Little House on the Prairie." A story suggesting that censorship and suppression of information are in the public interest would not be likely to turn up on "Lou Grant," although an *examination* of the censorship issue *is* a good topic for that show.

Eventually, you should be able to come up with a list for a show that indicates theme matter under three categories: "not likely to be used," "might be used," and "likely to be used." Obviously your best bet is to concentrate on material in the last category.

That decision will not be as easy as it appears. Most of the "likely to be used" themes will already have been used. You must come up with a new angle on a familiar theme. In a broad sense, that is what a broadcast writer must *always* do. You are not likely to come up with a theme that has *never* been used before on television. The medium is too voracious not to have tried anything that *can* be tried and that has a good chance of succeeding. Most of the themes that have not been used either deal with topics considered unsuitable for television or topics that have too little general appeal to draw an audience on a mass medium such as television. Few topics are still considered taboo if they are handled with good taste; however a good many topics have little audience appeal. Even a noncommercial station must give some thought to the number of people who will view a program. Your theme must have audience appeal.

Assume, then, that the theme you select is not likely to be entirely new. Your job is to take a familiar theme that fits the pattern of the show and treat it in a way that is fresh enough to hold an audience. Often the key is to develop interesting new characters.

CHARACTERS

An important distinction among programs is the use or nonuse of continuing characters. Most programs have a set of continuing characters. A few—"Fantasy Island" is an example—may have only one or two continuing characters. Some programs have no continuing characters and present a new cast and story in each episode. You need to understand this clearly. If continuing characters are used, *how* are they used? Do they simply provide a unifying theme for the show, with most of the action carried by new characters each week? Do the main characters in the series carry the action each time, or are the secondary continuing characters the ones who take turns carrying most of the action? For example, in "Quincy," most of the action centers on Quincy himself. In "Lou Grant," continuing characters such as Rossi often are the main characters in a story while Grant himself plays a less prominent role. In "Fantasy Island," Roarke and Tattoo serve mainly to tie the various stories together, usually taking only minor roles in the actual dramatic action.

If you intend to write for a program, you must understand how the various continuing characters are used in the stories. Again, there are always exceptions, but you are better off using the usual treatment a series reserves for its various continuing characters.

You also need to know *how* these characters have been portrayed. Because so much must be said in so little time, most television characters tend to be two-dimensional. In a drama, you usually have more time to develop characters because few dramas use a half-hour format. Moreover, in a well-produced series, the producers and script editors take advantage of the regular reappearance of some continuing characters to build up the traits associated with those characters. You need to understand those traits when you write for those characters. You should not have characters act in ways that are contrary to the image the audience has of them. Once in a while it is possible to have a character reversal in a script—a tightwad becomes a spendthrift, an ugly duckling becomes a sex symbol—but such changes are almost always temporary. The character must revert to "normal" by the end of the program. You cannot expect the producers to welcome a permanent change in the traits of a continuing character, which would present problems in the use of scripts that have not been aired and that show the "old" character. It causes headaches when the program goes into reruns, and it can give rise to more problems when the program is syndicated. Therefore, you had better learn to write for the character that has been developed. You must keep the character consistent.

Characters' Traits

Established writers can often obtain background material on major traits of various characters in a series from the producers. The Writers Guild also will provide material of this sort for some series. However, the beginning writer will gain much simply by watching the major continuing characters in a series and seeing how they are portrayed. This way you will learn not only the major traits of each character but also the techniques other writers have used to make those traits manifest.

Knowing those traits can also save you time. Rather than use precious time explaining these characteristics to the audience, you can simply include a few reminders and use the time you saved to develop interesting *consequences* of those characteristics.

Knowing your characters can also help you avoid writing action into the script that would be either out of character or difficult for the actor playing the part to perform. Suppose, for example, you wanted to write a "Lou Grant" script in which the character Animal turns out to have studied ballet as a young man and demonstrates his skills by giving an impromptu performance in the city room. Your first problem is that Animal hardly seems like the ballet-dancing type. But you *might* be able to pull it off as something never before mentioned about the character. It is not out of the question that someone who wants to be a photographer might also have an interest in the visual and compositional aspects of ballet, just as an athlete might study ballet to develop movement and coordination. The greater objection to using this theme in a script is that you have no way of knowing whether the actor who plays Animal could dance well enough to make the story convincing. Not every actor can perform every role. The more specialized the action you call for—dancing, singing, and so forth—the greater the probability that the actor you are writing for will have problems with the material.

Even if you know the actor in question has the particular skills you intend to write about, there is no guarantee that the producers will want to involve the program in the additional production work required—especially if the action seems only vaguely related to the known traits of the character. Certainly there are ways of faking action when necessary. But first you have to convince the producers it *is* necessary. And scenes that have to be faked always push the credulity of the audience to its limits. The scene in which the ingenue plops down at the piano and dashes off a Chopin etude that would tax Artur Rubinstein may have worked in 1930s movies, but it's not likely to convince many members of the audience today.

Adding New Characters

Writing in new characters with special talents is also unwise. New characters create problems in casting and production—problems the producers would probably rather avoid. Adding a new character is the kind of idea that is more likely to develop from a conversation between people connected with the show than from a story idea from a writer who is not regularly associated with the show. Therefore, when the producer of a series buys an episode introducing a new character, it is most often from one of the show's regular writers or staff members.

SETS

Another element you should pay careful attention to in any program you would like to write for is the program's sets. Two things must be kept in mind here. First, how many sets are regularly used in the program? Each set and each scene shot on location adds to the complexity and costs of production. Some programs make use of a large number of sets and locations, but most stick to a few regularly used sets plus one or two sets specially built for the show. If all action can take place on the regularly used sets, so much the better. Note that some programs work almost entirely with sets and avoid location shooting. Others use a mixture of both. There are budgetary and production reasons for decisions of this sort, and you should tailor your script to conform to these decisions.

Before you call for a set or location not regularly used on a show, give some careful thought to the production problems this may introduce. Of course, sticking to just one or two sets can be dull visually, but introducing new locations just for the sake of variety is not likely to help sell your script. Remember that most television pictures are medium shots and close-ups. In about 80 percent of the shots, you cannot tell if your characters are at the Fountain of Trevi or the city waterworks.

Whatever sets you *do* use, have them well pictured in your mind. It's not a bad idea to make a sketch of the floor plan of each set. Whenever you describe action for your characters, think about where they have to move on the set. Of course, it is the director's job to block out action and camera movement. But you must be careful that your script doesn't demand difficult or impossible action. This is particularly important if the action takes place on a regularly used set in a series because only minor changes can be made in such sets to accommodate action. Suppose you have your heroine look up from the desk where she is working and see a menacing face at the window. The only window on the set had better not be in back of her. Always keep the set in mind when writing.

Location Costs

"Star Trek" writer David Gerrold says that the first script idea he submitted to that program was rejected with the notation that it was a good idea for a $3 million movie but that its production requirements were far too expensive for television.[1] There is a lesson to be learned here. You must know something about the budget the program you are interested in has. You can afford more expensive ideas for some programs than for others. In almost any case, producers look most kindly on a script that is relatively inexpensive to produce.

All this means that any writer for broadcasting has to have a good insight into the basic techniques of production and some concept of the relative costs of those techniques. Once a script has been purchased, decisions about which techniques to use lie with the producer and the director. But they will not be likely to buy a script that presents production problems or requires expensive techniques to start with.

Let's take an example. Suppose your script calls for the hero to be chased through the Piazza San Marco in Venice by a would-be assassin. The producer has a number of alternatives, all involving tradeoffs between cost and visual effect. The scene could be shot on location—expensive. Backgrounds could be shot in Venice and the action performed in a studio.

[1]David Gerrold, *The Trouble With Tribbles* (New York: Ballantine, 1973), p. 25.

Backgrounds could be added by Chromakey if the show is done on tape. If done on film, the scene could be done as a process shot with the backgrounds added optically in the printing, or the scene could be shot on a set using rear projection for the background. Or, for either film or tape, a set could be built. (Some elements of a set would be needed for any technique except location shooting.) Possibly a San Marco set, left over from a previous production, might be found on a back lot somewhere in Hollywood. But you could save the producer money and headaches by having the action somewhere else—in a hotel corridor in Venice, for example. A few stock shots of Venice could be used to establish the location. Or better yet, if the series is being produced in Hollywood, why not find a location in the Los Angeles area instead of Venice? Or choose a locale that can easily be faked near the studio? Much of "Fantasy Island," for example, is shot in the Los Angeles County Arboretum. In most cases, the cheapest and easiest way to produce a program is to shoot it in a studio. So if you can limit your script to locations easily shot on studio sets, you will probably be making your script more salable.

PRODUCTION TECHNIQUES

Understanding production techniques is extremely important. For example, almost no dramatic programs on commercial television today are shot "live." They are either on film or on tape, with the number of taped shows increasing and the number of filmed shows decreasing. Nevertheless, if you are preparing a script for a college video production or a noncommercial station, you may have to plan on a live production.

Live Production

Shooting a "live" show places many limitations on the locations you can use and the action you can portray. Every action you call for has to be put in the context of both the layout of the set and the movement of the cameras. The tendency is for scenes to be static because every physical movement by a character introduces problems. It also stands to reason that most exteriors or scenes in known locations will present problems. Moving characters between sets at scene changes is a major problem, which must be thought out carefully in advance. In short, the "live" show is the most demanding for the writer.

Here is another example. Suppose you want to have a love scene. You could set it on a park bench. That's easy enough to set up with proper lighting and a little scenery. A beach scene would be much harder to set up. A scene on the living-room couch would be easiest of all—if you've ever wondered why that is such a popular spot for romance on television.

Suppose you want to shift the scene to the same couple meeting the next day in an office. You have set yourself an almost impossible transition for live television drama. You must have a completely different set, with different lighting and audio requirements, and you must somehow get each of the two characters onto that set. Each character will have to come in *after* the scene opens to allow them time to move from one set to the other. You also have to allow time for the actors to make at least minor costume changes, since this is presumably the next day. Unless there is an intermission in the show, making such a scene shift is highly impractical. You should restructure your script to avoid the scene change and the problems it creates.

Tape Production

In writing for commercial television—and most noncommercial television as well—you are not likely to face all the problems cited above because you will almost certainly be writing for videotape or film. *Some* of the problems of live television production do crop up in videotaped productions. Videotaped shows are virtually always multicamera shows. They are shot in long takes; frequently an entire scene is shot without a break. Pickup shots are usually done later to replace flubbed lines or insert close-ups where it was not possible to get them in the first shooting. The final product is assembled by the videotape editor under the supervision of the director or assistant director (and sometimes the producer). The transition problem of "live" shows is not a problem here because there is almost always a break between the shooting of separate scenes.

Nevertheless, the writer must think about the action *within* each scene. Are there movements that will be difficult for the actors or difficult to follow with the camera? Are there special shots required that will be hard to get? Video cameras are bulky and hard to move around. Do you really need that low-angle shot? Is the overhead shot so essential to the story that the producers will spend the money to rent a crane for that one shot? Where will the microphone go on that wide shot?

Sure, these are all basically problems for the director, but *you* created them, and scripts that cause *too* many problems are not likely to be bought. Moreover, creating problems of this sort indicates to the producers that *you* don't understand the medium for which you are writing.

Film Production

Programs shot on film give you the greatest freedom in writing. Film equipment remains more portable than video equipment, although the gap between the two is narrowing. Film programs are customarily made one shot at a time. Usually only one camera is used. Lighting, makeup, and microphones can be checked and changed as needed before each shot. Poorly done shots can be reshot until they are right. You have much greater freedom in the camera shots you want, the kind of lighting you want, and the locations you want to shoot. Even with film, however, you must understand the medium in order to write for it. Television films are usually shot on relatively low budgets and in short periods of time. That means that you still cannot write in material that will be expensive or time-consuming to shoot. To save time, some filmed shows are shot with more than one camera, using techniques similar to those of videotaped shows. For these programs, the restrictions on the writer are much the same as those for videotaped shows.

STUDIO AUDIENCE

A final consideration for the writer is whether the program is to be produced on a closed set or before a live audience. Relatively few dramatic programs are done before an audience. This is an advantage, since work can proceed faster and with greater freedom on a closed set. An audience limits camera movements, restricts the shots that can be used, and sometimes creates audio problems. Programs to be produced before an audience must use the simplest production techniques. In many ways, they run perilously close to being stage plays. You will very likely be limited to one or two sets. There may be minimal opportunity for costume changes. Lines and action must be such that the performers can memorize them quickly. Action needs to be kept limited.

Balancing these disadvantages is the kind of spontaneity that pervades performances before a live audience. The performers' timing can be greatly helped by the responses of the audience. For the writer, however, the presence of an audience is likely to be more of a hindrance than an advantage.

STORY TREATMENTS

Writers do not usually send complete scripts to a producer in the hope of selling them. The producer hasn't the time to read them, and the writer cannot waste time on scripts that may not sell. Sometimes a producer may wish to look at a couple of scripts from a new writer to see how well the writer handles material, but the first step in most script sales is the submission of one or more treatments—basic script themes. A well-known writer may have to submit only a story idea, and writers often submit several ideas for additional scripts along with one or more story treatments.

Essentially, two kinds of story treatments are involved. First the writer submits a brief treatment or story idea to the producer. If the producer likes the idea for the story, he or she then hires the writer to write a detailed treatment of the script. (The writer is paid Writers Guild scale for this complete story treatment.) The beginning writer should put every bit as much effort into the story idea submitted to the producer as into the treatment the producer pays for. The beginner cannot afford to submit just an idea or a sketch as an established writer might do. The beginner is an unknown quantity. The first treatment is one way the writer has of convincing a producer that the writer has both a good story and the talent to turn it into a good script.

If you are hired to write a treatment, the producer or the story editor almost always suggests additions to or changes in the original idea. The writer may also be sent some earlier scripts from the series to study as a guide to dialog or traits of important characters. Changes related to the program's mode of production also may be requested.

Pay attention to the producer's comments. They may not please you, but you must comply with them if you wish to sell the script. Begin from scratch by incorporating the producer's suggestions into the basic plot. The end result may be different from your original concept, but it must be just as carefully plotted and written. Remember, you still haven't sold the producer the script.

A treatment should run about ten pages. It outlines the general plot and treats important scenes in detail. Do not take the word "outline" too literally. The treatment should read more like a short story. Pick out two or three key scenes in your plot—probably the denouement will be one. Describe each scene in detail, giving some of the important dialog. Begin with clear descriptions of the major characters and the sets on which the key scenes are played. Use the dialog both to make key points in the plot and to help delineate characters. The dialog and the descriptive material help sell the story by giving the producer an idea of what the story will look and sound like, so paint a verbal picture. Link the scenes together with a good strong narrative.

Go over the completed treatment and see how it reads. It must read as smoothly as a short story. It must leave the reader with a picture of each important character and each major scene. You should be able to "hear" the dialog as you read it. Above all, the treatment should hold the reader's attention from start to finish.

In some ways, the treatment is harder to write than the script because you must express more in less time. But, the effort you put into turning out a good treatment is worthwhile. If the producer is happy with the story treatment, he or she will hire you to write a complete script of the story. And preparing a good treatment will not only improve your chances of selling the script, it will also provide the basic structure and some of the actual content for your completed script.

The Plot

The key to a good treatment (and a good script) is a well-constructed plot. There is a literary term, borrowed from the French, *piéce bien fait*, "the well-made play." The implications are slightly derogatory—a plot and action crafted to a formula that has been shown to be successful in previous plays. In an era when kindergarten finger painting is considered "creative," the ultimate sin in writing is often thought to be being "slick." If the opposite of "slick" is true originality, fine; too often, however, not being "slick" simply means being sloppy. Sloppy treatments do not sell.

Before you begin your treatment, have the basic plot of your script carefully thought out and written down. In a sense, most television dramas do follow a formula. It is this: The main character or characters must progress through a *series* of problems that block the way to solving the main problem of the story. In a murder mystery, for example, the main problem is to discover who committed the crime. But in the solving of *that* problem, the main characters are threatened and faced with other crises to deal with every step of the way. The tension builds from crisis to crisis until the denouement. In the same way, a drama progresses from problem to problem while working toward the solution of the major problem presented. In drama, the plot may be a tragedy, with the major problem *not* solved or solved in an unsatisfactory way for the main character. Tragedy, however, is not a major component of television drama. The television audience usually prefers to see the big problems solved at the end of the show. In a series with continuing characters, things pretty well *have to* be back to normal at the end of each episode. You certainly cannot have the main character die at the end of your script, nor can you do much else of a permanent nature to a character unless the producers have decided to write a character change into the series.

Even when a script deals with real tragedy—usually in an anthology series or with a minor character in a series with continuing characters—the idea is to find something that transcends the tragedy in the end: The family of a dead child learns to pick up the pieces and go on, the paraplegic learns that even in a wheelchair, life goes on. Rarely does a television drama end on a bleak note such as Dreiser's *Sister Carrie*, "Know, then, that for you is neither surfeit nor content. In your rocking chair, by your window dreaming, shall you long, alone."[2]

Basically, most drama in Western societies validates the values of those societies. Good is ultimately rewarded and evil finally punished. From the Greeks we take the idea that the character who comes to a tragic end has somehow brought that fate upon himself, usually through hubris—excessive pride. From the Old Testament we take the concept of life as a series of tests put before us to be overcome through adherence to moral law. These strains of thought push us strongly toward plots that end with either good defeating evil or the hero refusing to be broken by misfortune. Modern writers sometimes portray their characters as victims of the social system, and such stories may end with the main characters defeated by the system; here, too, the usual theme is the hero beating the system or motivating others to work to change the system. Almost never do we see on television an existential drama in which rewards and punishments are dealt out by blind fate for no reason at all. This goes too far from our basic concept of what constitutes a story. In the end, we expect a story to have some meaning, some message. A story about a man who works in a pickle factory and is one day accidentally killed when he slips and falls in front of a bus may be true to life, but it's not likely to sell.

In the final analysis, most dramas follow the pattern outlined at the start—a series of problems to be solved by the hero or heroine en route to solving a major problem. Ideally, each problem should seem more difficult than the one that went before. Each should seem to put the main characters farther from the solution of the major problem. The tension must build. Then, in the final minutes of the drama, the crisis is reached and resolved. The trick is

---

[2]Theodore Dreiser, *Sister Carrie* (New York: Modern Library, 1900), p. 557.

to make all this seem natural. The final problem must seem insurmountable, yet the hero must deal with it in a way that seems perfectly logical in view of all that has gone before in the story.

In his television film "The $5.20 an Hour Dream," Robert E. Thompson describes the struggle of a woman working in a factory who wants to move into one of the higher-paying jobs held exclusively by men. The villain in the film is the system—social traditions that relegate women to certain kinds of work, most of them low paid. Ellen, the heroine, must get *and hold* an assembly-line job no woman has ever held before. The major problem to be solved in this story is not getting the job but holding it. The writer makes the obstacles thrown in the heroine's path more numerous by choosing not to end the script with the woman winning the job. Instead, he concentrates on her problems in winning acceptance from the men on the assembly line, from the union, and from her employer. Complicating her problems at the factory are her problems at home as a divorcée trying to raise a daughter and work out her relationship with a younger man who provides her with male companionship if not much understanding.

The writer skillfully weaves all these problems into the plot. They are all real problems that someone in the heroine's position might face. Yet, taken together, they provide an enormous amount of conflict for a two-hour script. The trick the author uses is not the number of problems Ellen has to solve but the compressed time span in which the problems are dealt with—plus the fact that Ellen *does* deal with them, while in real life many of the problems would probably go unsolved.

We'll come back to the final script later. Here let's examine the basic elements. The writer opens the story by immediately introducing a problem that remains unsolved until the end of the program: Ellen's car is being held by a garage mechanic because she hasn't enough money to pay for the repairs that had to be made on it. This problem resurfaces several times in the story. At the end Ellen finally has earned the money to get her car back. In a sense, this is the problem around which the story is constructed. But it is not really the main problem Ellen must solve. Instead, it serves as a convenient symbol. Ellen's basic problem is too little money, and that in turn is the result of the *real* problem she must overcome—prejudice against her as a woman.

Next we find that Ellen's boy friend, Randy (aptly named), is not pleased with the problems of dating a woman with a daughter who always seems to be in the way. Then we find that Ellen's daughter, Kim, has taken up with friends Ellen does not approve of at the trailer court where they live.

We also learn that Ellen's ex-husband lies to Kim about gifts he wants her to think he has sent her. He is remarried now, and his new wife is pregnant. He says he cannot pay his back alimony, and the court offers no help to Ellen in getting anything from him.

Ellen makes her first pitch for a job on the all-male assembly line. Then we see Ellen and Randy on a date at a cheap joint. Randy clearly thinks there should be a quid pro quo for the money he spent on the date. Back at the trailer camp, Kim interferes and causes a fight between Randy and Ellen. Then Kim accuses Ellen of selling herself to Randy for money.

In Act 2, Ellen makes her pitch for the assembly-line job, and we meet Albert Kleinschmidt, the foreman of the assembly line. Ellen finds that the union refuses to back her request for the job. Ellen's stepbrother, who holds an administrative job at the factory, refuses to help her get the assembly-line job and advises her to find a new husband to support her. Ellen goes directly to management at the plant, where her hints of a civil rights suit win her a probationary transfer to the assembly line.

In Act 3, Kleinschmidt helps Ellen learn to operate the equipment. The men tease Randy about Ellen's job. The men on the line begin to give Ellen some grudging support, but one of them, Turkel, insists that the company plans to replace all the men on the line with women, at lower pay. Turkel sabotages Ellen's equipment. Kleinschmidt refuses to report the incident to management, and we learn that the plant management is looking for excuses to fire Ellen from the assembly-line job.

In Act 4, another assembly-line worker convinces a slow-witted workman, Bobby Jim, that Ellen is available for a price. Management has put a time-and-motion checker on the line to find excuses for getting rid of Ellen. This angers all the men on the line, but Turkel grouses, "They wouldn't be trying to get away with this stuff if it wasn't for you." Randy and Ellen have a fight over her job.

In Act 5, Kim finds she cannot attend a gymnastic contest without a male sponsor. When Kim's father refuses to take her, Ellen has to ask Randy. Randy agrees to sponsor Kim, but he makes clear what he expects from Ellen in return. At the contest, other youngsters tease Kim about her mother. There is a fight, and Kim is seriously injured. At the hospital, Randy blames Ellen and orders her to quit her job. She refuses, and they break up.

In Act 6, Bobby Jim, egged on by another workman, comes close to raping Ellen. They struggle and equipment is knocked over, halting the assembly line. Ellen refuses to tell the plant supervisor who caused the trouble. This wins the grudging admiration of the men on the line. Ellen is transferred to the swing shift. She learns she is to be tested on the different kinds of equipment on the line and will be fired if she fails. She rejects a chance to return to her old job.

In Act 7, we reach the major crisis of the story. Ellen is tested on the various machines. She does poorly, but is now defended by the other workers on the line. The supervisor refuses to allow Ellen to stand on a stool to reach some equipment, and the union shop steward refuses to come to her aid. Kleinschmidt then uses a ruse to show Ellen how she can handle the equipment without the stool. Ellen succeeds, but in the confusion she lets the assembly line get ahead of her and cannot complete the job. At this point, the men on the line sabotage the assembly line. Faced with the threat of a wildcat strike, the management men allow Ellen to keep her job on the line. In the final scenes, Ellen redeems her car from the auto mechanic, then gives encouragement to another woman who wants to try for a job on the assembly line.

Look over the plot, and you will see that Ellen has two or three problems to deal with in each of the first six acts. (The various "acts" simply indicate action taking place between commercial breaks.) In the seventh act she has to face a series of interrelated problems, culminating in her final victory. As the show progresses, the problems come closer together and become more serious in nature. The writer has compressed the action to the span of about one week, and we, of course, see it in about an hour and forty minutes, not counting commercials. Commercial breaks are one of the facts of life in writing for television. A good writer accepts them and tries to use them as logical breaks in the action instead of unwanted interruptions.

Writer Robert Thompson broke the action of the story into logical blocks of plot. Act 1 shows us Ellen before her assembly-line job. She is losing in every battle she has to fight. This helps us understand her powerful motivation to get the job and the added money it means. Act 2 sees Ellen rebuffed by everyone she approaches, but eventually her persistence pays off as she gets the job. In Act 3 Ellen survives her first day on the job and the sabotage of her equipment. We learn management is out to get her. In Act 4, the management representatives openly begin to monitor her work, and Bobby Jim is tricked into believing he can buy Ellen's sexual favors. In Act 5, resentment against Ellen leads to Kim's injury and the breakup of Ellen's relationship with Randy. In Act 6, Ellen is nearly raped by Bobby Jim, and she learns she is to be tested on her ability to operate all the machines on the assembly line. Act 7 shows Ellen surviving the tests on the equipment with the help of the other assembly-line workers, who have gradually been won over to her side.

Each act, or period between commercial breaks, makes a logical unit in itself. We never feel that the commercial has intruded on major action. On the other hand, the writer ends each act in a way that makes the viewer want to see what is going to happen next—after the commercial. At the end of Act 1, we are left wondering how Ellen will get the job. At the end of Act 2 we wonder how she will do when she starts the job. At the end of Act 3 we wonder how she will cope with the management plot against her. At the end of Act 4 we are left wondering when Bobby Jim will make his move against Ellen. Only at the end of Act 5 are we left with no specific hints about what may come next. Act 6 leaves us waiting to see how Ellen will deal with the test management has set up for her.

THE TELEVISION SCRIPT

Planning Your Script

When you begin sketching out the plot of your script, you should look again at the format of the show. How many acts will you have, and approximately how long will each be? Once you know this, you can begin outlining each act. First decide what is the major problem to be solved by the main characters and how that problem is to be solved. That most certainly will be your last act—although in some programs there may be a short "tag" after the last commercial that ties up loose ends. This is a frequently used technique in mystery programs.

List all the problems related to the major problem that the main characters will face in trying to solve the major problem. In "The $5.20 an Hour

Dream," Ellen's major problem was to get and keep a job on the assembly line. The related problems involved the effects on her daughter, the effects on her romance, the hostility of men on the line, and the hostility of management. Each problem was expanded to provide several crises. Use the same technique in planning your script.

Once you have compiled a list of problems that reasonably could arise, begin to arrange your plot so that each act presents a problem to be dealt with. Try to arrange it so that the more serious problems come near the end of the story and so that the frequency of the problems increases as the plot progresses. Then see if you can find logical ways to show at the end of each act what is coming in the next act. Sketch in a story line around these elements so that each act stands as a unit by itself. A problem has been faced, and the next problem has been introduced—to be dealt with in the next act.

With this much done, you are ready to submit a brief treatment of your story idea to a producer (or have your agent talk to a producer about it). If the producer then makes a contract with you for a full treatment of the story, you already have much of your work done.

Writing Your Script

If the producer decides to go ahead with your story, the expanded treatment will probably be returned with additional comments and suggestions. There probably will be conferences with the producer. There will be changes. There are *always* changes. It is important now to reach an agreement with the producer about the basic plot. Once the contract is signed, you are required to produce a script and, if requested, one rewrite. You can save a lot of time if you are certain of the basic story line before you begin writing.

No two writers follow exactly the same procedure, but you can work efficiently if you use essentially the same procedure used for the treatment in preparing the script. Decide what action is going to take place in each scene. Then begin to sketch in your dialog and action. The key scenes are usually the first and last ones. The first scene sets up the basic problem the story deals with and introduces the main characters; the last scene usually involves the solution of the problem that is the basis of the story.

Some writers believe that by the end of the first few minutes of a program, the audience should know basically what is going to happen in the rest of the program. You do not have to follow this rule, but certainly *foreshadowing*, the introduction of material that suggests to the audience what will happen later in the story, is a useful dramatic technique. Good writers do not waste time establishing the basic problem of a story in television writing. "The $5.20 an Hour Dream" opens with the garage mechanic presenting Ellen with the bill for the repair of her car. Ellen's first line (the second line of the script) is:

```
I know . . . but I just don't have that much --

but I will this afternoon.  See I'm going to court
```

```
and I'm going to get some back child support money

from my ex-husband.
```

There is no beating around the bush here. The author has told us at the outset that Ellen Lissik hasn't enough money to pay a $97.54 repair bill, that she's divorced, that she has a child to take care of, and that her husband is not meeting his child support payments. You couldn't get much more information into five lines of dialog.

Michele Gallery, in her "Lou Grant" script *Dying*, uses another technique of foreshadowing. The story deals with *Tribune* staffer Art Donovan coming to grips with the fact that his mother is dying of leukemia. The writer uses the story to examine different approaches to death and dying. Peggy Donovan's illness is only hinted at in the opening scene. Peggy tries to persuade the nurses to give a pain-killing shot to another patient. The nurses insist on following the instructions left by the doctor, and Peggy explodes:

```
Cut all the procedural crap.  I was a nurse when

your mother was in high school.  The man is dying,

so it's not like you're going to turn him into a

dope addict by giving him his shot two hours early.
```

Here again, dialog in the first few minutes of the show establishes the theme, although somewhat less clearly. The problem to be solved is how to come to grips with dying. We also know that Peggy is not young, that she understands medical problems because she was a nurse, and that she doesn't think the dying should suffer just to observe hospital rules. Because she is a patient, we may also guess that Peggy may have to come to grips with the problem of dying herself. In still another "Lou Grant" script, *Prisoner*, by Seth Freeman, the opening scene is a prison in which Charlie Hume of the *Tribune* is held. Hume is led to a gallows, then awakes, and we find the opening sequence has been a dream. Again, however, the viewers are given a clue as to what is to come. The program deals with human rights violations in a mythical Latin American republic, and we eventually learn that Charlie Hume was once held prisoner in a jail there.

What you plan for the first scene of your script, then, is all-important. It can foreshadow what is to come. It *must* hold the audience. One reason that foreshadowing is particularly useful in a television script is that the audience often uses those first few minutes of a program to decide whether to remain with it or switch to another channel. Giving the audience a hint of what is coming can help people make up their minds.

The final scene, of course, is the other crucial scene in a program. For this reason, many writers like to write this scene first. If all the elements are there, it is easier to decide where to plant the events that lead up to the denouement in earlier parts of the script. Some writers do the last scene, then the first, then construct a "bridge" between them. The last scene has to make sense. Take the crucial last moments in "The $5.20 an Hour Dream," in which Ellen has managed to move the heavy equipment without standing on a stool. Then at the moment of triumph, victory seems about to be snatched away. The assembly line is moving too fast for her to complete the work. Suddenly a fellow worker sabotages the assembly line and stops it dead. In a sense, this is a *deus ex machina* solution. We don't expect people to go around sabotaging assembly lines every day of the year. But the writer has carefully prepared us for that by planting two other stoppages of the line earlier in the script—once when Ellen's equipment is sabotaged and later when equipment falls into the machinery accidentally while she struggles with Bobby Jim. Dialog also suggests that management is not unfamiliar with sabotage on this particular assembly line. So, an unlikely solution has been made to seem likely.

The whole scene is a beautiful example of building to the final climax. It begins with Ellen facing a test she seems to have no chance of passing. Each time she squeaks by one part of the test, she is faced with an even more impossible one to pass. Even after the final test, the writer insists on one more, bigger crisis. The scene plays because the audience has been prepared for everything that happens by the earlier scenes.

In other scripts, the denouement requires less preparation. In Michele Gallery's "Lou Grant" script *Dying*, it is obvious from the time we learn she has leukemia that Peggy Donovan will die. The real question is how Donovan himself will take the death. Throughout the script, the writer has provided scenes that show Donovan first refusing to accept that his mother is dying, then gradually coming to terms with reality. In the final moments of the show, in the *Tribune* city room, Rossi asks Donovan how his mother is, and Donovan replies:

DONOVAN

Mother died Tuesday.

ROSSI

(STUNNED AND VERY EMBARRASSED)   Oh, no.   Please,

I never dreamed --

DONOVAN

It's okay.   Rossi.   Really.   The last month was

very tough, but very . . . (WANTING THE RIGHT WORD)

full.

LOU

Are you okay?

```
                    DONOVAN

    I'm fine.  Still very sad, but yeah.  I'm okay.

    I'd like to tell you about it later.

Lou nods, the phone at their desks rings.  Lou starts
to answer it.

                    DONOVAN (CONT'D)

    I got it.  (ANSWERING)  City desk.  Donovan.



Everyone picks up Donovan's cue, and Billie, Rossi and
Lou return to their desks.  Billie, however, makes sure
to go the long way around, so she can put a hand on
Donovan's shoulder, as we

                                            FADE OUT
```

Here the writer has opted not to give us a deathbed scene, a type of scene that has become something of a cliché. The point of the story is that death should not be overdramatized, and the writer makes that point by underplaying the death itself. In the previous scene we had seen Donovan with his mother, obviously coming to terms with the acceptance of her death. In the final scene we are assured that he has learned to deal with the problem. It is a simple and satisfying end to the program.

Subplots

Not all plots follow the simple development of a single idea. "Lou Grant" shows usually have one or more subplots that are indirectly related to the main theme. For example, in *Prisoner*, several story lines converge on the major theme of publicizing human rights violations in friendly countries. The script deftly cuts back and forth from Rossi and Billie tracking down the supporters and opponents of dictator Baroja of the mythical state of Malagua. Interspersed are scenes with Animal conducting man-on-the-street interviews. The writer uses this as comic counterpoint to emphasize the lack of knowledge of and interest in foreign affairs on the part of the general public. All these scenes play against the struggle at the *Tribune* to reach a decision about publishing an exposé of the Baroja regime. The writer sets out the major obstacle to be overcome early in the script by establishing that the *Tribune's* publisher, Mrs. Pynchon, is a personal friend of Señora Baroja. Señora Baroja is visiting Los Angeles, making it more difficult for Mrs. Pynchon to approve running the exposé. The decision to run the story does not end the script. The writer follows it with a confrontation between Señora Baroja and anti-Baroja protestors, one of whom turns out to be a member of her own family. The final scenes give us Señora Baroja's departure and the staff mulling over her farewell statements, trying to decide if they imply a change for the better in Malagua. The closing scene is Animal, pursuing his man-on-the-street story, now asking about nude sunbathing.

Obviously such a plot line does not fit the simple formula we suggested earlier. As is the case with many "Lou Grant" scripts, the writer is more concerned with developing ideas than with telling a simple story. When we first approached the writer, Seth Freeman, about using some "Lou Grant" scripts in this book, he was somewhat skeptical. When we said we were looking for examples of foreshadowing, advancing plot through dialog, and similar dramatic techniques, Freeman said something to the effect that "I don't pay much attention to things like that."

Obviously he does not have to. A skilled professional writer does not write from a set of textbook rules. He writes what years of experience have taught him works. But a beginner has to start somewhere. You need to learn some rules before you find out which rules you can do without.

In *Prisoner*, despite the skipping about from subplot to subplot, all the action builds toward the major question of whether to run the story or not. Each subplot contributes to the story. Rossi discovers that the pro-Baroja demonstrators are actually members of the Malaguan military. Billie learns more about human rights abuses in Malagua from the anti-Baroja demonstrators. Hume, whose nightmare opens the program, risks his career by denouncing the Baroja regime to Señora Baroja at a party given by Mrs. Pynchon. He writes his exposé of the regime, makes the final decision to publish it, and submits his resignation to Mrs. Pynchon—who, of course, refuses it.

The story does build from crisis to crisis. It does reach a final resolution of the problem set out. What makes the script harder to analyze—and perhaps more interesting—is that the crises are not all faced by the same character. In a sense, the major protagonist is Hume. Both the decision to write the exposé and the decision to publish it are his. But Grant, Rossi, Billie, Mrs. Pynchon, and Animal all contribute. Because there is no single character with whom the viewer can identify throughout the story, there may be less emotional involvement in a script of this nature. On the other hand, the lowered emotional involvement may make it easier to concentrate on the issues in a script of this sort.

Multiplots

Yet another type of plot is found in the "Fantasy Island" series. Here, two separate stories are intercut, sometimes interrelated by a basic theme such as "beauty is only skin deep." "Love Boat" is another series that intercuts two or more stories. If you analyze plots of this nature, you will usually find that the individual stories told have relatively straightforward plots, following the general rules we have outlined. The trick in scripts of this nature is when and how to make the necessary cuts from one story to the other. Usually the same rules that apply to the placement of commercial breaks will do for a cut from one story to another. But the segments must necessarily be shorter. The viewer must not lose track of the action in any of the plots. It is not unusual in these scripts to have some character or other review some of the action that has gone before to remind the audience of what has happened. This is not a bad idea in any script, since there are *always* people who tune in late or who were not paying attention at crucial moments.

Character Development

Development of character is as important to your script as development of plot. In some scripts, characters almost *are* the plot. In the "Lou Grant" script *Dying*, the entire plot depends upon the characteristics of the major characters, Peggy and Art Donovan. We need to understand them and how they think in order for the story to make sense. Drama, after all, is usually a matter of how someone comes to deal with a series of interrelated problems. *What kind* of person a character is determines how that person deals with his or her problems. If Peggy Donovan had been presented as a possessive mother, we would have had a different reaction to her impending death, and probably a different set of interrelated problems. Had she been portrayed as an indifferent mother who had little interest in her family, we would have yet another story. In the same way, the story would be different if Art Donovan had been portrayed as dependent, rebellious, jealous, or any of a dozen other ways.

What kind of person each character is must emerge from the action and dialog of your script. In television, there is precious little time to do this with subtlety. Drama does have some advantages over comedy here because most television dramas are at least an hour long, while comedies tend to be half-hour programs. You have a bit more time to develop your major characters.

You also have the advantage in some programs of having continuing characters. In the "Lou Grant" series, Grant, Rossi, Billie, Donovan, Hume, Animal, and Mrs. Pynchon are all continuing characters. The audience already knows some of their major traits.

Even for a series with continuing characters, each show is a new ballgame. There will always be new members of the audience, as well as old ones who somehow missed out learning the particular characteristics of a given role. So, to some degree, you must reestablish basic character traits in each script. At the same time, as has been pointed out earlier, you must not alter the traits established for that character in previous scripts.

What are some techniques writers use to establish character traits quickly for the audience? They can begin with the name. You need not lie awake nights brooding about it, but you should give some thought to the name you give your new characters. How about "Lou Grant"? Would "Louis Grant" conjure up the same image? How about "Lou Gruber"? Not the same man, is it? Do we need to ponder much over a character named "Animal"? Even the naming of a country can have implications. How about "Malagua"?

Sounds rather sinister, doesn't it? It's worse if you know enough Spanish to know that it means "jellyfish" in some parts of the Spanish-speaking world, or just "bad water" if you break it into two words. And it sounds suspiciously like a combination of Nicaragua and its capital city of Managua, where the dictatorship of the Somoza family was being overthrown at the time the script was written. In "The $5.20 an Hour Dream," Robert Thompson gave his main character the name Ellen, an ordinary, not very exciting name. Her last name is Lissik, which sounds foreign, an immigrant name, and in America we tend to associate immigrants with lower-paying industrial jobs—which fits Ellen to a T.

In Act 3, Thompson names the workers on the assembly line where Ellen works and gives a brief description of each. See how well the names and descriptions go together:

```
HOMER BURDEN,         a strapping 30-year-old black
                      who has the most physically
                      demanding job

HARVEY TURKEL,        a raw-boned hillbilly

JERRY "SQUAT" AIKEN,  a cherubic, just slightly
                      mean-spirited type

JIVE,                 a black whose solemn, almost
                      remote manner belies his
                      sarcastically given name

BILLYBOY,             a thin, bearded, anemic-
                      looking 25-year-old
```

Here we see the writer using the name as a means of helping to give the audience clues about the character, and also using the second of the writer's tools—the physical description. While many writers no doubt choose names without any conscious intent, it is interesting to note that most writers give full names to all their major characters—even when those names are never heard by the audience. Thompson, for example, gives Ellen's stepbrother the name "Harry Oblatt," but the name is never used in dialog in the script. Still, knowing the character's name helps the casting director choose an appropriate actor for that part, and helps the director and actor decide how the part should be played.

The writer usually backs up the name with a description. In many cases this is essential. The character of Jive would very likely be miscast if the writer had not given us a description. For important characters, the description is usually given in considerable detail. Take Thompson's description of Albert Kleinschmidt, the sympathetic foreman of the assembly line on which Ellen works.

```
This is ALBERT KLEINSCHMIDT, the foreman of the
assembly line.  He has a square face and square
shoulders, but a trim, narrow waist, and his work
shirt is tailored with sewn-in pleats to accen-
tuate the tautness of his body.  He is a decidedly
short man (barely, if any, taller than Ellen), but
his shoulders, arms and neck are roped with smooth
muscles -- the kind that come from working with
barbells.  His hair is short, his work outfit and
even his clothes are spotless, and -- particularly
in comparison to the others in the bar -- he is
scrupulously clean, even to his short-clipped
fingernails.  He looks to be in his late thirties.
```

Part of the description is essential to the plot. Kleinschmidt must be about the same height as Ellen so that he can show her how to handle the equipment without standing on a stool in the last act. But beyond that, the writer has given us a very precise picture of what Albert Kleinschmidt should be like. The name and demeanor are all decidedly German. Kleinschmidt is a no-nonsense, hard-working type who is in control of any situation. He is a strong, self-disciplined man who lives by the rules. The dialog reinforces what the audience may have guessed from the character's appearance and name. In his first line, Kleinschmidt politely corrects Ellen. She had started to call him "Al." "Albert Kleinschmidt," he says, reinforcing the impression of Teutonic precision and formality. He is no ordinary workman—the kind of character who would insist on being called "Al."

Very quickly we are given confirmation that he's a man who can handle almost any situation. Describing his workmen, he says, "Last month I had one of 'em go off his nut and come at me with a wrench." There's no suggestion Kleinschmidt had any trouble dealing with the situation.

At the end of the scene, we get another suggestion of Kleinschmidt's ability to deal with whatever happens. Another patron at the bar makes a leering suggestion to Ellen that there are other ways she can earn money than by working on an assembly line.

```
            BALD BAR DRINKER

    And so do some other things.  (TO ELLEN)

    I know a way you could make some extra

    money, sweetie.

Kleinschmidt jabs a stumpy finger toward the drinkers
and glares at them.

            KLEINSCHMIDT

    Nobody asked your opinions.  Nobody was

    conversing with you.
```

```
Ellen glances back gratefully toward Kleinschmidt,
then -- though still flustered by the comments -- she
ignores the pursuing gazes and hurries out of the bar
and O.S. . . . CAMERA HOLDS for a beat longer on Klein-
schmidt, who continues to glare at the two bar drinkers;
then turns back to his game.
```

The action establishes Kleinschmidt clearly as someone who stands up for his rights and also stands for the old-fashioned virtues. He will not let a woman be insulted. He does not like the idea of a woman working on the assembly line, but he will treat Ellen with respect and defend her against her tormentors.

Dialog. The dialog, too, fits Kleinschmidt's character. It is controlled and formal. He does not blow up and swear or make threats. Earlier he apologizes to Ellen for using a phrase that probably would have been stronger were it not for the restrictions on language in television.

Despite Kleinschmidt's clearly being a notch above the ordinary work-men in the plant, the writer consistently keeps Kleinschmidt's dialog working class. His verb forms are resolutely lower class: "There's always openings," "one of "em . . . come at me with a wrench." So are his pronouns: "Who for?" The auxiliary verb "have" disappears: "I got trouble enough."

English usage, of course, is one of the key ways that a writer has to indicate social class and regional background for characters. A writer must have a good ear for such usage. What is involved is not simply the correct or incorrect usage of certain words. It is also the *placement* of the words. Take this line of Burden's: "I ain't never thought that little thing was going to last this long even." It is not simply the incorrect grammar, but the word sequence here which indicates we are dealing with a dialect. The dangling "even" at the end of the sentence is simply not typical of standard middle-class American speech.

There are no simple rules for writing in dialect. A writer simply must have an "ear" for it. It is not accomplished by writing distorted pronunciations of words in phonetics in the script. Burden has a line that begins: "There's big and there's big fat, that's different. Last team I tried out for, . . ." You *don't* show that's dialect by writing: "They's big an' they's big fat, tha's diff'nt. Las' team I tried out fo', . . ." That kind of Uncle Remus dialect would be justly offensive to any black actor—and would not come close to contemporary black speech. Moreover, it is almost impossible to read. A writer may indicate an unusual pronunciation of a word *now and then*, but dialect is written through the selection and placement of words. Leave the pronunciation to the actors.

Sex. There are dozens of means besides dialog that the writer can use to indicate things about the character being portrayed. We have already noted names and descriptions. Simply the sex that you choose for a character can say much. People tend to think in stereotypes. That's so much the worse for society, but so much the better for the writer because the writer can use those stereotypes to help build a character. "The $5.20 an Hour Dream" is built around sexual stereotyping and its effects on our society. Ellen is stereotyped because she is a woman. When she tries for a job that doesn't fit the stereotype, she runs into problems. She also finds that there are stereotypes for people who don't fit the regular stereotype. Some of the workmen suspect she is a lesbian. Others think she is a part-time prostitute. She can't fit the stereotype of "working mother" because that is reserved for less grimy kinds of work.

The very stereotype that Thompson is dealing with in this script also serves writers in other scripts. Obviously no writer should feel proud that he or she is perpetuating a stereotype. But the stereotypes are still there in the mind of the public, and the writer either uses them or goes to extra lengths in the script to explain *why* a character does not fit the mold. The day may be coming when you can make your lead character a woman who is a professional baseball pitcher without suggesting there is something unusual about it. The sooner that day comes, the better; in the meantime, you must deal with the fact that people do not expect women to play professional baseball. Your choice of a character's sex, whether you like it or not, says certain things to the audience about that character, so it is important that you take that into consideration when you create a character in a script. Suppose, for example, that it had been Billie's mother rather than Donovan's mother who was dying in Michele Gallery's *Dying*. Or suppose that it had been Donovan's father instead of his mother that was dying. It would not be the same story. We would expect the characters to react differently.

Occupation. Occupation, too, helps define a character. The fact that Peggy Donovan in *Dying* had been a nurse tells us something of her ability to deal with her approaching death. Kleinschmidt is a foreman, not just an assembly-line worker. If Peggy Donovan had been an ice skater instead of a nurse, the audience would have expected a different response to the knowledge of her illness. If Kleinschmidt had been the commanding officer of a military unit and Ellen were asking to go into combat with the unit to collect combat pay, we would expect a different reaction from Kleinschmidt—at least his manner of reacting would be different. You need to think very carefully about the occupation you want your character to have. Remember, too, that different occupations imply different working hours. This may be only a minor problem, but you may find halfway through your script that you have your character doing something that her or his normal working hours would usually preclude.

Physical Description. We noted earlier that the physical description of a character is important. The producers may later decide to cast performers who look quite different from what you have described in your script, but if you paint a verbal picture of a character, it will help you keep the character consistent. Certain characteristics can help the audience get a better picture of your character. Is the character tall or short? Fat or thin? What color and type of hair? If it's a man, has he a beard or a moustache? What is the character's race? Does the character speak with an accent?

How does your character dress? Neatly? Sloppily? Expensively? Sensibly? Flashily? To look sexy?

Are there any special physical traits? Does the character limp? Is the character hard of hearing? Blind? Nearsighted? How does the character walk? Hesitantly? Confidently? Stealthily? How does the character speak? Rapidly? Deliberately? Haltingly? With a lisp? Does the character interrupt others who are speaking?

Are there any mannerisms? Frequent checking in the mirror? Constant brushing of dust off clothes? Frequent adjustment of clothing? An unusual way of holding a cigarette? Would the character sit on the edge of a desk or on the floor?

You can overdo it, of course. If your character has traits that draw attention to themselves, they should be there for a good reason. Either they should help us understand the character or they should contribute to the plot. Don't make a character walk with a limp or speak with a lisp if it serves no function. True, characteristics of that kind might be developed in a character who appears frequently in a series, but for a character who appears in a single episode of a program, you may divert the audience's attention from important elements of the story with little added to your story by the distracting character trait.

Traits can often be shown in dialog as well as action. In Truman Capote's script for the offbeat John Huston classic *Beat the Devil*, there is a character who is a chronic liar. The trait is emphasized by the character's verbal trait of starting almost every speech with "As a point of fact . . ."

In short, try to think of every character in terms of all that that person conveys to the audience through actions and speech. In a pinch, a character trait can be introduced through dialog such as: "John? Don't be fooled. He's afraid of his own shadow." Some such verbal confirmation of any trait is not a bad idea in any script. But the audience will be convinced only when dialog and action demonstrate the desired character trait.

Let's sum up, then. Study the program you want to write for and learn its format. Learn the kinds of stories that program prefers to use—and those it won't use. Block out the time segments of the show and begin to sketch in your plot. You may find it useful to write the last scene first, the first scene second, and then fill in what goes between. Make sure that your final crisis and its solution are of major proportions, that they come near the end of the story, and that they provide a quick and dramatically satisfactory solution to the problems presented.

Introduce your main characters quickly, and delineate their problems clearly in the first act. It is useful to give the audience an idea of what to expect in the first minutes of the show. Do not use trivial problems; do try to find problems the audience can empathize with. Be sure you have a clear idea in your own mind of the important traits of each major character. Present new problems of increasing magnitude in each succeeding act. Try to end each act except the last one with a new problem looming on the horizon.

Prepare a well-written treatment of the story for submission to the producers by your agent. Pay careful attention to the suggestions of the producer and write a new treatment to those specifications if your story idea sells. The treatment must be a well-crafted short story combining good dialog and skillful narrative and descriptions. Finally, when you get the go-ahead, expand your treatment into a completed script.

It takes time and thought to work out a good television drama. But the finished product is often something that can make far more of an impact on your audience than any other broadcast writing. Keep at it, and you'll find that the work pays off.

MINISERIES

Somewhere between the regular television drama, with its hour or 90-minute format, and the soap opera, with its five-days-a-week format, lies the miniseries. The most successful television program of all time, "Roots," was a miniseries. "Shogun," another miniseries, also set records. The idea of the miniseries is to use several successive episodes to tell the entire story instead of telling it all in a single show. This allows time for more thorough development of plot and better development of characters and subplots. Initially, broadcasters were somewhat skeptical about the format. They preferred weekly series programs and, to a lesser degree, one-time specials. The success of "Roots" changed all that. Today networks frequently schedule miniseries, and independent stations have found that by using miniseries they can compete with network stations. Sponsors such as Mobil and Xerox have sometimes established their own "networks" of stations to show miniseries. There is no doubt that the miniseries is now an established form of drama for American television.

The major difficulty in discussing miniseries is the extreme fluidity of the format. The episodes of a miniseries may run one a week for several weeks, they may run on successive nights in the same week, or they may run on several nights of several weeks. The individual episodes are not necessarily of the same length and may not have the same number of commercial inserts. This creates a problem for the writer, who must know what blocks of time are to be filled.

Once you have established how many episodes there are to be and how each will be split by commercials, you can begin to block out your show. You can begin by trying to plan a major crisis for each episode of your story. If the main plot line does not seem to fit this, you can use one of the subplots, but you should have some major crisis to be resolved in each episode. It goes without saying that you should end each episode with an even more imposing problem to be dealt with in the next episode. Within each episode, you try to have a minor crisis to be solved in each time block, with a new problem looming at the end of each time block. Here again you can use subplots to create interest in the story, and you need not involve your major character in each sequence.

It is also all right to use some of the time blocks simply for plot development. For example, a developing romance between two characters need not face a problem at each step. Because you have more time to develop character and plot, you can involve your audience in the lives of your characters without always having to rely on crises. If you have used foreshadowing in your plot, you may be able to move your characters through seemingly blissful scenes while keeping the audience aware that the problems to be solved are growing. In "Shogun," for example, it is clear from early in the series that the romance of the English sailor with a married Japanese woman can only come to a tragic end in feudal Japan. The more deeply they fall in love and the more they become involved with each other, the greater the problem that they must ultimately face. The love scenes do not themselves function as crises, but the undertone of inevitable disaster makes each love scene build toward a crisis certain to come.

The writer has to assume that a substantial portion of the audience may have missed a previous segment, so it is customary to begin each episode of a miniseries with a brief series of flashbacks summarizing the action to that point. Also, in order to entice the audience to view the next program, episodes usually end with a tag that shows scenes from the next episode. (In some ways this harks back to the format of film serials that used to run in theaters.) You must set aside time blocks for this opening and closing material. Then you need to determine what time blocks remain for you to use for your plot.

You can use the additional time available in a miniseries for many useful purposes. You can show more about the major characters, making them less one-dimensional. You can develop and add subplots; they help sustain audience interest. You can introduce additional characters. This again can make the show more interesting to the audience. It is unfortunate, but true, that a good deal of the time in some miniseries is filled with padding. For example, instead of dissolving from the hero saying, "I'm going back to the hunting lodge," to him walking through the door of the lodge, they show two minutes of him driving mountain roads. Of course, it is possible to add greatly to a story by giving thought to visual elements that do not inherently advance the plot. Shots of landscape and scenery, under the right circumstances, can add to the mood of the story. Action scenes can sometimes add greatly to the quality of a story without advancing the plot much. The fox hunt in *Tom Jones* is a splendid example. With the help of a good director, you can sometimes make use of these devices within the longer framework of the miniseries. But usually you should use the extra time you have for the purposes outlined earlier: increasing the depth of characterizations, adding interesting new characters, and adding subplots. Don't resort to padding in your script. Such padding as may be needed for purposes of giving the program the correct running time (and some usually is necessary) can be added in the final stages of production.

Most miniseries have been adaptations from novels, although some original scripts have been produced as miniseries. Candidly, the chances of an unknown writer selling a project as expensive as a miniseries are not very good. The chances are somewhat better if you are working with an adaptation of a novel that has already proved itself successful than if you try to promote your own script. Unfortunately, it is very difficult for an unknown writer to obtain the rights to adapt a major novel.

If you think of the 30-minute television script as being the television equivalent of a short story and the 90-minute drama as the equivalent of a novella, then the miniseries is the equivalent of a complete television novel. It multiplies the demands on your ability to plot and develop character and dialog. The need for discipline in excising every unneeded element remains. Even if you have a hundred hours for your story, you still should have a valid reason for every line in it, but you can allow yourself the luxury of developing the needed elements much more fully in a miniseries.

DOCUDRAMAS

The idea of basing a drama on factual events is almost as old as drama itself. Certainly some of the Greek tragedies drew from historical events. Shakespeare's historical plays are among his most powerful. Nevertheless, most writers tend to distinguish between historical drama and "docudrama." As early as 1898, long before the term "documentary" had been applied to film, French film pioneer Georges Meliès was producing what he termed "actualités réconstituées au studio," studio re-creations of such news events as the sinking of the battleship *Maine* and the coronation of Edward VII. But a change came over the thinking about such re-creations of actual events after British film scholar John Grierson coined the term "documentary" to describe Robert Flaherty's *Nanook of the North*. Grierson stressed that the documentary demanded the use of "actuality" material—film or phonographic recordings of the actual events being described. Grierson's dogma did not immediately take hold in the United States. Radio regularly used dramatizations under the title of "documentaries," and film series such as the March of Time used a mixture of actuality and dramatization. However, by the late 1940s Grierson's concept had pretty well won out. Not that historical drama was out, but the term "documentary" was now used only for actuality programming.

Some programs straddled the line between the two forms, notably the "You Are There" (later, "CBS Is There") series. Starting on radio, the series switched to the new medium of television. "You Are There" dramatized historical events, using actual historical documents as the source of all lines spoken by the actors playing the major characters—except the ubiquitous CBS reporter.

Unfortunately, the technique did not remain in hands as scrupulous as those of Robert Louis Shayon, who wrote most of the "You Are There" scripts.

New programs came onto the scene in which more and more fictional material was interpolated into scripts.

The first uses of the term "docudrama" were limited to historical dramas presented as if they were documentaries, essentially grafting fiction onto the "You Are There" technique. The term "docudrama" has since been applied indiscriminately to almost any dramatization of an actual historical event.

The technique has both its defenders and its critics. Former Writers Guild President David Rintels has argued that in order to create the proper mood for a historical drama, the writer must often rewrite, rearrange, and interpolate material into history. An example of this approach can be found in Ernest Kinoy's docudrama "Collision Course," which was about the conflict between General Douglas MacArthur and President Harry S. Truman. Writer Kinoy included a scene with dialog of the meeting between the President and the general on Wake Island. The actual meeting was held behind closed doors. Only Truman and MacArthur were present, and no one but Truman and MacArthur knew what the two said to each other. Was Kinoy justified in writing such a scene? Kinoy defends the dialog in the scene, saying, "I knew what Truman said he said and what MacArthur said he said and the result of the meeting."[3]

Still, many people worry about this casual "creation of history" by writers. *Saturday Review* critic Karl Meyer has called docudrama "as crooked as a camel's back."[4] And TV critic Cecil Smith calls it "a bastardized word for a bastard form of drama."[5]

The question, of course, is how much "docu" and how much "drama." How much is a writer entitled to invent and add to an actual historical situation? It is the opinion of the authors of this book that everyone would be better served if the term "docudrama" were reserved for the type of program exemplified by the old "You Are There" series. However, that is clearly not what is happening. We fear that the ultimate result will be a recapitulation of the early history of American radio documentaries in which facts play a smaller and smaller part and fiction a greater one until "docudrama" comes to mean simply a drama that has some tenuous factual basis. Even more disturbing is the muddling of fact and fiction in the minds of viewers, particularly youngsters who may think they are seeing a factual presentation of history.

It took a long time to establish Grierson's insistence on actuality as the basis of the documentary in America. The result of accepting that doctrine has been to give the documentary a great aura of authenticity. There is, in our opinion, a degree of dishonesty involved in pulling the documentary's cloak of authenticity over fictionalized historical dramas by calling them "docudramas." Grierson made it quite clear that he took the term "documentary" from the school of historical researchers at the University of Chicago and other academic institutions who had determined to free the writing of history

---

[3]Cecil Smith, "A Dialogue on Television's Docudramas," *Los Angeles Times,* March 8, 1979, III, p. 34.
[4]Ibid., p. 1.
[5]Ibid., p. 33.

from interpretation and supposition and limit it to the firm scientific basis of ascertainable fact. That derivation of the term "documentary" makes its cooption into the term "docudrama" all the more inappropriate.

Whatever the case, the docudrama is a viable form in today's television. The writer's job in preparing a docudrama begins with scrupulous research. You must know every element in the story and every conflict in the versions of it. If recent events are involved, you can often interview people actually involved or close to the story. But it is likely that your first stop should be a library.

Dramatic Structure

Unless you accept Rintels' thesis that you can rearrange history (and we hope you don't), your problem in the docudrama is constructing a plot that moves from problem to problem in a way that holds the audience's interest. Your main characters' lives may not have been lived according to the ideals of dramatic construction. The trick is partly in picking the elements in the historical event you intend to cover. Remember, with television you can compress or stretch out time to suit your needs. If you are wise, you will choose the most climactic event in the story as the end, or nearly the end of it. In the docudrama "Evita Peron," the story ends with Evita's death. The writer could have continued the story through the unsuccessful attempts to have Evita canonized by the Roman Catholic church, Juan Peron's growing battle with the church in Argentina, and his ultimate overthrow and exile. It could even have carried the story through to Peron's triumphant return and the return of Evita's body from its hiding place in Italy to Argentina. But the theme was Evita, not her husband, and not her corpse. The program ends with her death and the thousands of mourners filing past her casket.

If you place the most dramatic point of the story at the end, you have solved part of the problem of dramatic construction. The next job is to arrange the other key events in the story so that they fit the time blocks of the program. In a life like that of Evita Peron, there was plenty to work with. Scenes could be built around her illegitimate birth and the death of her father, her liaisons with important army officers, her romance with Peron, outsmarting attempted coups, dealing with the crumbling Nazi regime, building a corrupt charitable foundation to buy support, the rebuff of Evita's attempt to hold political office in her own right, and ultimately her death of cancer at 32.

Character Development

Unfortunately, in solving the problem of dramatic structure in the docudrama there is a danger of losing character development. Docudramas tend to be episodic, which makes it difficult to make a character develop evenly. You can show the main character at 16 in one scene and at 30 in the next. That creates no problem for the plot, but it does not help the audience understand what changes have taken place in the personality of the character. Indeed, in ordinary dramas, we rely on a great many artificial devices to explain character. Many of them show up only rarely in real life. In "Evita Peron," the script focuses on Evita as an illegitimate child and her early discovery that the quickest way out of poverty was to sleep with the right people, as explanations for her later behavior. But it is entirely possible for a historical villain to have had a perfectly normal childhood and perhaps to have endured nothing that explains later actions.

Still, whatever the realities of life, audiences expect some understanding of the motivations of characters, and that may prove to be the most difficult thing to demonstrate in a docudrama—at least if you stay true to the facts. Sometimes you can interpolate very brief scenes that do not contribute to the dramatic buildup of your plot but do serve to add to our understanding of key characters.

Flashback

Another technique that you can use in docudramas, and in other forms of television drama, is the flashback. This gives you greater control over the dramatic construction of your story by allowing you to place historical events in the sequence that best fits your needs. Often you can begin your story near the end, so to speak, and then develop it in flashbacks to earlier events. Too much use of this technique can confuse your audience —especially if the flashbacks are not in chronological sequence—but judiciously used, it can let you build your script toward a dramatic climax without being tied to the strict chronological development of the actual event.

The docudrama is a good format for students to practice their craft on because it demands that you study the dramatic structure of a story and work with it. It is not an easy form to work with. It is challenging. And it can be humbling because it is a constant reminder that truth is usually more dramatic than any plot you can invent.

SOAP OPERAS

The most durable form of broadcast drama is the soap opera. Nine of the 13 major soaps have been on the air for more than 14 years, five for more than 20. Sociological treatises have been written on their implications, and learned psychologists have duly studied soap opera fans to find out why they tune in day after day. The reason, according to some, is that the programs provide answers for the problems the audience members encounter in their own lives. Others believe that people unhappy with their own lot (and who isn't, every now and then?) are pleased to see lives even more wretched than their own. In addition to these scholarly conclusions, it would be impossible to overlook certain added attractions of the contemporary soap opera—notably sex. There is an inordinate amount of tumbling into and out of bed in the modern soap opera, and it might be more appropriate to call some of them "sheet operas."

Here is a description of the plot of "Young Lives," a syndicated soap opera that was offered for sale at the 1981 convention of the National Association of Television Program Executives (NATPE): "Rachel likes Brad, who's been making eyes at Melanie lately, so Rachel told Melanie's mother that there wouldn't be a chaperone at Brad's party that weekend. Meanwhile, John was in the back of Roger's van with Jan, and Coach Hamilton caught Dirk with a marijuana pipe in his locker."[6]

There you should get a glimpse of some of the basics of writing a soap opera. Given time to steam things up, the writer could probably get Melanie's mother in the back of the van with Brad—or maybe the coach with Roger. You need a large cast with at least four to six important continuing characters, at least one of whom should be noble, put-upon, betrayed by other characters, and regularly shafted by fate. At least one of the other continuing characters should be a thoroughgoing villain with fewer scruples than a cobra. And several of the characters should show the sexual proclivities of alley cats.

However, it's not all brain tumors and hot tubs. The soap opera demands more careful plotting than almost any other form of broadcast writing. The writer is denied the symmetry of other forms of drama. There is no real beginning. There is—if the show is successful—no end, only an interminable middle. The writer builds from climax to climax as in other forms of drama, but never to The Climax.

It goes almost without saying that in this, of all, forms of dramatic writing, you must present your main characters with a series of problems to be solved. The difficulty is that the solution of those problems must *not* wrap up the story. There must be another, more horrible-seeming problem arising even as the previous one is laid to rest.

Plot Structure

The dramatic construction of a soap opera plot is complex. Soap operas on television usually run one hour, some more. Within that hour, you usually have six commercial breaks. Sometimes the last segment of the program previews what is coming the next day, and a few shows still preview the action of the preceding program in the first segment of the show. You must, of course, know the format of the program, and sketch out your plot around it.

It has been said that the viewer should be able to miss a week of a soap opera and still not feel lost when returning to the show. That may exaggerate a bit, but it is true that the writer of the soap opera must somehow find things for his characters to do and say without advancing the plot very much each day. Yet, the building from dramatic climax to dramatic climax must be sustained in order to keep the audience interested. That is why the plotting of soap operas is an art unto itself.

How is this achieved? Says one expert, "Little action, much sentiment." You must be endlessly inventive in creating subplots. The five guidelines of soap opera plotting are said to be gossip, manipulation, humor, individual

[6]David Cook, "Storm Brewing Over 'Young Lives,' " *Los Angeles Times,* March 19, 1981, VI, p. 12.

concerns, and communication. The problem of plotting is facilitated somewhat by the relatively large number of continuing characters present in a soap opera. Your plot can run almost like the "voices" of a Bach fugue. (Or perhaps, better, like a Stravinsky composition in which each part proceeds independently with its own rhythm.) You can cut back and forth freely between subplots while advancing your main plot by millimeters each day. The main plot need not reach a climax in each program, but one of the subplots should, and the program should end with hints of more complications for a major character.

The total number of characters in a soap opera can be staggering—although only a few appear in each episode. In 1981, "All My Children" listed 49 characters, "Another World" 34, "As the World Turns" 27, "Days of Our Lives" 26, "The Doctors" 27, "Edge of Night" 21, "General Hospital" 46, "Guiding Light" 33, "One Life to Live" 35, "Ryan's Hope" 18, "Search for Tomorrow" 23, "Texas" 28, and "The Young and the Restless" 33, which averages about 31 characters per series. That is an enormous number of characters for the writers to keep track of, and it is important to keep files on each character so that there are no slip-ups. Writers sometimes do lose track of what has happened to their characters in soap operas. For example, when Erica Cudahy in "All My Children" started taking birth-control pills, listeners wrote in angrily saying that Erica had been surgically sterilized on the program three years earlier.[7] But the large number of characters is essential to provide the needed number of subplots to keep a series moving.

The interplay of plots is not always dictated by the writer's preference. Very often a character has to be written out of the script for some time because of illness, a vacation, or other commitments. Indeed, characters often die of terminal contractual difficulties. More than one producer has come back from an acrimonious session with an actor's agent and instructed the writer to have the character played by the actor cast beneath the wheels of a conveniently passing train. Fortunately, death is often a reversible condition in the soaps, and writers have found all manner of tricks to bring back, Lazarus-like, a supposedly dead character.

Whatever the reason, you must have many plots running simultaneously, and you must have the flexibility to change one at a moment's notice. Remember, a creature as minuscule as a flu virus can bench a major character for weeks.

Here is a typical week's plot for "As the World Turns," one of the best-known soaps: James Stenbeck has hired Margo Montgomery to help with the training of his horse, Caliope. James's wife, Barbara, suspects James has other types of horsing around in mind for Margo. Caliope races and, contrary to Barbara's hopes, wins. When Barbara, who remained home in Oakdale, calls James's apartment near the track in Florida, Margo answers the phone. That does not improve Barbara's estimation of the situation.

---

[7]Barry Siegel, "The Soapers, Daytime TV: Faith, Fervor, Fanatic Fans," *Los Angeles Times*, July 29, 1979, I, p. 24.

Meanwhile, James wants to take Margo out and tells her to wear some of the clothes his wife has left at the Florida apartment. Later James tries to give Margo a new Mercedes, but she turns it down. James says his marriage is on the rocks and that he loves Margo. Margo says she will not be James's mistress.

Meanwhile, at the office of Grant Coleman, Lisa Coleman is visiting Grant when Joyce Hughes arrives and invites Lisa to her and Grant's wedding. Lisa blows up. Later, at Lisa's apartment, Grant says he will have nothing more to do with Lisa if she can't be civil to Joyce. Lisa demands to know if Grant really loves Joyce. Grant storms out.

Cut to Dee Dixon, who is being served with a subpoena to be a defense witness in the rape trial of Dr. John Dixon. Cut to lawyer Maggie Crawford asking fellow lawyer Tom Hughes about his relationship with Dee. Cut to Dr. Bob Hughes proposing to Lyla Montgomery. Before she can answer, Dr. John Dixon calls to say he is coming over to talk about the rape trial. Lyla does not tell Bob Hughes who called. After Bob leaves, John arrives and threatens to damage Lyla's reputation if she testifies against him.

Cut to the courtroom. Tom Hughes and Maggie Crawford make their opening remarks in John's rape trial. Maggie says she will prove that Dee lied when she said John raped her.

Meanwhile, Nick Andropolous is accusing Andrea Korackes of stalling in signing her divorce papers. Back to James and Margo. James tells Margo he will divorce Barbara. Back at home he finds fault with Barbara. Barbara finds out that James has given Margo a promotion.

This recap covers only part of the action in the program. The main plot lines are James Stenbeck's pursuit of Margo and Dr. John Dixon's rape trial. Additional plot lines involve Grant Coleman's decision to marry Joyce Hughes because she is dying of a brain tumor (a disease slightly more prevalent than the common cold in soap operas); a mysterious secret project that James is working on with a Professor Wilson in Egypt; a valuable necklace hidden in Greece for which Andrea Korackes had the map; Carol Stallings' growing infatuation with Steve Andropolous, who is after the necklace; Nick Andropolous, who is after Steve and the map Andrea gave him; and Eric Hollister's growing passion for Professor Wilson's daughter, Hayley, who has a mysterious lung infection.

That really skims the surface, and leaves numerous subplots untouched, but it should give you an idea of the intricate plotting called for in soap operas. Clearly you need a framework within which you can construct all these plots. There needs to be some connection that brings together the various lives in your program. "General Hospital" gives one obvious approach, relating the people whose lives are somehow connected to a large hospital.

Note that, despite the large number of characters, everyone has an easy-to-remember name, and no two characters have the same first name. The audience needs to be able to keep them separated in their minds, and so do the writers.

Usually each episode ends with some substantial problem facing a key character so that the audience will be sure to tune in the next day to see what will happen. The last show of the week should be particularly filled with unsolved problems so that the audience will be waiting anxiously to tune in Monday's episode.

Production

It is useful to understand how soap operas are made. Normally, a series turns out about 260 episodes a year. Usually, several episodes are taped on the same day, so a week's programs are usually taped in two or three days. A typical script runs almost 100 pages. It is not unusual for an actor to have to learn 30 pages of dialog for an episode. Each episode is usually rehearsed three times, then taped, with very few retakes. This means that you will have to write a script that is relatively simple for the performers to learn and that can stand a good deal of improvising—a script in which it will not hurt if the player substitutes some of his or her own lines when the real ones can't be recalled. The script must also be relatively easy to produce. Action must take place on the sets that are regularly used for the series.

Because there is so much writing to be done, soap operas are usually written by teams. These are always staff writers; freelance material is never used. Care must be taken to stick to the basic themes that have been established for the series. Some series, such as "Guiding Light," are owned outright by sponsors—in that particular case, Procter & Gamble—and the theme is set by the sponsor. For "Guiding Light," it is family members facing disease and accidents and involved in romantic triangles. If you want to practice writing a soap opera, watch one for several weeks and determine first what the specific themes are.

Soap operas usually have long lives, and they provide steady employment for the writers who work for them. The soaps are popular with the networks because they are highly profitable. Weekly costs run around $300,000, which is cheap for television, and the networks usually make back the week's production costs from a single episode's advertising. The three networks gross over $750 million a year from soap operas. A half-hour soap opera brings in around $31.2 million a year and costs only about $6.2 million to make. Top performers may make over $100,000 a year, and writers make about $4,000 a week.

Audiences

At any given minute, about 30 million viewers are tuned in to soap operas. Some 71 percent of the viewers are women, mostly between 18 and 49. Most have high school educations and have family incomes between $10,000 and $20,000. The makeup of that audience should enter into your thinking when you write soap-opera plots. Some of the newer soap operas, such as "Ryan's Hope," have a better-educated audience and have more men in their audiences. These shows tend to be more topical in their material than the other soap operas are. The characters sometimes have drug problems, and the outcome of sex, which is usually pregnancy in the older soaps, may be venereal disease in some of the newer ones.

Not all soaps are daytime programs. Many would classify programs such as "Dallas" as a soap opera. Others would include the distinguished British import "Upstairs, Downstairs" in the soap classification. However, the usual concept of a soap opera is what broadcasters call a "strip show," that is, one that runs in the same time slot five days a week.

Most young writers will not have the chance to start out writing for a soap opera—unless it is a series prepared for a college station. Nevertheless, it is a major form of television writing, and it is worth your while to experiment with the form. It is a challenge to you as a writer, and will certainly help to develop your ability to plot dramatic scripts.

Television comedy usually means situation comedy. From time to time, television comes up with comedy of a different sort—a "Laugh-In" or a "Saturday Night Live"—but in the United States the great bulk of television comedy is situation comedy. The "sitcom" has a continuing cast of characters, some basic theme, and usually a half-hour running time. Its customary format consists of a first act, a commercial, a second act, a commercial, and a tag. A few open with a teaser before the first commercial. The script must almost always give plenty of exposure to the stars of the show and should use some, if not all, of the continuing characters. It is fairly common to introduce one new character in an episode—someone who appears only in that episode.

The writer's job is to take the theme of the show and prepare a script that fits that theme and makes use of the main continuing characters. It has to be done within the time frame of the show.

THEMES

Themes are usually general: "One Day at a Time"—a divorced mother and her two daughters trying to remake their lives; "Barney Miller"—day-to-day activities in a New York City detective squad room; "Taxi"—the lives of a group of New York cab drivers; and so on. There are certain other factors related to the theme that you need to watch for. For example, all three of the programs listed above tend to use "message" stories. Most of the scripts make some sort of comment on social problems. Beyond that, you should note the sets used in the programs. Nearly all the action in "Barney Miller" takes place in the squad room or in Miller's office. The physical limitations of the show are very much like those of a stage play. "Taxi" takes place primarily in the garage, by the dispatcher's cage, but often shows other locations. "One Day at a Time" usually takes place in the Romanos' apartment, but sometimes shows other locations. All these differences have to be kept in mind when you begin to plan a script for one of these shows.

CHARACTERS

It is also important to know which characters carry most of the action. While Barney Miller is nominally the star of the series that carries his name, action is divided fairly evenly among the main continuing characters, and episodes frequently feature interaction between one of the continuing characters and a noncontinuing character. In "Taxi" a different continuing character is usually featured each week, and frequently a noncontinuing character is brought in. In "One Day at a Time," stories mostly feature Ann Romano, with secondary emphasis on one or both daughters.* Noncontinuing characters frequently arrive and provide the problem to be solved in a particular episode. In a program like "WKRP in Cincinnati," the action tends to involve most of the continuing characters in each episode, although noncontinuing characters frequently appear.

The writer has to give careful thought to these differences. Retaining the theme and key characters is an important element of situation comedy. The writer should not tinker too much with what the public—and the producer—have come to accept as the customary form and style of the show.

THE PLOT

Plotting a situation comedy can be difficult. You need to think of a problem that you can introduce to the audience quickly, develop rapidly, and solve by the end of the show. Moreover, that problem has to carry the weight of the vehicle for 50 or more jokes or funny lines. "Barney Miller" plots are sometimes (although by no means always) fairly slight. On the other hand, "One Day at a Time" almost always has a well-developed story line, with a problem introduced and dealt with, if not solved, by the end of the episode.

Plots can, and often do, deal with serious problems, even though the problem always provides opportunities for some funny lines or action. Some

*Since this was written, the older daughter has been written out of most of the scripts.

contemporary situation comedies border on tragicomedy. Whatever the nature of the basic problem for the plot, the writer must be sure that it can be developed in a humorous way.

You must begin your script for a comedy program—or any other type of program—by viewing the particular show until you are sure you understand the program's theme and characters. Once you feel confident about this, you can begin to look for a plot idea by imagining a typical day in the life of one of the main characters. What does he or she do? Whom does this character meet? Think about the character working, eating, shopping, and going about day-to-day activities. What problems might develop that could be the basis of a plot?

A less subtle approach is simply to look about for a social problem that the show has not yet tackled—since that is the basis of so many comedies today. How can the main characters of the program become plausibly involved with that problem? Often you may have to use a noncontinuing character. Suppose, for instance, you decide to stick your neck out and do a program on veneral disease. You're not likely to have one of the main characters contract one of these diseases, but a main character could provide advice and help to a noncontinuing character with some such problem.

You may have other ideas for a plot. Be careful of the one-gag plot. Inexperienced writers often sit down and think, "Gee, wouldn't it be funny if . . ." and come up with some hilarious idea—but one that will not sustain a half hour of jokes. What you see as a plot may be nothing more than one elaborate gag. Tricky and elaborate plots are *not* characteristic of situation comedy. The plot is simply a story line around which to group your jokes.

Never content yourself with just one plot idea. Don't leave your typewriter until you have at least four or five ideas, preferably more. Then begin to elaborate on each of them in turn and see which ones seem to be giving you the best opportunities to be funny.

Next, begin to consider how to introduce, develop, and resolve the plot within the program's time frame. In a series that centers on one character, you will usually have to set out the basic problem before the first five minutes of the program are gone. You can elaborate on this, bringing it to some sort of crisis before the second commercial and then building it to the final crisis and solution in the second act.

However, if you are working with a program that gives fairly equal weight to several different characters, you may need only a relatively weak plot line to string together segments involving the various characters. In such a case, you can introduce at the start of the show what the unifying theme will be, but you do not have to concern yourself so much about when specific events occur in the script. We'll call these two techniques "tight plotting" and "loose plotting," and take a look at each one.

Tight Plotting

For a tightly plotted story, first answer these two questions carefully: What sort of jam does the main character get into? How does he or she get out of it at the end? Here you have the "bookends" of your plot. Pay particular attention to the way the problem is to be solved at the end, because this must be both quick and funny. If it isn't, you probably should put the story aside and work on another one.

Now, working backward, sketch in the major crisis of the plot, which should come immediately before the solution. Then sketch in a lesser but funny crisis for just before the second commercial. Now, before adding any further complications to the plot, begin writing down all the gags you can think of that fit each of the crises you have outlined. If the situations do not help you to generate plenty of gags, then you may need to consider another plot. If the situations *do* give you plenty of ideas for humor, you may need little more plot than you have already provided.

Let's examine a script. In this case, we'll look at one by Paul Wayne and George Burditt for the series "Three's Company." The basic theme of the series is the adventures of a young man who poses as a homosexual so he can share an apartment with two girls without arousing the suspicion of the landlord—a theme that would have been out of the question for a television series a few years ago. The script we examine is called *Helen's Job*, and it features one of the continuing supporting characters—Mrs. Helen Roper. (Mr. and Mrs. Roper were spun off into a series of their own later.) What's the plot? Mrs. Roper is goaded into taking a job, discovers she doesn't like it, and has to find a way to get her husband to ask her to quit, so she can save face. Solution: She declines to cook for her husband and threatens him by telling him they will have to have expensive meals out every night. It doesn't sound very exciting, but remember, the plot is only the vehicle for the humor. It has the necessary requisites: The problem can be stated fairly quickly, the crisis is simple enough, and it can all be resolved neatly and quickly.

Let's see how the plot is fleshed out. The final crisis before the problem is solved: Mr. Roper likes the money and wants his wife to keep on working. A crisis to end Act 1: Mr. Roper tells his wife he will not allow her to go to work, and Mrs. Roper announces that she intends to take a job anyway.

The first task the writers have is to introduce the basic problem. They begin the show with the Ropers bickering over Mrs. Roper's allowance. This is introduced within the first two minutes of the story, simply by Mrs. Roper raising the issue. Her husband resists. She says she resents being dependent upon him for money. He says it's his money. She threatens to get a job. By now, about six minutes have elapsed. Mrs. Roper goes to borrow some syrup from Jack, Janet, and Chrissy, the *menage à trois* who are the central continuing characters of the series.* The two women urge her to be independent, and Janet tells her about a job opening. Roper joins them and orders his wife not to take the job, bringing us to the crisis that ends the first act.

At the opening of the second act, the writers begin to build toward the final crisis. Roper tells Jack and the girls he's enjoying life with Mrs. Roper working, although it's clear he is putting up a brave front. He is certain she will

*Since this was written, Chrissy's role has been written out of the series and she has been replaced by a new character.

come begging for forgiveness. Roper leaves, and Mrs. Roper arrives to confirm that she hates working. Jack seeks out Roper in a local bar and convinces him that Mrs. Roper likes her work and that she is being approached by other men at work. The ruse works. The jealous Roper returns to the trio's apartment ready to urge his wife to give up the job.

Here the writers demonstrate their skill in building the plot. Obviously the story could end here—but it lacks a major crisis, and the solution to the crisis is too drawn out. The story would run out of steam if it ended here. (It is also short, but we are assuming that a good writer could fill the necessary time if this were the plot line selected.) Instead, the writers turn to a well-established trick of plot development. Just when the solution seems to be in sight, something occurs that makes the happy solution of the problem seem even more impossible than before. Jack overplays his hand trying to convince Roper that Mrs. Roper will be making a great sacrifice by quitting her job. He tells Roper that the manager of the cafeteria where Mrs. Roper is working is so pleased with her work that he is raising her pay to $150 a week. Roper immediately decides that that is too much money to give up and says his wife should keep on working.

Here the writers are playing on a known trait of the continuing character, Stanley Roper: He is known to be tightfisted. However, the writers do not rely on the audience's remembering this from previous programs. Instead, they remind the audience of it in Roper's dialog at the opening of the program, when he and Mrs. Roper argue about money. That the trait of tightfistedness has been established over many programs makes it easier to introduce into this episode, but the writers are not relieved of their obligation to reestablish the trait for this episode.

Now we are ready for the final resolution of the problem, which the writers manage to pull off in only 15 lines of dialog. Mrs. Roper talks about eating out at expensive restaurants, and Stanley's cheapness now works to her advantage. He begs her to stay home and agrees to give her the increase in allowance she asked for at the beginning. The last minute of the script is used to add a few jokes that are part of the usual banter between the Ropers. In the tag, Janet, Chrissy, and Jack, whose meddling caused most of the trouble, express regrets for having interfered in the Ropers' lives and wind up with a visual gag that results in Jack's being doused with a glass of milk. The tag really has little to do with the plot, but it puts the main characters of the series on camera at the closing, and it expresses a mild "message": Don't meddle in other people's lives. And, of course, it ends the show with a laugh.

Exploring the Plot. The script has a well-planned plot. It allows for the following "scenes" in which different characters engage in dialog. Each new combination of characters provides new opportunities for humor. First comes the war of the sexes between the Ropers. Next a short scene in which Chrissy's dumb blonde traits are exploited in dialog with Jack and Janet. Then Mrs. Roper enters and relates her problems with Stanley. An exchange is developed between the two girls taking a feminist position, and Mrs. Roper holding out for the virtues of being a housewife. (Just as Stanley's tight-fistedness has been established early, Mrs. Roper's lack of real interest in working is also established early.) Jack states the message that is pressed home in the tag: "This is none of our business." Roper enters, and he and Mrs. Roper resume the center of the stage with an argument that ends with Mrs. Roper's decision to take the job Janet has just told her is open.

In Act 2, Roper and Jack discuss Roper's life without Mrs. Roper at home. Roper leaves; the girls return for a short scene in which Jack tells them Roper doesn't mind the new situation. Then Mrs. Roper arrives to announce she hates the job. In a scene primarily involving Mrs. Roper and the girls, the battle between housewife and working woman is replayed. Then comes a scene between Jack and Roper in a local bar. (This may be a slightly unusual facet of this script because it calls for a set not regularly used in the series.) Next comes the scene with the Ropers and the trio—all taking fairly equal parts. And the final scene before the tag ends as the episode opened, with the Ropers alone at home.

This continual regrouping of the characters is useful in keeping the gags coming. It permits the writers to use not only the basic plot line but also the differences in outlook of the characters to provide added humor. Comedy writer Abe Burrows has written, "In radio and television you have to bowl the audience over in the first thirty seconds of your show. If there's the smallest hint of dullness, the audience switches to another station. The slogan in TV is 'Grab Them Quick!' "[1] The writers of "Three's Company," and of most comedy shows, know that rule. The script opens with a sight gag of Stanley Roper carefully seasoning his scrambled eggs, bite by bite. There are six verbal gags in the first two minutes of the script. Then the pace slackens to one or two jokes per minute as the plot is developed. In the next scene, the writers give us four gags in the first minute, and then they slow the pace to allow more plot development. At no point in the script do we find more than a minute passing without at least one joke. When things are really rolling, the gags come every five or six seconds.

Obviously, you can't depend upon plot alone for this much humor. It must be developed from the traits and personalities of the characters on the screen. In most cases, it will be developed in dialog between two of the characters. Sometimes this consists simply of the old comedy standard of one character providing the "straight" line and the other the gag. However, a clever writer can make several successive lines funny by having each speaker top what was said by the other in the previous line. Here's an example from the script we are analyzing. The comedy is relatively low-key, but each line is designed to draw a laugh. Roper and Jack are discussing Roper's lunch, which Roper says was "great."

JACK

Really? What did you have?

[1] Abe Burrows, "The Making of 'Guys & Dolls,' " *Atlantic,* January 1980, p. 44.

                          ROPER

Peanut butter sandwich.

                          JACK

We must exchange recipes sometime.

                          ROPER

Nothing to it. All you need is two

slices of bread, some peanut butter.

And a knife.

                          JACK

Gee, I wish I had time to write that

down.

                          ROPER

What do they teach you in that cooking

school?

Here, Jack's sly digs are being played against Roper's comments, which are obtuse but with an underlying intent to put Jack down. The script does not tell us whether Roper does or does not get the full drift of Jack's comments. The lines could be played either way and still be humorous. The lines are not big laughs, but they keep the audience chuckling.

   By now, you should get the basic idea of the tightly plotted comedy. The plot line is simple but well thought out. It moves from crisis to crisis, finally reaching the major crisis and then quickly moving to a simple resolution of the problems. Use the plot line to develop "scenes" involving interplay between characters. We're using "scenes" here in a fairly broad sense—not just a change in location or time, but simply any change in the major characters carrying on the dialog. It is from these interchanges that most of your funny lines and action will come. The jokes must come at frequent intervals. The number of jokes may slack off a bit during the development of the plot—but there still must be some jokes.

Loose Plotting

In a loosely plotted script, there is less attention paid to the development of plot line and more to the interplay between characters. There is always *some* plot, but there the buildup of crises may be absent, and the solution to the problem may pack little punch. Take this plot line from *Operation Mercy,* written by Michael Morris for the short-lived "The New Temperatures Rising Show":

The staff is suspicious of Dr. Paul Mercy's behavior and the purpose of a planned trip to Rochester. At the end of Act 1, the staff tricks Mercy into admitting he is going to the Mayo clinic to have "pollips" (so spelled in the script) removed from his throat. Mercy says he is afraid he'll let the staff see that he's afraid of this minor operaton, so he wants to have it done elsewhere. The staff insists that Dr. Mercy have the operation done at his own hospital. Dr. Mercy winds up in the children's ward, where he finds the children are equally scared. In the morning he is hauled off to the operating room, and in the tag, we learn he came out just fine.

Obviously, there is less plot to deal with in this script. Rather, it is designed to let the main characters engage in funny lines and action. The major crisis, if there is such, is Dr. Mercy screwing up his courage to be led off to the operating room. Even at this point, the crisis and solution are minor points because Mercy goes off to the operating room still scared. In this series, Mercy is no hero in the ordinary sense. He is humorous and interesting because he is cowardly and generally nasty to people. The humor is not so much in what he does as in how he does it—which is true of most comic characters.

Around that fairly flimsy plot line, the writer created the following scenes. First, a short dialog between Nurse Kelly and Dr. Noland. Next, a scene with Dr. Mercy and his sister Edwina, as Edwina signs in a patient at the hospital. The writer introduces two props for the plot here: Dr. Mercy nervously cracks his knuckles, and he keeps taking throat lozenges. Then come two short scenes, perhaps added to pad out the script, in which Mercy exchanges words with a patient and an orderly. Next comes a scene between Dr. Noland and Dr. Mercy, which introduces one of the children Mercy will room with later. Then follows a scene between Nurse Kelly and Dr. Noland in which Noland begins to guess why Mercy is going to Rochester. Next is a scene with Noland and Edwina in which Noland further confirms his suspicions. Then comes a scene between Noland and Kelly in which he gathers more evidence on Mercy's condition. Finally comes a scene played primarily between Mercy and Noland in which Mercy confesses.

All those scenes are in the first act. You can see that the writer is working for fast pacing in this script because of the dizzying number of scenes. You might also guess from this that the program is designed to be shot on a closed set, probably with single-camera technique, certainly with extensive off-line editing.*

In the second act, Noland and Mercy continue their debate, and Mercy agrees to be operated on in his own hospital. Then comes a scene between Mercy and Edwina while he signs himself into the hospital. Next a scene

---

*When the director selects among cameras and other video sources while a performance is being taped, it is called "on-line" editing. When videotaped segments are edited together and special effects or audio material are added by the videotape editor after the actual taping of a performance, it is called "off-line" editing.

between Nurse Kelly and Dr. Mercy in which he expresses more worries. Then a scene with Mercy and another patient in his room. Then a scene with Mercy and five children in the children's ward. Finally a scene with Mercy and Noland as Mercy is rolled into the operating room. The tag is a conversation between Mercy and Noland sometime later.

Exploring the Plot. If all this seems to make little sense, stop and look it over carefully to see what the writer has done. There are four major characters—Noland, Mercy, Edwina, and Kelly—plus the children and some other minor characters. Dr. Mercy has a scene with each of them, including the children and the other patient in his hospital room. Noland has scenes with each of the major characters. Kelly has scenes with Mercy and Noland. Edwina has scenes with the same two men. The writer has used his relatively small cast to provide nine different sets of people engaging in dialog—not counting Mercy's dialog with his fellow patient or with the children. Each new combination allows new opportunities for jokes. The greatest number of scenes is between Dr. Mercy and Dr. Noland, but there are only four major scenes between them.

In comparison, in the tightly plotted "Three's Company" script, there are far fewer combinations. There is dialog between the Ropers, between Mrs. Roper and the girls, between Roper and Jack, and between Jack and the girls. Chrissy and Janet are treated almost as a single entity. The writer develops the dialog more thoroughly.

It may not always be the case, but in general the loosely plotted script has to provide more interplay among different characters. Because there is little plot to keep the audience occupied, the dialog has to keep the audience laughing. While "The New Temperatures Rising Show" was not successful, do not assume that tight plotting is always essential to a successful comedy series. Barney Miller is a good example of a series in which most episodes have relatively loose plots. The interplay of the main characters carries the show.

In the "New Temperatures Rising Show" script, there are two to four gags a minute through most of the show. Since little time is required for plot development, more can be devoted to humor. More is not necessarily better. What makes an audience remember a program as funny is a combination of writing talent, acting and directing skills, and the context in which the program appears. Sometimes a poor script may succeed and a good one fail. Skilled performers may be able to save a weak script. On the other hand, a very funny show may fail because of low ratings if it is scheduled against an extremely popular show, and a sophomoric one may succeed if it faces little competition in the same time slot. At any rate, it seems certain that a comedy show needs to produce at least one gag per minute of playing time. Most will do considerably better than this. But quantity is not the determining factor. It is the mood you create in which to tell the jokes that gives a program a feeling of being funny. That probably is why tightly plotted series seem to hold up better than loosely plotted ones.

HUMOR

What *is* funny? That's the question comedy writers are always trying to answer. There is no real answer. What's funny in one time and place can be tragic in another. There has probably been humor as long as there have been human beings. People have written humor and funny scripts for actors going back at least to the ancient Greeks. Here are a few techniques that you can consider when preparing a script.

Situations

The Misperception. One or more characters of a comedy often labor under misperceptions. Usually these are resolved by the end of the program, but in some cases they can be a continuing element of the program. For example, Stanley Roper's belief that Jack Tripper in "Three's Company" is a homosexual is an integral part of the plot. When the Ropers were spun off for a new series, a new landlord, played by Don Knotts, was introduced to continue the concept. In this case, the deception is deliberate on Jack's part. It is also a fairly common comedy situation to have the misperception entirely accidental.

In the British series "Fawlty Towers," Basil Fawlty mistakes a deadbeat guest for the hotel inspector in one episode and showers him with service while maltreating the actual hotel inspector. Misperceptions may carry through the script or may be the basis of a single gag. Again in an episode of "Fawlty Towers," after a series of earlier misperceived events far too complicated to explain here, Basil Fawlty, clad in his underwear, winds up crouching over a prostrate bellboy when guests arrive and draw the conclusion that there is open perversion in the hotel lobby. At times, the misperception may be double, with two characters, each having the wrong idea about the other. A fairly ancient plot line is the boy courting the girl because he thinks she is rich only to find out she is courting him for the same reason.

The Imagined Predicament. In its extremes, the misperception becomes the imagined predicament. Many comedies have been built around the somewhat morbid idea of a character mistakenly believing he or she is dying. Numerous supposed catastrophes—loss of job, eviction, and such—can be the basis for comedy.

Fooling the Audience. With misperceptions and imagined predicaments, the audience is usually let in on the gag. However, it is possible to keep the audience in the dark, letting them learn at the end that they've been taken in, too. This is a fairly risky procedure because it cannot contribute much to the story until the end. It usually serves to provide some zany ending to the story.

Reversed Roles. This gimmick is an old favorite for comedy. Thorne Smith's old story "Turnabout," in which a husband and wife find they have mysteriously assumed each other's bodies, has been made into several movies and television productions. The film *Goodbye, Charlie* had the theme of a lecherous male punished by being reincarnated in the body of a beautiful woman. Opera abounds in "trouser roles," roles to be sung by women who are supposed to be men posing as women. Octavian in *Der Rosenkavalier* is one such role. Cherubino in the *Marriage of Figaro* is another.

Most modern comedies take a more plausible approach of simply having two people trade roles, such as a husband staying home to care for the children while his wife works. Variations of this theme are easy to develop in an era when women are assuming more and more roles once held by men, while sexual stereotypes for both sexes are disappearing. (Note, however, that it is the *existence* of these stereotypes that sets this theme up for comedy.)

Reversal of sex roles is an obvious and easy approach, but role reversals can take place between any two characters, regardless of sex. The theme is almost always the same: People do not appreciate their own jobs or the difficulties of another's job until they've tried it. In many cases, the role reversal can be on the part of a single individual, instead of a switch between two persons. The "Three's Company" script we examined earlier has elements of this in it, with Mrs. Roper trying to become a working woman instead of a housewife. In that script, however, the change of role is not made out of envy for the other role, which is often the basic motivation in comedy scripts. Mrs. Roper is pretty clearly pushed into taking the job, which gives the script a different slant—the emphasis being on meddling in other people's lives, not on envying other people's jobs.

A change of character traits is often the theme of comedy scripts. A greedy character becomes generous. A mean character becomes kindly. All of these can be a basis for jokes. *However*, if you are dealing with a continuing character in television, you must have the character revert to "normal" at the end of the script. Otherwise, the traits that have been established with the audience for that character cease to be of use. More important, the change may create confusing inconsistencies when the program is presented in reruns, which may not follow the same sequence as the original episodes of the series did.

Unorthodox Viewpoints. Again, what makes these a basis for comedy is stereotyping. We expect old people to act a certain way. We expect ministers to act a certain way. We expect women to act one way and men another. Any character running counter to these stereotypes can be funny. The character of Dr. Mercy from "The New Temperatures Rising Show" is a good example. He is not only antithetical to the steroetype of a doctor, he is antithetical to the basic concept of a lead character in a series. He is an antihero. He is crass, money-grubbing, spiteful, and cowardly. The writers even deliberately give him bad jokes to tell:

INT.   ELEVATOR -- DAY

3   The elevator doors close. In the elevator 3
                  with him is an ORDERLY, a MALE PATIENT
                  fresh out of surgery, lying on a stretcher,
                  and a NURSE holding a bottle of glucose
                  that feeds into the man's arm. Paul
                  picks up the chart lying at the patient's
                  feet.

                            PAUL
                  Oh, I see you're one of Dr.
                  Noland's patients.

                        PATIENT
                      (sedated)
                  He took out my appendix.

                            PAUL
                  That's Noland . . . he'll take
                  anything that's not nailed down.

         Paul laughs at his own joke; then sobers.

                        PAUL (Cont'd)
                  Just a little hospital humor.

It's only fair to point out that the role of Dr. Mercy was tailored to the actor who played it—Paul Lynde—who had developed the kind of character portrayed in the series over a quarter of a century of playing similar roles. Nevertheless, the basis of much of the humor is that the character does not fit our cliché image of a series hero.

Humor, of course, often explores certain underlying suspicions we have about leaders and heroes. Thurber's short story "The Greatest Man in the World,"[2] which has also been adapted for television, tells of a man who becomes a hero and turns out to be just the opposite of everything heroes are supposed to be. He is vulgar, greedy, self-centered, and lecherous. Ultimately, he has to be murdered so the truth will not destroy the image the media have created for him. Underlying that theme is the suspicion—or hope—we hold somewhere in the corner of our minds that no hero is quite as noble as portrayed. In the case of Dr. Mercy, the American public has grown increasingly aware that not all doctors are Marcus Welby; jokes about lazy, greedy, or incompetent doctors are fairly common. The medical profession is one of the most influential in our nation, however, and a writer is probably well advised to balance off every incompetent doctor with a dedicated one somewhere in the script, lest there be angry letters from medical associations and trembling in the continuity acceptance department.

[2]James Thurber, "The Greatest Man in the World," in *The Thurber Carnival* (New York: Harper & Brothers, 1945) pp. 112—117

Funny Actions. These can consist of doing something ordinary in an unordinary way, or they can be odd actions that no one does ordinarily. It is surprising that there is not more visual humor in television. The reason seems to be primarily that it is harder to think up. Not, of course, that you cannot think of *some* actions that are funny—but it is difficult to find funny actions that fit the characters and plot of a given story. Moreover, the visual humor has to be *good.* There are a few comedians who are true clowns and can pull off slapstick humor, but most actors fail unless the action is original and well thought out. Some visual humor can be funny because it is expected. During the time Chevy Chase appeared on NBC's "Saturday Night Live" he could be expected to fall through or off something every week—usually at the opening of the program. The fall was funnier because it was anticipated by the audience. A pie in the face continues to be *somewhat* funny because the audience has a general idea what is going to happen from the moment the pie is picked up. But pratfalls and pies in the face are far too familiar to the audience to get much of a laugh without some special angle.

Think of some of the classic visual gags and try to analyze why they work. Think of Jack Lemmon straining spaghetti through a tennis racket in *The Apartment.* It works because it's an everyday task done in a way that no one would think of doing. Somehow it fits with his character as a somewhat maladroit bachelor. On the other hand, most of the visual humor in Marx Brothers films works because the characters are so eccentric we are willing to suspend belief and accept them doing such ridiculous things as being chased through a department store on roller skates. The "Three's Company" script we have examined uses visual humor in the tag. Here, the writer uses words to build us up to an unexpected visual happening:

                              J ACK

           Now drink. But - be sure and drink

           from this side of the glass . . .

        (POINTS TO SIDE NEAREST HIM)

           And never from this side of the glass.

        (POINTS TO SIDE FARTHEST FROM HIM)

                            CHRISSY

           Why can't you drink from that side?

                             JACK

           Because if you drink from that side

        (DRINKS FROM FAR SIDE AND AS HE TILTS GLASS, MILK

SPILLS DOWN HIS SHIRT FRONT)

        · . . . It'll spill all over you.

Dialog

Most comedy, of course, is verbal comedy. If you construct your plot carefully, you can play characters off one against the other, allowing for all sorts of verbal interplay. Here are a few of the types:

Put-downs. In the "Three's Company" script, Mrs. Roper inquires of Stanley if he thinks her new nightgown is sexy. Roper replies, "Please, Helen, not while I'm eating!" This works so long as it is in keeping with the character speaking and so long as the victim is not too sympathetic a character. The audience can become annoyed if sympathetic characters are the targets of too many cruel remarks. At the least, some sort of retribution is expected.

Retorts. One of the most common types of funny line, the retort is usually a line that responds to a put-down. In the put-down cited earlier, when Stanley Roper tells his wife, "Not while I'm eating," she snaps back, "Or when you're sleeping, or when you're working or while you're sitting or standing or. . . ." She is alluding to Stanley's lack of interest in sex, which is one of Roper's characteristics used for humor in the series.

Analogies and Descriptions. In a program titled *My Kingdom for a Horse* in the "Sanford and Son" series, Fred Sanford dresses a horse in baggy pants in the hopes of passing off a gelding as a stud horse. Fred asks his son Lamont how the horse looks and Lamont replies, "Like Al Capone." Describing her first day working in the cafeteria, Mrs. Roper says:

                MRS. ROPER

        Did you ever see the movie "Earthquake"?

                CHRISSY

        The cafeteria looked like that?

                MRS. ROPER

        Only when things quieted down after the

        rush hour.

Or, here is Dr. Mercy comparing his illness with that of another hospital patient, Mr. Margolies:

```
                    MARGOLIES
        I'm a three stone gallbladder.
        And you?


                    PAUL
        I'm a double Pollip.
```

Malapropisms. A standard element of humor, these are usually linked with dialect of some sort. Comedian Norm Crosby has made a career out of monologs full of malapropisms, such as his description of Samson and the "uncircumscribed Philistines."

Perhaps the greatest contemporary source of malapropisms is Archie Bunker, who, like Crosby, confuses "circumcised" with "circumscribed," and who loves to eat "smashed potatoes." "Bunkerisms" sometimes go beyond being malapropism. For example, Dr. Sigmund Freud becomes "Dr. Sigmund Froost" on the tongue of Archie Bunker. The writers often set the audience up for a Bunkerism by having Bunker preface it with the phrase "one of them what ya call your," as in "she's one of them what ya call your 'lemians.' "

Backhanded Compliments. These are comments intended to be complimentary by the persons making them, but sounding awful to everyone else. Often they tie in with some character trait of the person making the compliment. When hillbilly programs were popular, they abounded in comments like, "Miss Emmy Lou, you're purtier 'n a plate of hog jowls and collard greens."

Double Meanings. Many, of course, are not suitable for use on the air. In the old "Here's Lucy" series, in an episode entitled "Mary Jane's Boy Friend" by Fred S. Fox and Seaman Jacobs, Mary Jane's boy friend cracks a very poor joke. Mary Jane says loyally, "Don't you just love him? He's so full of fun!" and Lucy responds, "Yeah, he's full of it."

Pretty clearly, what Lucy thinks he's full of is not fun. The ambiguity of the pronoun "it" lets the line provide two meanings—one funny. Thousands of words in English have more than one meaning: *Bill:* "The high school band played Beethoven last night." *Dan:* "Who won?" And then there is the often-quoted review of an actor playing King Lear: "He played the king as if someone were holding the ace." In both examples, the humor comes from the different meanings of "play." And, finally, of course, there is Henny Youngman's old standard, "Take my wife . . . please!"

Keep in mind that the audience must fully understand both meanings of the words used. The first use of them must seem logical in the context, and the second use must be unexpected.

Dialect. This rich old resource of humor must be used with caution these days. It must never appear that you are demeaning a group by making fun of the way its members talk. Moreover, most dialect writing, like most other forms of stereotyping, falls far short of the actual speech of the group it is supposed to represent. For example, if you go through scripts of the series "Sanford and Son," you will rarely find anything in the lines to indicate that the characters are black. The dialog could just as well be read by whites or members of any other group. There are some jokes, of course, based on race, and some entire episodes whose plot depends upon the race of the main characters—but there is little in the writing itself to indicate any dialect. There are a number of reasons, the most obvious being that most blacks speak about the same English as anyone else. There are regionalisms and buzz words in the black community, but the mass media have pretty well standardized American English.

Even where differences do exist, those that can be used are limited because words used in a mass medium must be understood by the mass audience. So dialect can be faithful to actual speech only to the extent that actual speech in the dialect is close enough to standard English for a mass audience to follow it. Probably, Mark Twain was giving a fair impression of the English spoken by black slaves when he wrote these lines in Huckleberry Finn:

> Well, 'twarn't no use to 'sturb you, Huck, tell we could do sumfn—but we's all right now. I ben a-buyin' pots en pans en vittles, as I got a chanst, en a-patchin' up de raf'. . . .

If blacks ever really did speak that way, they certainly do not today, and would be properly offended at anyone who tried to portray a modern black with such dialog. (Granting that the slave, Jim, knew enough English to make "all right" two words, which few students and even script writers do today.) But compare that with these few lines from "Sanford and Son."

```
                         FRED

        That makes you a horse thief, Calvin.

                        CALVIN

        No it doesn't either.  Perkins stole him.

        I bought him from Perkins.

                         FRED

        That makes you a horse thief once removed

        . . . and once a horse thief is removed,

        he gets from ten to twenty.
```

Writing dialect is more an exercise in the understanding of speech patterns than in the actual pronunciation of words. Of course, the actors will change the pronunciation of some words, but the writer is likely merely to confuse things by trying to spell out word changes phonetically, *except* where a particular pronunciation of a word is essential to the joke. Writer Leo Rosten points out that the whole emotional tenor of language is colored by race and culture. Summing up some differences, Rosten writes: "The English understate: Mediterraneans exaggerate . . . . Where the English frown upon the display of emotions, Italians and Moroccans and Jews act out their 'natural' conviction that emotions are *meant to be verbalized, embroidered, and shared.*"

Rosten draws his examples from the Yiddish. Characteristics of the speech patterns he discusses includes the following: "Emphasis by transplanting a predicate adjective: 'Funny, he isn't' " meaning emphatically that the man is not funny. "Dismissing an idea out-of-hand by framing it as a question: 'I should invite him to my son's Bar Mitzva?' " meaning definitely he should *not* be invited. "Sarcasm via the addition to a straightforward sentence of 'only,' 'just,' or 'merely': 'Why did he leave her? She only tried to poison him—once a week.' "

Rosten cites dozens of other characteristics of Yiddish that could be adapted for use in writing dialect. Note that none of those just mentioned (or any not cited here) stress *pronunciation.* It is word order and word emphasis that create the dialect.

Rosten pays special attention to word emphasis in a sentence. He points out that each of these sentences means something different, although all use exactly the same words in the same order:

> Did *I* send flowers to the hospital?
> Did I send *flowers* to the hospital?
> Did I send flowers to the *hospital*?[3]

Probably, by placing the sentence in the appropriate context, you could even milk additional meanings out of it:

> *Did* I send flowers to the hospital?
> Did I *send* flowers to the hospital?
> Did I send flowers *to* the hospital?

Note how the writer in *"The New Temperatures Rising Show"* used tricks of word placement to provide a Yiddish dialect for Dr. Mercy's temporary roommate, Bernie Margolies:

```
                    PAUL
          Mr. Margolies, getting agitated
          is not good for me.

                    MARGOLIES
          And for me, it's good?  Three
          times last night they woke me
          up to give me sleeping pills.
```

[3] Leo Rosten, *A Treasury of Jewish Quotations* (New York: McGraw-Hill, 1972).

```
              PAUL
    I'll make a note of your
    complaints.


              MARGOLIES
    Where are you going to get all
    the paper?

Paul presses the buzzer frantically.


              MARGOLIES
    Go ahead ring.  You know what
    you'll get from ringing?  Muscle
    cramps, you'll get.  They won't
    answer.  But I must congratulate
    you for hiring the handicapped.
    Who else would give a job to
    deaf nurses?
```

Word Distortion to Illustrate Character. If you do use this technique for a gag, you must spell phonetically what the actor is supposed to say. "Saturday Night Live" made fun—some would say cruel fun—of Barbara Walters's difficulties with the letter *r.* Actually, the pronunciations used were almost identical to those used by the character Elmer Fudd in the old Bugs Bunny cartoons. Fudd used to suffer endless abuse from the "cwazy wabbit." On "Saturday Night Live," "Babwa Wawa" (played by Gilda Radner) would discuss "vewy impo'tant pwoblems." A good many people would question whether it is in good taste to ridicule someone who has a speech defect, even though stammering, lisping, and other speech defects have been fodder for comedians for centuries. Probably the writer is on safer ground if the pronunciations are affectations. Whenever a female character pops on camera calling everyone "dahling," the audience will immediately assume the role is meant to be that of a supercilious snob, and probably a comic one. (The late Tallulah Bankhead made "dahling" a trademark. Most of the stories about her are a bit rich for use in a textbook, but one apocryphal story had her answering the door of her bungalow at Hollywood's Garden of Allah, stark naked, with a monkey sitting on her shoulder, and booming out in her near baritone to the astounded caller, "What's the matter, *dahling,* haven't you ever seen a monkey before?")

Spoonerisms. This form has definite limits. Either it is good for one or two gags treated as accidental slips of the tongue or it is necessary to create a character who has as a trait the frequent making of spoonerisms. "Colonel Stoopnagle and Bud" was a radio program that played on this theme, as did the various printed Stoopnagle stories. Books have been written about William A. Spooner, the Oxford don whose muddling of the English language gave us the name spoonerism. He is reputed to have dismissed a student from Oxford with: "You have deliberately tasted two worms and you can leave Oxford by the town drain."[4]

4Mary Blume. "The Inspedible W. A. Crooner," *Los Angeles Times Calendar,* September 11, 1977, p.67.

One obvious problem in using spoonerisms is that the audience must figure out what was actually meant. This can be tricky. The spoonerism is customarily made by transposing the first letters of two words in a sentence. However, Dr. Spooner is reputed also to have transposed entire words, "I remember your name perfectly, but I just can't think of your face." This is easier for the audience to follow, but may slip by some viewers as easily as it slipped by Dr. Spooner. After all, it almost sounds right. Generally speaking, when you use spoonerisms, you are going to have to give the audience a little time to think about the meaning of the statement—and that can be risky in comedy. Spoonerisms sometimes play in scenes about drunks: "Bartender, you fulled my glass too fill!" It is difficult to make them carry much of the burden of comedy.

Puns. Reputed to be the lowest form of humor, the pun remains popular. But for most broadcast humor, it is often too difficult to set up the background for a pun. Very often the pun is a sort of intentional spoonerism, transposing the first letters of words to give them new meanings or transposing whole words in expressions. However, while the spoonerism may result in nonsense words, the words created by transposition in puns should have meanings of their own. There is, for example, the old story of Chan, the Chinese teak dealer, whose goods were being stolen. Tracking what appeared to be the footprints of a boy, he discovered that the actual culprit was a bear—a boy-foot bear with teaks of Chan. Such puns always bring a groan, and that is what they are intended to do. Part of the humor of the pun is the labored wording required to achieve the goal. The audience mutters, "Oh, no!" but it does chuckle.

Silly Rhymes. Again there is relatively little time for this sort of humor because it is too difficult to find a plausible reason for interjecting it into a plot. When used, it normally is found in variety-type humor rather than in situation comedy. Classics in funny rhymes were those presented by the late Ernie Kovacs as the lisping, effeminate poet Percy Dovetonsils. British comedians like Benny Hill often insert rhymes, usually risqué, into their routines. The obvious advantage to rhyme is that it has built-in foreshadowing. The word required to complete the rhyme is usually obvious—and often dirty—and the humor frequently stems from the clever way in which the person reciting avoids using the improper rhyme. This can be either by substituting an unexpected rhyme, which is usually funniest, or by turning the unacceptable word into the stem of a longer word, such as:

> In the midst of botany class
> The teacher fell on her as-
>   pidistra, proving it cant
> To call it a "Cast Iron Plant."

There are hundreds of other forms of verbal humor, but the material in this section should give you an idea of some fairly common ones.

Parody and Satire

These are among the favorite devices of student writers. Unfortunately, they are among the most difficult forms of comedy to write and perform, and as a result, often fall flat. Parody makes fun of some verbal style. Every year, a Los Angeles bar holds a contest for the best parody of the style of Ernest Hemingway. Hemingway has always been a favorite of parody writers because his style was both distinctive and easy to imitate (although not easy to imitate while trying to write a complete story or book). You can parody Hemingway's style because his style was glorious and well known. You'd have less luck parodying the work of Virginia Woolf because, although her style is distinctive, her work is not widely read.

Parody for broadcast writing is often a parody of specific programs or popular films. It can also be a parody of a type of film or program. "Saturday Night Live" frequently parodied television news programs. The "Carol Burnett Show" used to parody both specific films and styles of film. Parody is a form that lends itself best to revue-type programs rather than series. However, a few series may have a theme that is actually designed to be a parody. "WKRP in Cincinnati" is essentially a parody of Top-40 radio stations.

Satire, on the other hand, makes fun of social and political customs. Often the technique is exaggeration or carrying something to a ridiculous extreme. In the "Here's Lucy" script *Mary Jane's Boy Friend,* writers Fred S. Fox and Seaman Jacobs fill some time in the script by satirizing self-improvement programs. Mary Jane has a tape-recorded lecture that she listens to and responds to for several minutes:

```
              MAN'S VOICE (RECORDED)

   You are lovely . . .

              MARY JANE

   (RECITING)  I am lovely.

(LUCY, STILL LOOKING AT HER BOOK, HAS TO REACT TO THIS.
HER EYES WIDEN.)

              MAN'S VOICE

   You are very, very lovely . . .
```

This continues for three pages of the script until Lucy finally asks Mary Jane to move to another room.

Satire and parody both depend upon overemphasizing material. This is where it becomes tricky. The line between really funny exaggerations and simple slapstick clowning is easy to cross, and the result is always something less funny. Because we live in an era of blatant excesses, it is difficult for a writer to know when the line has been crossed. Henry Morgan, whose satirical humor did much to change the style of comedy in radio during the 1940s and '50s, had these observations about some television programs that doted on satire:

> "Saturday Night" is an absolute horror. . . . There's no taste and very little talent. Aykroyd (Dan) is good. So is Gilda Radner. The rest stink. I really think it's the worst-written show on television.
>
> "Monty Python" . . . is either very, very good or very, very bad. The thing that bothers me today is that everything seems to be so unstructured. You buy a book and it hasn't been edited. You watch a film and it hasn't been directed, it hasn't been written. That's why everything is so rotten.[5]

Non Sequiturs. In everyday life, we assume that specific causes lead to known effects and that two and two should equal four. In non-sequitur humor, the tables are turned. The answers do *not* logically follow from the questions, and the resulting twisted logic amuses us. Goodman Ace used to write wacky non-sequitur dialog for his wife, Jane, in their old radio series, "Mr. Ace and Jane." Here's a sample:

JANE: Hello, dear. (<u>DOOR CLOSES</u>)

ACE: Well, Jane, what brings you downtown this early?

JANE: Just fine. Hello, Mr. Norris. How are you?

NORRIS: I've been a little under the weather lately, Mrs. Ace.

JANE: Yes, isn't it?[6]

The Unexpected Answer. If you analyze most comedy dialog, you will find that the fact that the response to a statement is a surprise—whether logical or illogical—is what brings on the laughter. Take this exchange between Fred Sanford and his son Lamont in the *My Kingdom for a Horse* episode on "Sanford and Son":

LAMONT

WHAT'S THAT HORSE DOING IN THE KITCHEN???

FRED

I don't know . . . you saw him last.

[5]James Brown, "Rumpled Satirist Hasn't Lost a Step," *Los Angeles Times Calendar,* April 22, 1979, p. 104.
[6]Goodman Ace, *Ladies and Gentlemen—Easy Aces* (New York: Doubleday, 1970), p. 87.

```
                    LAMONT

POP . . . I WANT AN ANSWER!!!

                    FRED

Well, it's very simple . . .

                    LAMONT

I DON'T WANT A LIE!!!

                    FRED

It's getting harder.⁷
```

Sometimes, the explanation of an unexpected answer is what gets the laughs. Asked why her husband hasn't returned a phone call, Jane Ace says she's just taken four showers. Asked what that has to do with it, she explains, "The phone always rings when I'm in the shower."

SUMMARY

There is no way to list all of the possible ways to write comedy. What we have listed in this chapter should give you some idea of the range of verbal and visual humor you can call upon. Comedy writers usually work closely with the performers who will be reading their lines. Changes are frequent. One danger in writing comedy is that by the time the material has been rehearsed and rewritten many times, good material begins to seem stale. Comedy writers can easily lose perspective. It is a good idea to have someone read or view your material fresh. That will help you decide whether a joke you have lost faith in really is a failure or whether you have simply seen and heard it too many times in the rehearsal.

Keep in mind, too, that in television comedy you must grab your audience at once. Scripts often open with visual humor. The reason is fairly simple. Any verbal humor requires some preparatory dialog. Visual humor, if well planned, can be instantly funny to the audience. Concentrate heavy doses of humor at the start of the program, just before the end of the first act, and at the end of the show. This will help to hold your audience at critical moments when they might consider switching channels. Never let more than 60 seconds pass without giving the audience something to laugh at.

---

⁷"My Kingdom for a Horse," September 6, 1974.

TELEVISION COMMERCIALS 5

and
Public
Service
Announcements

Preparing any commercial requires careful thought and planning by the writer. It is one of the most difficult forms of writing to do successfully. You have only seconds to say what you have to say—yet you are expected to accomplish more in those seconds than most writers have to do in a half hour or more. The writer of drama or comedy has only to entertain and involve the audience. Often there is a message to be conveyed, a hoped-for change in attitude on the part of the viewer, but as long as the script holds the audience, no one blames the writer for failing to change the way the viewers think and act. Not so with the commercial. The whole purpose of the commercial is to affect the way the viewers think and act. Your goal is to sell the product. A commercial that fails to sell is not a good commercial. Every advertising man can tell you grim stories of commercials that the viewers loved—but that failed to get the viewers to buy. Conversely, there are hundreds of tales of poorly produced, unimaginative commercials that sold the product. In the days when cigars were made by hand in city storefronts, the wrappers sealed with a lick of the operator's tongue, tobacco tycoon George Washington Hill is supposed to have pushed his Cremo Cigars with the radio commercial, "There is no spit in Cremo!" Hill didn't care what people thought about the commercial as long as they thought about Cremos when they went to buy cigars.

ESTABLISHING THE GOAL

Your first real job, then, is to know what your commercial is expected to do. Not all commercials "sell" in the most obvious sense of the word. There are, for example, *institutional commercials,* designed to create a favorable impression of the sponsor. Some sponsors, telephone companies for instance, have no competition. They may be interested in encouraging you to increase your use of the telephone, thereby increasing sales, but they don't have to worry about getting you to use *their* telephone system instead of someone else's. Telephone companies are *regulated* by state and federal boards, however, and a major concern is that the public have a *good image* of the telephone company. A far greater concern than getting you to increase your use of the telephone is producing advertising that keeps you satisfied with the telephone company itself. If the public is *not* satisfied, the telephone companies are in for a difficult time with their regulators. *Institutional*, rather than *product*, advertising is the main job in producing commercials for such organizations.

Some products and services are intimately tied to the image of the producer; again, what is advertised is the institution rather than its product or service. Banks, for example, are hesitant to advertise their services in the same way a grocer might advertise fruit. Much depends upon an image of stability and conservatism—although that concept in bank advertising has changed somewhat in recent years. Still, the idea of the commercial is usually to sell the image of the bank as a safe place for your money. You emphasize the institution, not its services.

Public service announcements call for another approach. Here the goal is not so much to sell a product as to sell an idea. The public service announcement may seek to "sell" in the sense that it motivates the viewer to contribute money or services to the organization involved. Or the goal may be behavior modification, to get the audience to think and act in a different manner. Because very special problems are involved in preparing public service announcements, we have prepared a separate section on that topic at the end of this chapter. It suffices to note here that, while the services rendered are the most important aspect of any charitable organization, very often it is the image of the organization that must be "sold" to the public.

A somewhat similar problem gets a very different treatment when you are advertising items for mass consumption. There is, in fact, little difference between many major products. Somewhat as in institutional advertising, you must sell the *brand,* but in this case, the product is always emphasized. Usually there is some kind of superiority implied for the product. For example, corn flakes are corn flakes. It is doubtful that there is much difference in food value or taste from one brand to the other. Yet your job is somehow to suggest to the audience that it will be more satisfied if it buys *your* brand of corn flakes.

Brand advertising and institutional advertising are usually *delayed response* types of advertising. The sponsor does not expect the viewer to rush right out of the house and make a bank deposit or buy a box of corn flakes. Some other advertisers want to see immediate results. Usually these are small-volume advertisers, such as used car dealers. They deal in *direct response* advertising. If the viewers do not buy the advertised product within a short time (usually one day), the ad has failed.

You must have a good grasp of the basic purpose of your ad before you can begin to write it. Be sure you understand: Am I selling a product, a brand name, or an institution? Is my goal immediate response or delayed response? Have the answer to those questions clearly in mind before you think about writing the ad.

STUDY THE PRODUCT

You should also carry out some careful research on the product. Use the product if possible, or try to talk to people who have used it. Check out competing products as well. Make a list of the things you like and dislike about the product you are going to advertise, and do the same with its main competitors. What does the competitor's product contain that might make a person quit using it and try something else? What would make someone want to try it?

Sometimes the most obvious approaches turn out to be unsatisfactory when you think them over carefully. For example, if you have two products that are essentially the same, except for brand name, you would think that you could stress the fact that your product is cheaper. But you had better think that approach over very carefully. Suppose the audience believes that a cheaper product is an *inferior* product. "You only get what you pay for" is an old saying, and many successful advertising campaigns have been built on that concept. One well-known brand of Scotch whisky was first marketed in the United States with the proviso that it must be sold at 10 cents a shot more than regular bar Scotch. The *New Yorker* magazine abounds in what someone once called the you-cannot-possibly-pay-more-for-this-item type of ad. So you have to be careful about advertising a product on the basis of its being cheaper. If you use that approach, it has to be couched in terms that also stress quality. One such ad goes, "The finest you can buy . . . at a surprisingly modest price."

You must also be careful about making any statement that suggests price is the *only* difference between your product and others of the same type. You want the buyer to feel that she or he is getting *better* quality than can be supplied by the competition. Remember, if you tell the audience, "All products in this category are the same, so you might as well buy ours because it's cheaper," there may be a cheaper brand than yours on the shelves tomorrow. (Of course, that is the way the economic system is supposed to work, but you won't find many clients who are interested in that approach.)

If you are an advertising copywriter for a large firm or advertising agency, you will probably have data supplied to you by a research staff that studies very carefully what the public thinks about your product and its competitors. But research does not do the writer's thinking for him. It simply tells him what to think about. Suppose the research staff tells you that people are not switching to your product because they think it is old-fashioned. However, the researchers also tell you that people who do use the product buy it for the same reason, they *like* its old-fashioned image. How do you attract new buyers without losing the old ones? How do you say the product is new, but old-fashioned? If you pay attention to television advertising, you will see that a great many advertisements do exactly that.

```
                    DAUGHTER

        Mother, you've been using that same

        old ZOTZ detergent since I was a

        baby.

                    MOTHER

        Wrong!  This is new, improved ZOTZ,

        with wonder-working triglyph, to get

        clothes cleaner than ever before.

                    DAUGHTER

        New ZOTZ?

                    MOTHER

        Like old ZOTZ, only even better.

        . . . And they say you can't improve

        on perfection!
```

THE PRODUCT'S APPEAL

A major decision to be made in planning a commercial—often one made in consultation with the research department—is what appeal the ad should make. Every advertisement should appeal to some basic human need. Different writers have compiled different lists of these basic needs, but the underlying concept is the same. You will not have great success if you simply say to the viewer: "Buy this product!" You must make the viewer feel: "I *need* this product." That may be a conscious decision on the viewer's part, or it may be a subconscious response to your message.

All human beings have certain basic needs. If you identify your product with one of those needs, you have made a much stronger appeal. Some, although by no means all, of those needs are security, sex, self-esteem, variety, and play. Let's examine them.

Security

Everyone needs to feel safe. You need to feel safe from physical attack, be it by nuclear weapon or neighborhood bully. You need to feel secure against the elements—warm, dry, and on firm ground. You need to feel secure against hunger. You need to feel economically secure. You need to feel that your property is safe from theft and damage. When you get right down to it, very few people *really* want to "live dangerously."

Franklin D. Roosevelt, no amateur at motivating the public, used the "Four Freedoms" as a major theme in World War II, as a means of uniting the people behind the war effort. They were Freedom of Speech, Freedom of Religion, Freedom from Want, and Freedom from Fear. The appeal to security in those "freedoms" is direct and obvious. It helped to motivate people to accept the ultimate paradox, that they must risk their lives and security in order to obtain security in the future.

Banks and savings institutions are obvious examples of sponsors whose services appeal to the need for security. One western savings institution reportedly paid the late John Wayne $1.3 million to do a series of television ads. The choice of Wayne was masterful. Wayne had a dual image with the public. On the one hand, he was identified with political conservatism. (Not even a radical is likely to put his money in a radical bank.) On the other hand, Wayne's movie image was that of the hero—one willing to risk his life to *protect* others. How could your money be safer than having John Wayne standing over it with a six-gun? And finally, of course, Wayne had enormous personal popularity.

Visually, this series of advertisements—which won many advertising awards—was stunning. The ads stuck to the western theme that was the subject of so many Wayne films. Full use of color photography put Wayne in scenery as dazzling as that of many of his movies. The western theme also tied in to the name of the sponsor, Great Western Savings and Loan.

The psychological appeal of the commercials, however, was not to Wayne in the image of a gunslinger. That would hardly do for a savings institution. The theme instead was that Wayne, the successful actor, who had made millions—but invested some unwisely—now put his cash where it was safe, in Great Western. It played beautifully against Wayne's two-fisted image of his younger days and the conservative image of his later years. Wayne had had recurring bouts of cancer, and the audience certainly knew he had few years left to live. Yet here he was, in his declining years, regretting the errors of his youth and urging all to benefit from his mistakes and tuck their savings safely away at Great Western. It was a masterful appeal to the need for security.

A rival savings and loan institution promptly hired comedian Bob Hope to do its commercials. ("Today, the stars are making the commercials and the unknowns are making the movies," said Hope.) The theme was similar to that used for Wayne. Hope, a man in his late seventies, who had made millions, was emphasizing the importance of putting money in a safe place—this time California Federal Savings and Loan. Hope's theme was not that he had invested his money unwisely before, but that it was harder to save money now than it had been when he was making "Road" pictures. Where the Wayne ads had played up Wayne's western image, the Hope ads, naturally, played up Hope as a comedian. "I get very serious when it comes to saving money. . . . Today, with everything going up, including my golf score, you need a hedge against inflation." Bill Larkin, a Hope gag writer, helped the agency (Jensen and Ritchie) write the scripts. Hope described an account at the savings and loan as "about as good as you can do unless you're married to a plumber."[1]

As with any good advertising campaign, research preceded the preparation of the scripts. The target audience was people over 50 years of age. This was an audience that had known Hope most of its life, and was facing the basic problem of how to protect savings and investments built up over the years against rampant inflation. The need for security was a particularly strong motivation for this group, which would soon be facing retirement and the need to survive on carefully invested savings. Actually, Hope's message wasn't a very promising one. Money in a bank is not likely to hold its own against inflation—even in the high-interest accounts being advertised by Hope—but the alternatives held no guarantee of doing better. In a no-win situation, the audience could at least laugh along with Hope and agree that the bank was about the best solution "unless you're married to a plumber." (Note, by the way, how that joke points up a threat to the security of the viewer. When you need a plumber, you usually can't put it off regardless of the price.)

Sex Appeal

While security is a major appeal in the making of a commercial, probably the most common appeal is to sex. That has a great many different meanings, of course. There are both overt and covert appeals to blatant human sexuality in some advertisements. A famous shaving cream ad of some years back featured burlesque house music and a beautiful blonde urging, "Take it off. Take it all off!" A Bell Telephone advertisement stresses friendship and family ties, but the theme "Reach out and touch someone" can also have sexual connotations.

Actually, it's on this secondary level of sexuality that television ads are more likely to operate. It is an appeal to being "liked" and "loved," not necessarily to actual sexual gratification. It may seem unfair to combine this form of "love" with plain old sex, but the appeal is often only a matter of degree, as in the Bell Telephone ad.

Yet another appeal to sex tends to combine our first category, the need for security, with sex. A good many ads play upon sexual insecurity. Use this product, and you will be more sexually desirable, more masculine, more feminine, more whatever. Such ads often appeal to sexual stereotypes. Drink our beer and be one of the boys. Bake our cake and be loved by your husband. Wear our girdle and be sexually attractive. There is nothing inherently masculine about guzzling beer, and not much sexually stimulating

[1]Martin Rossman, "Hope Stars in New 'Road' Show," *Los Angeles Times,* January 30, 1979, III, p. 15.

about cakes or girdles, but they fit with certain images we have, and the ads play on those images.

Self-Esteem

Closely related to the sexual need is the need for self-esteem. While the appeal you work on in using sex is "use our product and you will be loved and desired," the appeal to self-esteem is "use our product and you will be respected and looked up to." You can find both approaches used in automobile ads. In some ads—usually for "sporty" models—you see the owner of the automobile surrounded by admiring members of the opposite sex. In others, the automobile may be pictured in surroundings of wealth and elegance. The vehicle is a status symbol. You may only be the third assistant screw-sorter in a nut-and-bolt factory, but you can hop into the car and you are instant royalty—or so the ads try to suggest. This is a concept deeply ingrained in the American psyche.

Appeals to self-esteem work best with easily identified products. It may be an appeal to security to know that you have bought the best of some category of products—but to be looked up to for buying it, people have to recognize it. Suppose, for example, you wanted to market the most expensive (and presumably best) men's socks in the world. It would be difficult to appeal to self-esteem because no one really pays much attention to men's socks. Your best appeal is probably to security because the wearer of the socks probably just wants to be able to put them on and not have to think about them again until he takes them off. But if you were selling a wristwatch, you could appeal to self-esteem. The owner of the watch is going to be looking at it throughout the day, and others will notice it as well. You can probably buy a perfectly good watch for $20, so if you pay more than that, it is at least partially because the watch gives you the feeling "I am important" or "I have good taste" every time you look at it—and you assume everyone else who notices it will feel the same way.

How would you make this appeal? You might show the watch in expensive surroundings or being worn by seemingly important people, or you might have famous people do commercials wearing the watch. "Gee! If Sir Laurence Olivier wears one, it must be good!"

It is also possible to play this appeal in reverse. You can appeal to self-esteem by making the buyer feel she or he is too smart to be taken in by regular advertising. For years, Volkswagen played up its image as an ugly little car. Rather than playing down the "beetle" nickname, the ads encouraged it. When new models arrived, the American name given to the line was not "Mustang" or "Grand Prix" or some of the flashy names chosen for other cars, but "Rabbit," something that is small and fast. Again, one felt the designers at Volkswagen had gone out of their way to make the car a little uglier than necessary. The idea was to have an identifiable product that would give the driver the feeling "I'm too smart to be taken in by all the advertising and chrome trim. I am a terribly smart person for buying this modest, inexpensive, but well-made little car." The image was so successful that most buyers ignored the fact that the Volkswagen had ceased to be inexpensive when it came to purchase price.

Two very similar television campaigns were waged using the appeal to self-esteem by two major stock brokerage houses. In each, the viewer saw a series of people—some famous, some just actors—who had apparently just been notified of a successful stock transaction. In one, the theme of the ads was "Thank you, Paine Webber." In the other it was "You look like you just heard from Dean Witter." In the second, the theme was sung. The basic idea is the same for both series of ads: Smart people, some of them well-known, make money by dealing with this brokerage firm. It is interesting to note that the appeal was not to security here. It would seem logical that the investor would want to feel her or his money was secure. But that might also raise in the investor's mind the thought that any investment has its risks. Instead, the ads suggested, *"smart investors use us."*

Variety

Yet another appeal for you to consider in planning your commercial is variety. We all get tired of the same old stuff. "New," "improved,"—such terms abound in commercials. As we mentioned earlier, a balance has to be struck between the security that people find in familiar things and their natural curiosity about new ones. Seven-Up made a direct appeal to curiosity with its slogan "Try it, you'll like it!" This was backed up by a series of highly imaginative "psychedelic" commercials, trying to create a new image for the product. There was no change in the product itself (balancing the security of the familiar with the appeal of the novel). The entire approach was to get people to *think* about Seven-Up as part of new and exciting times.

Another soft drink, Dr Pepper, improved its sales with a series of humorous ads in which resisting people were coerced in one way or another to "try" Dr Pepper, and, of course, liked it. The theme was that Dr Pepper was "misunderstood." At least one ad in this series also made some use of sex with a tongue-in-cheek ad that kept the viewer guessing for a few moments what it was the young man was urging the young lady to try for the first time.

Play

The last basic appeal in our list is perhaps the most important—the desire for play or entertainment. If your commercial does not entertain, it is probably in trouble. We say "probably," because as was pointed out at the start, there are some examples of perfectly awful commercials that sold products very well, and many very entertaining commercials have failed to sell the product. One example of the latter was a commercial produced by Seven-Up during the period it was stressing the idea that it was the "Un-Cola." The basic appeal was to novelty—try something besides a cola drink—but the approach of the particular commercial involved was humor. The commercial consisted of a parody of an Ingmar Bergman movie—complete with subtitles. It was a clever, amusing idea, but . . . . In the control room of a major San Francisco network television station, about 15 minutes after the commercial had run, someone looked down at the program log and asked, "Did we run the Seven-Up commercial?" Not one person there could remember. When the people being paid to run your commercial can't remember it, you are in trouble.

Successful appeals to the natural inclination to play must be more than simply clever or funny. They must link the product firmly with the need to play and be amused. Pet food commercials often achieve this while also combining an element of the need for love. Pets usually provide their owners with both amusement and love. For sponsors, they provide a market of 15 million dog owners and 25 million cat owners—each cat putting away about 180 pounds of cat food a year—or at least having that much put out for the cat by the owner.

Nine Lives cat food appealed to this combination of love and humor in its series of ads with Morris the finicky cat. Morris became such a hit that people sported Morris T-shirts and hung Morris calendars on their walls. When Morris finally went to that big sandbox in the sky, he was eulogized by major newspapers and network television news programs. The theme of the ads was always the same. Morris would amuse the audience by expressing distaste for some attempt by his owner to please him. But his determination to be finicky was always overcome by the apparently irresistible appeal of Nine Lives cat food. Humor here was the "hook" that attracted and held the audience. The message, of course, was, "If you have a finicky cat (Is there any other kind?), he'll eat if you feed him Nine Lives."

There are many other ways to appeal to the natural instinct for play, and most of them are easier than planning commercials with animals. (One producer has estimated that it takes 2,000 feet of film to get one usable foot of film when shooting animals.) The "Pepsi Generation" ads were another example of appeal to play—with some other appeals thrown in. They consisted of a montage (series of quick shots) showing people playing and enjoying themselves. Some were shown drinking Pepsi-Cola, and the word "Pepsi" was frequently repeated in the musical background.

Consider these basic needs we have discussed. Usually you can make one or more of these appeals the basis for your commercial. To do so, you need to know the product, the audience, and the effect the sponsor desires to achieve. When you have decided upon these, think how each appeal might be used to achieve the best effect. Make a list, and winnow it down to the best appeals. Sometimes you will find only one seems suitable. At other times, you may be able to use virtually all appeals. Examine them all carefully and pick the best.

GETTING THE MESSAGE ACROSS

Years ago, researchers studying the effects of a government campaign to fight bigotry isolated a series of problems that anyone must face when getting a message across to the public. It's good to keep these in mind as you work on your commercial. They are selective attention, selective perception, and selective retention.

Selective Attention

People do not pay as much attention to things they do not want to hear as they do to things they want to hear. Thus, your first job is to gain attention. To do so, you should open the commercial with something the viewer believes she or he wants to see.

One reason for keying your commercial to basic needs is because you know there is general interest in them. There is considerable advantage, too, in using famous people in ads because the audience recognizes them and watches to see what they will do. The savings and loan commercials using John Wayne and Bob Hope discussed earlier are good examples of making use of prominent people to attract your audience.

Selective Perception

Once you have overcome selective attention, you have the more difficult job of overcoming selective perception. This is where the best skills of the writer are called for. Selective perception is the tendency of people to distort things to fit their preconceptions. People have been known to watch a commercial and go away convinced it advertised a competing product. First, exercising selective attention, they were not watching very closely, and then, exercising selective perception, they simply substituted the name of a favorite product for the one advertised. There are several ways you can help solve this problem with your writing.

First, make sure your copy is free of any ambiguity. Do not leave anything in the script that might be interpreted some other way than you intend. For example, "You'll never forget eating at Chez Maladroit" can have more than one meaning. You may never forget it because the food or service is awful. One poorly thought out restaurant commercial used to advertise that the food was so good that doctors recommended it to their patients. The unintended implication was that when you ate there, you would be surrounded by a bunch of sick people.

A second way to avoid selective perception is to make use of repetition. It is an old rule of thumb that you should repeat the product name at least three times in a commercial. That rule was designed for radio. For television, you can easily get the sponsor's name before the audience many more times. It can be spoken by the announcer, used by characters in the commercial, shown on the screen both as a title and as some permanent part of the set. It can be repeated in musical backgrounds. And, of course, you can show the product itself—which in most cases you will want to do. Often you can show the product in use. By keeping the sponsor's name before the audience through every channel available, you help cut down on the risk of selective perception.

Selective Retention

Finally, there is the problem of selective retention, which simply means that people remember things they agree with best. Repetition again is helpful. In the incident involving the parody of an Ingmar Bergman movie mentioned earlier, there was only fleeting reference to Seven-Up and the "Un-Cola." Apparently it wasn't enough, however clever the commercial was. Repetition could have helped.

Use of familiar characters helps overcome all three problems of selectivity. People wanted to watch Morris the cat, they associated Morris with his product, Nine Lives, and they remembered Morris when the commercial was over. This helps to explain why advertisers keep using a character in television commercials if the audience seems to like or at least remember that character. Mr. Wipple has been warning people not to squeeze the Charmin toilet tissue for over 15 years at this writing—more than 300 commercials. It's been 13 years since Mrs. Olson has run into a neighbor who knew about Folger's Coffee. Madge the manicurist has soaked people's fingers in Palmolive Liquid in 250 commercials over the past 12 years. And Josephine the Plumber retired after 12 years of cleaning up people's sinks with Comet.

Obviously one thing to keep in mind when creating a commercial is that it is useful to create or use a character that can continue in subsequent commercials. (Nine Lives had several Morris lookalikes ready to follow in his paw steps when the original Morris passed away.) The audience identifies and remembers continuing characters.

Another way to help people remember your commercial is to have a slogan or theme to go with it. Mr. Wipple's "Don't squeeze the Charmin" is a good example. The "Pepsi generation" is another. Repeating these themes in each script or in the musical accompaniment drills them into your audience's mind.

Keeping your script simple is still another technique to help the audience remember it. Harry McMahan, the man who selects the "100 Best Commercials" every year, says the present generation is "bored with details." Top commercials today, he says, usually have fast-paced action, strong musical effects, and tight editing.

POLITICAL ADVERTISING

Such students of animal behavior as Konrad Lorenz have established that most animals have inherently aggressive elements in their makeup. These aggressive tendencies are expressed in competition for mates and in the establishing and defending of territory. While many scientists do not agree, it seems likely that human beings share these aggressive tendencies and desires to establish territory. Nevertheless, these tendencies do not have to be expressed in antisocial ways. Freudians, for example, would argue that most of our "animal" instincts, including aggression, are "sublimated." We find socially acceptable outlets for them. Instead of competing with clubs for mates, we compete in business for money, power, and prestige.

It is impossible to look at our society—or any society—without finding hundreds of activities that seem to substitute for aggression and territoriality. Each year, some 35 million Americans watch the Super Bowl. From 1970 to 1980, eight of the 25 largest television audiences were for Super Bowl games. Football combines aggressive action (often resulting in the injury of players) with territoriality—gaining or losing yardage. The losers do not suffer the fate of losing gladiators in the Roman arena or the losing team in Aztec ballgames (who were beheaded), but we place great stress on winning.

Important among higher animals is the ability to form groups to gain or defend territory. In human terms this translates into teamwork. We often join a team to compete, whether it is on the football field or in the business field, and we love to be on the winning team. Part of this competitive team behavior centers on the selection of leaders for the teams.

Historically this was done by combat. Later, leadership might become hereditary—as long as the royal family could fight off ambitious competitors. From Confucian China came the concept of choosing officials through testing of their abilities. In Europe, some tribes chose leaders by the amount of noise that each contender's followers could make by pounding on their shields with swords. In the Church, advancement was often through merit, although family ties helped.

Of course, the concept of electing leaders by vote had been with us since the time of the ancient Greeks. However, it was not until this century that the concept of allowing virtually all adult citizens to vote was firmly established in the West (and women still cannot vote in some Swiss cantons). Outside the Western democracies, with few exceptions, the vote—if it exists at all—is strictly limited, and those allowed to run for office are even more strictly restricted. In the United States, we have made elections major national events in which the media play an increasingly dominant role.

Political Advertising and Human Needs

Political advertising, like all other forms, is directed to basic human needs. What are some of the needs that can be appealed to in political advertising? One need that can be played upon is the very team spirit we have been talking about—the need to compete, the need to select leaders. Be warned, studies show that political campaigns do not really "swing" a great many votes. Most people come into the campaign with their minds already made up on the major issues to be decided. They may not choose to admit it openly (most people would prefer to tell everyone—including themselves—that they are going to consider all the issues carefully before they make a decision), but elections do not occur in a vacuum. The issues build up over time. An election focuses attention on certain issues, but the voters have probably already formed some opinions on most of the issues. Moreover, most of us have political predispositions acquired from family, friends, and business.

In some respects, then, the political advertisement functions like the cheerleaders at a football game. It keeps the faithful supporting the team of their choice and keeps the team fighting hard. It is unlikely that any fan ever switched to another team because he or she was convinced by hearing what the opponents' cheering section was shouting. It is not quite as unlikely that a political ad will make a convert, but it has to be admitted that you cannot expect to change many minds with a 30-second spot.

What you try to do is to keep those who have made up their minds to vote for your candidate sufficiently convinced and excited to work for the candidate, contribute money, or at least get out and vote. You also hope to restore to those who may be faltering in their support a sense of obligation to stick with the party or candidate. This is particularly important for groups whose family, ethnic, or socioeconomic origins may incline them to one political viewpoint, while their present status influences them to vote for the other party. A similar problem may arise when some specific issue tends to throw a group that has traditionally supported one party into support of the other party.

The appeal to conflict or team spirit is one approach that you can use in political advertising. The incessant use of the word "we" in political rhetoric is not accidental. The attempt is to make everyone feel part of the team, perhaps by the recitation of lists of groups who have benefited or will benefit from the victory of the candidate or party. We have tagged this approach the Walt Whitman technique, following the observation of a friend who once said that the way to write a Walt Whitman poem is to begin "I sing of . . ." and then copy fourteen random pages from the yellow pages of a telephone book. This can sometimes be cast as a series of rhetorical questions about the opponent. "What has my opponent done for the farmers? What has my opponent done for the auto workers? What has she or he done for the Asian refugees, the small business people, the elderly . . . ?"

Get the bad guys—on the other team—is another appeal. Perhaps one of the strangest appeals to "our team can beat the bad guys" took place in Los Angeles in the 1960s. One of the candidates for mayor found an issue that allowed him to elect himself captain of the team for all the housewives in the city. For years the city had had an ecologically sound system of garbage collection. Different types of garbage—metal cans, glass, wet garbage, and so on—had to be kept separate for separate collections. This was a chore for those at home taking care of the house. The candidate launched his campaign by calling in the press for a news conference and publicly throwing a tin can into a can of wet garbage—a misdemeanor under the city law. Then he promised, if elected, to repeal the laws requiring the separation of various types of garbage. In today's energy-short world, that appeal might not work, but this was before the energy crisis, and the candidate was swept into office considerably aided by the garbage issue. (One of the authors of this book was sensibly restrained by a news editor from beginning a story about the election, "In Los Angeles, where garbage is news—and vice versa. . . .")

The candidate had formed a team and created a shadowy team of opponents—the city administration, the garbage collectors, somebody out there—to fight against. Well-planned media coverage kept portraying the candidate as leading the fight against the sinister garbage collection conspiracy. It was an appeal to the need for conflict—albeit a rather odd one.

Of course, political ads can make use of other needs as well. For example, the need for security can be used in political advertising.

One famous commercial used in a presidential election had to be withdrawn because opponents felt it gave a grossly unfair picture of the man against whom it was directed. The commercial, showing a child playing with flowers followed by an atomic explosion, implied that electing that candidate would lead to atomic war. It is hard to find a more obvious appeal to the need for security than that.

In fact, the political campaign presents the copywriter with a difficult problem. Politics is the one field in which the consumer can never do real comparison shopping. You vote for what the candidate says he *will* do. An incumbent, of course, can point with pride to his accomplishments—just as his opponent can view with alarm the incumbent's failures. But you really do not know that someone else in the same job would have done better or worse. Political writers simply divide their time between being crystal ball gazers and Monday morning quarterbacks. And what constitutes a "good" or "bad" decision by an officeholder always depends on who is making the evaluation and whose ox got gored.

So, in an area in which the word "best" manifestly has no meaning, the copywriter's job is to prove that his candidate is best. The voter has to feel that he will be safer—or at least will not be less safe—if your candidate is elected. Safe from *what* depends upon the election. One of the writers of this book was hired to prepare a series of television "political announcements" (no one likes to call them "commercials") for a slate of candidates in a city election.

The choice of television as the best medium for the campaign was debatable. The city in question was a bedroom suburb of a large midwestern city. It had no television station of its own, so the announcements would have to go on one or more of the stations in the urban center nearby. Most of the viewers of the announcements would not be voters in the election. Given that most of the city's working population were commuters, radio announcements in "drive time" would have been a logical choice for political spots. Radio was in fact used, but the candidates felt (probably correctly) that they could make a more lasting impression on the voters with television spots.

The appeal of the campaign, of course, was to the need for security. In this case, the idea was that each member of the slate running for city council and mayor would contribute uniquely to protecting something valued by the citizens of the community.

Ray Hurley (not his real name), a former newspaperman, had done much to promote the history of the community. His role would be to protect and preserve historical sites in the community. But he wanted to show *all* the historic spots of the community in one 30-second spot. Originally, he had wanted to show four different locations in the 30-second spot. This was eventually cut to one—about all that could be handled in the short time span.

Running with him was a local contractor, whom we have called Larry Mullins here. Mullins was to represent economic growth for the community, protecting jobs and keeping taxes low. His 30-second spot was filmed on the site of a new shopping center he was building in the city. He was shot wearing a hard hat, posed in front of a crane.

The most important member of the slate was the candidate for mayor—a handsome young lawyer. We shot him in his law office, poring over law books, indicating that he was a hard-working citizen who knew what the law was all about.

The copywriter usually does not have a free hand in preparing political scripts. The candidate, obviously, has the major say in deciding what he or she will say to the public. However, the copywriter has to polish that material up for the speakers—and above all put it in a usable television format. The major problem faced by the writer in preparing the spots was getting what the candidate wanted to say into a 30-second framework. It is generally agreed by communication researchers that the 30-second spot is as effective as, or more effective than, other forms of political advertising on television. From a cost standpoint, it was almost essential to use the short format for the campaign. But—as critics of this type of political advertising have constantly pointed out—it leaves little time to present the issues to the voters.

None of the candidates for whom the announcements were prepared had done any television spots before, although two of them had appeared on television panel programs. The greatest difficulty was encountered with Hurley, the retired newspaper columnist. He, of course, wanted to write his own copy—and he did. It was a beautiful little speech—but it ran three minutes. He did not want to cut it. That was the "editor's" job. "Shoot it this way," he insisted. "You can edit it down later." Eventually the candidate won his way, and the ultimate result can be determined from this letter the writer sent to the head of the campaign committee shortly thereafter (names of persons and locations have been changed):

Dear Mr. Roy,

Enclosed is our billing for services to date.

I am encountering some difficulty with the editing of Mr. Hurley's 30-second spot. In order to get his copy to fit the 30-second time frame, I've cut heavily. I still need to make one additional cut. The copy now reads:

> This is for real—historic Midvale—The old spring—Midvale is for real in history, tradition, solid citizenship. It doesn't need tinsel, cellophane, whoopla, and commercialism. Midvale needs a real team for this City Council election—Ray Hurley asks your vote for Roy, Mullins, and Hurley—and that's for real too.

I can either delete "Historic Midvale" in the first line, or delete the final phrase. In terms of the meaning of the spot, it would be better to cut off the final "and that's for real too." However, this creates some visual problems. There is no time left to fade to black if we do this. The screen would have to go black immediately after he says "Roy, Mullins, and Hurley," or we would see his lips mouthing "and that's for real too" during the first part of the fade to black. I'd appreciate knowing how Mr. Hurley feels about this. . . The only other alternative is to change the spot from 30 seconds to one minute.

Sincerely,

In this case, the writer had failed in his duty by not insisting that the copy be edited to time before shooting began.

STORYBOARDS

Preparation of a storyboard is a normal routine for most commercials. Storyboards can be useful in all forms of television production, and are used to some degree in other types of television, but their greatest use is to be found in the preparation of the commercial.

One reason is simply that it is an easy task to make up a storyboard for a commercial. Since the average network commercial today is only 30 seconds long, you could illustrate every second of a commercial with a storyboard and still not use up much paper. However, a more important reason is that the high cost and compact nature of the commercial make it important that every second of it be thought out carefully in advance.

A storyboard consists simply of a series of frames, shaped like your television picture, with a place to number the frame and space below to write the copy for the action shown. The space may also be used to describe the action in greater detail. At a large agency, the art department usually sketches in the pictures for the storyboard. Elsewhere, the writer may sketch in what she or he had in mind to go with the copy. These need not be polished drawings. They need only be clear enough to show what the screen will look like while specific lines of copy are being read. (Naturally, when storyboards are prepared for showing to a sponsor, an artist is usually called in to give the storyboard a professional appearance.)

But the storyboard can be a wonderful tool for the writer's personal use—and this requires no more drawing skill than the ability to draw stick men. For almost any writing assignment, the writer will benefit from taking the time to sit down and sketch out the major action of the script. New ideas often occur to you while working with a storyboard, and unforeseen problems sometimes become obvious.

For the commercial, you should prepare the most detailed storyboard possible. Every intended change in the visuals should be indicated. Figure 5.1 is a storyboard for one of the commercials described later in this chapter.

Figure 5.1 A Typical Storyboard

PRODUCTION TECHNIQUES

When you have analyzed the needs your commercial should appeal to, and have sought appropriate means to cope with viewer selectivity, you are ready to decide which technique to use in presenting the commercial. Much of this depends upon budget and available facilities. For example, it is pointless to consider an animated cartoon if you have a small budget. Animation is a very costly procedure. It is equally pointless to write a commercial that calls for special effects that are not available to you. And, of course, you must have agreement with the sponsor on the length and number of commercials to be produced. Over three-fourths of network commercials today are 30-second commercials. Most studies indicate that the 30-second spot does just as good a job as a one-minute commercial. Perhaps a few years down the line, you may find yourself doing 20- or 15-second commercials. You must have a decision on the length before you begin, just as you must know whether the commercial is to be a "one-shot" commercial or if there will be several in the series.

Here are some of the most common techniques used for commercials. We have included in this list both those that can be produced at the smallest station and some that can only be produced by specialized production centers.

1. One or more slides with the announcer's voice over. These are cheap to produce, but rarely very interesting. If you are to overcome selective attention, try to make the slides visually stimulating. Prepare these scripts using live television format. Be sure that there is adequate time to read each slide if more than one is used. If there is printed material on the slides, it should be no more than four or five words. Repeat key elements both visually and verbally. A recorded musical theme can sometimes help, but it must be chosen with care so that it does not detract from the spoken material.

VIDEO	AUDIO
FADE IN:	ANNCR
SLIDE #1: Sundae	Go on. Live a little. . . .
	How about a hot fudge sundae
	. . . smothered with whipped
	cream . . . and pecan chips?
DISSOLVE TO:	
SLIDE #2: Soda	Or a strawberry soda . . .
	with two big scoops of ice

```
                              cream?  How long's it been,

                              huh?

DISSOLVE TO:

SLIDE #3: Banana Split        There's still a place where

                              it's really just as good as

                              you remember. . . .

CUT TO:

SLIDE #4: Benson Logo         Benson's Old Fashioned Ice

                              Cream Parlours. . . .

                              There are 38 Benson's Ice

                              Cream Parlours in the

                              metropolitan area. . . .

                              There's one near you. . . .

                              Because you deserve it.

FADE TO BLACK                              END
```

2. The direct pitch; announcer on camera. This is perhaps one of the most unappealing forms of commercials, but ironically it is often one of the most effective.

It consists simply of the salesman standing there in front of the camera, urging the audience to buy the product—and usually demonstrating or exhibiting the product. Often the announcer is a nasal-sounding man with a New York accent selling potato peelers or a used car salesman who sounds recently imported from Oklahoma. It doesn't matter. This form of commercial really does sell—especially if the goal is direct rather than delayed response. As writer, you must prepare a script that is convincing, and you must have the commercial very clearly thought out in your mind. It does not happen by accident that the camera cuts from a medium shot of the announcer to a close-up of the potato peeler at the right moment. That must be rehearsed—and before it can be rehearsed, it must be in the script.

First think of the product and what it is you want to *show* about it. Then think of what you want to say about it. Remember that you will want to back up words with pictures. That means giving thought to visual continuity. Don't prepare a script that requires the camera to skip rapidly from one shot to another and back. Try to get everything said that relates to close-ups in one block of copy. What follows is *not* a good script:

VIDEO	AUDIO
	ANNCR (Cont'd)
CU: Masher	. . . and this potato masher
MS: Anncr	that I'm selling this week
CU: Masher	also extracts juice from
	oranges.
MS: Anncer	Think . . . for just three
	ninety-eight!
CU: Masher	And it even tenderizes those
	inexpensive but tough cuts
	of meat. . . .

The writer is calling for too much switching of camera shots. This is distracting. It would be better to demonstrate the many wonders the potato masher can perform in one shot, and keep the other information on another shot.

While most commercials today are 30-second spots, the direct pitch is more likely to be a one-minute spot because it is too difficult to get much done in 30 seconds. (However, skilled announcers who do this sort of commercial can usually pack a lot into a short time. You may be able to estimate 180 or more words per minute for your copy instead of the customary 150.) Here's a simple example:

VIDEO	AUDIO
FADE IN	HENRY
LS: Henry	Hi! I'm Henry Miller of Henry's
	Budget Men's Store on Broadway
	here in downtown Midville.
MS: Henry	This week at Henry's we're
	having a sale that beats
	anything we've ever done
	before.

WIDEN SHOT TO SHOW Coat	This men's sports jacket I'm wearing . . . only 39-95. Think of that . . . . And look
CU: Coat material	at this material . . . Looks almost like real Harris tweed. . . . For so much less.
MS: Slacks	And these genuine polyester flannel slacks -- 19-95! Now how can you do better than that? The same slacks are 30-dollars and more at stores all over town. . . . But at Henry's -- just 19-95.
MS: Henry	(REMOVING JACKET) This wash and wear shirt I'm wearing -- they're on sale too. Would you believe only 5-95? Even this
TIGHTER ON Tie	tie I'm wearing -- and every tie in the place, just 3-dollars.
LS: Henry	(STARTING TO UNBUCKLE BELT) Even our complete selection of men's fashion underwear is . . .

VOICE
(Off Camera)

Hold it, Henry!

HENRY

Oh . . . well, I guess you'll

```
                        just have to come in and see

                        for yourself.
SLIDE: Logo & Address   (OVER SLIDE)  Henry's Budget

                        Men's Store.  Forty-eight

                        South Main Street, in

                        downtown Midville

FADE TO BLACK                           END
```

No one would call this script an artistic masterpiece, but it may work for the kind of immediate response usually sought in this sort of ad. The weak attempt at humor at the end helps a bit. However, the commercial would be much stronger if it had something at the beginning to attract and hold the audience.

Sponsors often place ads like this in relatively low-rating programs. This is partially because it is cheaper, but also because the program competes less with the commercial. One advertising executive who places a lot of ads of this type likes to use the late movies. Viewers, he says, are then simply killing time, and are far more susceptible to the advertising message in this type of show.

3. Announcer with studio set. You can considerably improve the type of ad discussed above by putting your announcer in some sort of a set. This adds relatively little to the cost, and makes the ad more interesting visually. Henry, for example, could have had a couple of chairs and a rack of clothes. Or the clothes could have been on hangers in various parts of the set. Take care, however, that you keep in mind the amount of movement you are adding to the script if you use such a technique. It is more interesting visually, but it takes more time and is harder to produce. Usually you will have to reduce the amount of copy the announcer reads. It is even possible—but usually not advisable—to use more than one set. This requires very careful planning.

4. Studio announcer with Chrornakeyed background of film, videotape, or slide. An alternative to the use of a set is the use of Chromakey for the background. This is simple, cheap, and allows for a wide variety of effects. You can use slides or other nonmoving visuals for the background, or you can use film or videotape. The latter two, of course, are more expensive. The writer needs to give very careful thought to the technical aspects of the commercial in this case. (Of course, you should *always* give careful thought to the technical side.) Remember, the only way the announcer can see the Chromakeyed background is on a monitor. The Chromakey material, the camera angles, and the movement of the announcer all have to be planned very carefully to make sure that the announcer does not walk in front of something the audience is supposed to see. You also want to make sure that your background does not detract from what is being said. Always use visuals to *reinforce* what is being said verbally. Also be sure that the crew and equipment at your station can handle the technical effects you are calling for.

VIDEO	AUDIO
FADE IN	RICKY
LS: Ricky KEY VTR: Snow scenes	Hey! It's ski season again! And just in time, Ricky's Ski Shop is having a sale to help you get outfitted in style.
MS: Ricky	I'm Mike Ricky . . . and at my shop in the Louisberg Mall, you'll find anything you ever needed for skiing.
PAN RIGHT TO PUT RICKY AT LEFT EDGE OF FRAME & KEY SLIDE: #1: Boots	Why not give your feet a real treat with these Sno-Freek ski boots . . . made of real unborn llama skin . . . and this week . . . only 65-dollars
KEY SLIDE: #2: Skis	And how about these super-fast Kidney Skis -- a steal at 95 dollars....

In this example, Chromakey was used to provide shots at the opening to interest the viewer. Then it was used to show the merchandise being advertised. Nothing fancy was tried. The announcer remained stationary. Camera movement was used to keep him at left frame, while the Chromakeys of the merchandise were being shown. If you have visualized the entire script, it should be easy to work out. Remember, the television writer is writing pictures as well as words.

5. Filmed or videotaped message by the announcer, shot on location. A more elaborate production would be filming or videotaping the commercial on location. For the political spot announcements, it was decided at the outset of the campaign to shoot on location, showing the candidates in their community and at their jobs. Film was chosen as the medium because it then provided greater portability of equipment than did videotape for production. Today, with increasingly portable video equipment, the announcements would probably have been done on videotape. The obvious advantage of videotape is that you can view it at once and decide if retakes are needed.

The writer should always visit shooting locations before writing the script. You may get some new ideas—or you may decide it's not a good place to do the commercial. For example, you may discover the location is in the flight path of a nearby airport, and any sound recording will be interrupted every three minutes by planes roaring overhead.

Location shooting is usually more expensive than studio production, so you need to be sure that what you are getting is worth the added cost and trouble. Remember, too, that anywhere you shoot, there must be access to ample supplies of electricity, and that your crew and cast need decent food and a place to go to the bathroom. Anything that is not available will have to be brought in at added expense.

It is a good idea for the writer to be on location with the crew when shooting. If changes are called for, you can make them quickly and be certain that they don't create new problems.

Most location shooting in television is divided into two very different classes. Either the commercial is a very expensive one, produced by a major advertising agency for a major sponsor, or it is a relatively low-budget commercial produced by a station or local agency for a local sponsor. If you have the money, you can, as one automobile manufacturer did once, shoot your new model sitting in splendid isolation atop a sandstone pillar in the middle of the Grand Canyon. *That* costs money. When you start out as a copywriter, you are much more likely to be doing the far less expensive (and far less interesting) commercial of this type:

VIDEO	AUDIO
FADE IN ON Ed in front of Mustang	Hi, neighbors. Ed Pitman here to tell you about some of the bargains we've got this week at Friendly Ed's used car and van lot on Highway 92 in Colby.
CU: Ed	I know a lot of you are looking for an inexpensive little car that just won't eat you out of house and home for gasoline.
LS: Mustang	Well, just look at this little

	1979 Mustang . . . only
	30-thousand miles on her, out
	here at Friendly Ed's, and in
	showroom condition.
MS: Ed	And you're going to be
	surprised when you hear <u>how</u>
	<u>little</u> it costs. Just 35-82.
	That's right . . . 35-hundred
	and 82 dollars. Or just
	12-hundred down and 36 easy
	months to pay.
LS: Ed PAN LEFT AS HE MOVES	(WALKING CAMERA LEFT TO NEXT
	CAR) And if you think that's
	good, how about this 1980 Honda
	Civic, 64-thousand miles and
	only 22-hundred dollars!
SUPER SLIDE: Ed Logo & Address	You can't beat that, and we've
	got hundreds of them. Come on
	down and see for yourself.
	Friendly Ed's, just south of
	the Colby city limits on
	Highway 92 . . . Friendly Ed's.
FADE TO BLACK	<u>END</u>

That is not the kind of thing I am studying television writing to learn, you say. Agreed. But *that* is also what pays the bills for a lot of television stations. Many writers have started out writing just this sort of copy. It is also the kind of commercial most easily produced with the facilities available at many universities. Work on it. It is far from being as easy as it looks. And it is a good way to begin learning to think about your visuals and your copy together.

6. Dramatized commercial, taped in the television studio. This method can be effective for selling a product—if the performers and production facilities of the television studio are equal to it. You can write your script much as if it were a television drama or comedy. You need to pay very careful attention to the descriptions of action and camera movement. Spell out in detail every shot you want. Dialog must be particularly simple and clear. The challenge, of course, is to delineate the characters of your performers in just a few seconds. In that sense, no form of television production makes tougher demands on the writers and the actors. One reason for the longevity of some of the commercials we discussed earlier—Mr. Wipple squeezing the Charmin in 300 separate commercials—is that the audience understands the basic traits of the continuing characters, so no time is wasted explaining what the characters are doing. When you begin to write advertising copy, you probably will not have a chance to work on a continuing series of commercials at first, so you have to give much more careful thought to ways of making your characters seem plausible without wasting time. One way is to use familiar types—housewives, doctors, and so forth.

Commercials of this kind may be shot either with a one-camera or a multicamera technique. The writer will need to know that at the outset. If you are using a single-camera technique, you have a great deal of freedom in the action you set for your commercial. If you use a multicamera technique, you have to give very careful thought to number of sets to be used, movements by characters, special camera shots, and special effects you may desire. Here is an excerpt from a single-camera commercial, followed by an example of some of the changes that would be needed if the commercial were done as a multicamera production:

FADE IN:

INT. KITCHEN -- DAYLIGHT

(WIDE SHOT OF KITCHEN. MOTHER AND FRIEND ARE SEATED AT TABLE, HAVING COFFEE. DOOR BURSTS OPEN, FATHER AND SON ENTER, CARRYING FOOTBALL. THEIR CLOTHES ARE FILTHY.)

                    SON

          (SHOUTING) We won! We won!

(TWO SHOT: MOTHER AND FRIEND. MOTHER SMILES, THEN ROLLS EYES IN DISMAY.)

                    MOTHER

     They won . . . and my clean wash

     lost! How will I ever get out that

     ground-in dirt and grime?

                    FRIEND

     That's no problem. ZOTZ will wash

those dirty clothes cleaner than new.

(WIDE SHOT: WHOLE GROUP.)

MOTHER

Even <u>those</u> grimy clothes?

FRIEND

You bet! Come on, let's try it

DISSOLVE TO:

INT. LAUNDRY ROOM -- DAYLIGHT

(TWO SHOT: MOTHER AND FRIEND. MOTHER IS EXAMINING
CLOTHES.)

MOTHER

They really are clean! ZOTZ really does....

There is no problem here because the production is being handled as a
one-camera production. But the transition from kitchen to laundry room will
not work with a multicamera commercial unless there is a break in the taping
to move from one set to the other. To handle the material as a multicamera
production, the writer might choose to combine all action in a single scene on
a single set.

VIDEO	AUDIO
FADE IN: MEDIUM SHOT	(LAUNDRY ROOM. MOTHER AND FRIEND ARE EXAMINING LAUNDRY.) FRIEND I don't know how you do it. Your clothes look cleaner than new.
LS	(SON BURSTS THROUGH THE DOOR. HE CARRIES A FOOTBALL. HIS CLOTHES ARE FILTHY.) SON We won! We won! FRIEND

>   And it looks like your clean
>
>   clothes lost.
>
> TWO SHOT   MOTHER
>
>   No problem. Yesterday these
>
>   looked just like that.
>
>   FRIEND
>
>   I don't believe it.
>
>   MOTHER
>
>   It's true. New ZOTZ does it
>
>   every time.

The second version is not as effective as the first, but it can be done as a multicamera production, saving both time and money. The first version could be done as a multicamera production if the two scenes were shot separately, then edited together off-line later. However, that defeats some of the advantages of multicamera shooting.

7. Dramatized commercial on videotape or film at a major production center with full use of post-editing, optical, or electronic effects. If you have a large budget, you can plan your dramatized commercial for production at a major television or film production center. In such circumstances, the sky's the limit. It is possible to portray on the screen almost anything you can imagine. If you want cats to dance a gavotte in your commercial, it can be done. If you want detergent packages to fly through the air, it can be done. The question you must ask yourself is: Do I need that effect? There is a danger that you may make the commercial so tricky that people forget its main purpose—to sell.

8. Fully or partially animated commercials. This technique requires that you spell out in great detail exactly what action is required. This is one case in which the descriptive material is usually longer than the dialog. You also must be more detailed in explaining exactly what the actors are to do with their voices. Remember, the animated characters can not usually convey the variety of emotions that real actors can. The voice has to carry a greater burden. Your dialog, too, must be clear in its meaning. Think out the relationship between the picture and sound track very carefully. Prepare a detailed storyboard so that you are sure you know what the audience is seeing and hearing at every moment of the commercial.

It is very important for the performers providing the voices in an animated film that you paint a clear picture of the role they are playing. In the majority of instances, sound tracks are recorded first, then animation done to match the sound track. That means that the actors have to handle all their interpretation and timing on the basis of your description and the storyboard. One director demanded 125 takes of a sound track before he got what sounded right to him.

Remember, too, that animation can be too "cute" for many products. It is true that the scope of animated commercials has been greatly expanded in recent years. They are not all funny. They are not all for children. But cartoons are generally associated with children's shows and humor. So you had better have a very good commercial if it goes outside these bounds.

And, of course, keep in mind that animation is expensive. The less movement and action demanded in your script, the less expensive it will be to produce. It is a good idea to discuss your plans with the animators if you can. Often they can suggest ways for you to change the action and save on the cost of animation.

9. Concealed camera interview. The last technique to be discussed is the "documentary" approach. This can take several forms. In some cases, actors are used to give the impression that the material is unscripted and delivered by unrehearsed interviewees. This comes close to violation of Federal Trade Commission rules and professional ethics. In some cases real actors are used, but they are not given scripts and are asked to improvise. In yet other cases, nonactors are selected and interviewed before the camera. And finally, there is the hidden-camera format in which the interviewees are not supposed to be aware that they are on camera. Obviously, the script writer has less of a job here.

Obtaining material for this type of commercial is expensive and time-consuming. For example, 300 people were interviewed in order to select eight for a series of Bell Telephone commercials. The people interviewed were not told the material was to be used in a commercial, and only their voices were recorded. Later, when the eight to be used had been selected, camera crews were sent back to photograph them. The original voice recordings were used nonsynchronously over the filmed shots of the speakers.

The writer's job in these commercials is to tie the material together with a very few words from the announcer. It may be a slogan to go with the series, it may be only the name of the sponsor. The writer also has to decide how to use the nonrehearsed material. How much, which takes, what visuals to go with it. Despite the small amount of actual copy to be written, this is one of the toughest kinds of writing for the copywriter.

TELEVISION PUBLIC SERVICE ANNOUNCEMENTS

Every television station is required by Federal Communications Commission (FCC) regulations to devote a certain amount of time to public service announcements. Noncommercial stations, of course, have no other form of announcement.* Most large charities have their own staffs to produce advertising, or they hire a major advertising agency. Advertising agencies or

*FCC rules are changing. By the time you read this book, there may no longer be a legal requirement for public service programs, and noncommercial stations may be carrying some types of advertising.

individuals in the business sometimes donate their services to produce public service announcements, and the Advertising Council of America is an organization sponsored by the advertising industry which maps and produces advertising campaigns for worthy causes.

For the beginning writer, public service announcements are sometimes the first opportunity to write for the broadcast media. You may have a chance to prepare material for your school, your church, or some organization to which you belong. If your college has a noncommercial television station, you may be able to help prepare public service announcements for it.

Do not assume that a public service announcement is somehow not a commercial. You have the same problems to work out whether you are selling a product or selling an idea. Indeed, the preparation of a public service announcement is often more difficult than the preparation of a regular commercial. After all, if you are selling a product, some of your audience probably has some *need* for that product or can *benefit* from its use. No one really *needs* to give money or time to a charity. There may be psychological benefits, but the main idea is to benefit *others*. You are selling an idea that everyone usually agrees with in principal but that few are eager to make sacrifices for. Moreover, you probably will have a much smaller budget to produce your public service announcement than you would have for a regular commercial.

Stations are free to devote as much or as little time to public service announcements as they think they safely can and still not incur the displeasure of the FCC. The more entertaining the commercial is for the audience and the easier it is for the station to use, the better is your chance for getting it on the air. Don't expect a station to do your producing for you, and don't expect that you will get a choice time slot. You have to write an announcement that will get the maximum response from whatever audience it is able to reach.

Researching the Cause

When you begin to prepare a public service announcement, conduct essentially the same research you would for a regular commercial. First determine what it is that the organization hopes to achieve from its ads. Does it want donations? Does it want volunteers? Does it want to modify the behavior of the audience? Does it simply wish to inform the audience of certain facts? Too often, organizations are not very clear about what they hope to do with television advertising, and frequently they have a sort of vague hope that most of the ends above can be achieved. That's wishful thinking. You must have a single specific purpose in mind for each series of television ads you prepare.

You need to have the same kinds of audience research that big advertisers conduct. Unfortunately, only big charities can afford such research. Very often you will have to rely on your own instincts and a bit of checking up to determine what sort of image the charity may have with the audience. It comes as a surprise to many people that the public is not well disposed toward every charitable organization. There is, after all, nothing easier than finding some reason *not* to give money, give time, or change your life-style.

People often, for example, have the suspicion that most money in a charity goes to administration rather than to the work for which it was intended. In a few cases, this is true. Religious charities are sometimes suspected of diverting funds to church uses instead of the charitable activity for which they are solicited. And this, too, is sometimes true. In some cases, solicitation for funds has gone on long after the actual financial needs of the charity were met. In yet other cases, most of the money solicited has gone to professional fund raisers who are hired by organizations to solicit funds for them. The public is well aware of these problems and understandably casts a suspicious eye on most charitable organizations. Moreover, many major charities opt out of joint fund-raising efforts such as the United Way. The potential donor, who has already contributed to the joint fund-raising effort, needs a good explanation why more should now be given to some particular organization. On the other hand, because individuals disapprove of some of the organizations that receive funds from joint efforts, they may refuse to contribute to joint fund-raising campaigns as well. Too often a failure—real or simply rumored—by the charitable organization to help someone in need of the organization's services, leads to a lifelong distrust of that organization. "They may spend millions on research, but they wouldn't give my cousin ten cents when she was dying and couldn't afford to pay for the treatments." "They say they're a charity, but when I was in the hospital, they charged for everything they did."

So, you must begin your campaign with some research to find out what image the public has of your organization. You probably cannot change those preconceptions with your public service announcement, but the announcement must be prepared with them in mind.

Basic Appeal

Next, analyze the appeal to be made—money, services, or whatever. You'll find that it is far easier to get information across to the public than to get the public to make contributions of time and money. And it is easier to get contributions of time and money than to get people to modify their life-style. In fact, many students of communication would write off the last idea entirely.

Like any other form of commercial, the public service announcement, or PSA, must appeal to some basic human need. Some appeals are to self-preservation: "The life you save may be your own." However, it is probably better to appeal to self-esteem and love for others. We have lumped the latter category under "sex," although this is obviously not an appeal to carnal desires but to the basic loving relationships between human beings. It is the philosopher's distinction between *eros* and *agape*. You appeal to the protective love of a parent for a child and of one friend for another.

Self-esteem can be appealed to by simply making subtle reminders that those who support worthy causes grow in the esteem of others. People like to feel unselfish and giving. You must give recognition to this in subtle ways. You provide images in your advertising with which the viewers can identify. And you publicize badges, armbands, or other symbols that persons can wear to show they have participated in your charity.

Since curiosity is a natural part of most human behavior, you will find that supplying information to the public is not as difficult as it might first appear. People usually like to learn new things, especially if those things affect them personally. Where most information campaigns fall down is in trying to impart too much information to the public through the broadcast media. Anything that requires the learning of several new facts must be backed up with written information in a pamphlet or in some other source. This in turn requires that you use part of your PSA to motivate the audience to write in for the pamphlet or pick it up wherever it is available. This is much more difficult to achieve. Therefore, if you can concentrate your television campaign on informing the public of just one or two important facts, you will have a better chance of succeeding.

Where more than one or two facts are involved, you must adapt your techniques. For example, the American Cancer Society does not really expect the public to learn the warning signs of cancer from a television listing of them. Instead, the viewer is told if he or she has one of those symptoms to contact a doctor, and the viewer is urged to send in for a pamphlet listing the warning signals. It would be foolish to expect the public to memorize the various symptoms of cancer in the span of a 30-second—or even of a one-minute—commercial.

Identification

Much of the success of your PSA will depend upon your ability to get the audience to *identify* or *empathize* with others. To identify with a person is to feel that you are somehow living the other person's life. In a film, sometimes the viewers may feel that they *are* the hero or the heroine. That is identifying. Empathizing is simply being able to put yourself "in someone else's shoes." That sensation: "I know how he must feel right now." Empathy is more common and easier to achieve. If you can put your viewers in the role of the victim of some crisis, or in the roles of the victim's family and loved ones, you are well on your way to getting your audience to respond to your message. But you must be extremely careful. You must not make your audience feel that the experience is so distasteful that they want to forget about it. It is not by accident that PSAs tend to stress hope and to show victims overcoming, or at least coping with, their problems.

Understanding the Audience

You must constantly be in tune with the sensitivities of your audience. Remember that a *mass* audience contains people with all sorts of fears and dislikes. For example, one of the authors of this book was preparing a film on diabetes. When the film was viewed by an older, far more skilled, practitioner in the preparation of PSAs, his immediate response was, "Take out the scene of the insulin shots."

"But that's an essential part of it," the writer argued. "Diabetics must take insulin injections daily. The audience should understand. That's the point. To get the audience to understand."

"The point," said the older and wiser critic, "is to get the audience interested in the problems of the diabetic. Millions of people can't stand to see someone getting stabbed with a needle. It doesn't matter if it's insulin or acupuncture. You show people getting stuck with needles, and you'll lose a substantial part of your audience."

Sample testing of two versions of the film—one with injections, one without—proved the old pro was right. A surprising number of people became squeamish during the shot of the injections. The shot was removed from the film.

Even stronger reactions arise when you deal with something like blood. It doesn't take much more than seeing the word on paper to upset some people. Showing the drawing of human blood in a PSA is a sure way to lose a big segment of your audience.

People involved in the treatment of various diseases and social problems sometimes complain that the nice-looking, well-spoken "victims" shown in PSAs are a far cry from the real thing. They are right, of course, but the goal of a PSA is not *cinema verité* but the motivation of the audience to support your cause. The reality of some problems is often too ugly to thrust into the living room on the television screen. You must leave the audience with hope, not despair or revulsion. It takes skill and experience to know when you have crossed the line that separates showing a problem to an audience from frightening that audience off. Until you have that skill, you are best advised to err on the side of caution.

Budget

Most PSAs must be done on low budgets, so you must write your script accordingly. Special process shots, animation, and other expensive procedures are reserved for a few major charity drives that can afford them. Many talented people will volunteer to help in the preparation of PSAs, but that too can be a mixed blessing. It is one thing to demand 43 takes to get a shot right when you are paying your crew and actors. It is another when everyone is working free. That again suggests that you must keep the production of the PSA simple.

Remember, too, that one job of any commercial, including a PSA, is to entertain. Even humor can have its place in some PSAs. You must involve the audience in the same way that a drama or comedy involves the audience. The audience must be *interested* in what you are saying. You may have a *serious* message, but that is not an excuse to have a boring message.

PSAs are usually prepared in a number of different versions. There are two reasons for this. One is that you get more for your money if you can edit one commercial into several different forms. For example, a commercial may be designed so that it can play as a television PSA or so that the sound track by itself will work as a radio PSA. The other reason is that there is no certainty what the time slot will be that each station puts your PSA into. One station may have room for a 30-second spot, another may want a one-minute spot. A careful writer, then, will prepare a one-minute script which can, through editing of the videotape or film, be cut down to 30-second, 20-second, and even 10-second versions. Usually, these various versions are supplied to a station in a package so that it can run the one that best fits its schedule. Often the best way to prepare such a script is to begin with the shortest version that contains all the elements that are essential to your script. Then add material to each longer version, working in descending order of importance for the facts you supply. Here's an example:

VIDEO	AUDIO
FADE IN:	GOV. DOOLITTLE
MS: Governor CG: "Gov. Ernest Doolittle"	I'm Ernest Doolittle. Two thousand citizens of this state will die next year because of euphorbia. Please give so we can find a cure for this dread disease.
CUT TO: Logo	
FADE OUT	END

VIDEO	AUDIO
FADE IN:	GOV. DOOLITTLE
MS: Governor CG: "Gov. Ernest Doolittle"	I'm Ernest Doolittle. Two-thousand citizens of this state will die next year
CU: Governor	because of euphorbia. We still don't know what causes this disease, but your Euphorbia Foundation is funding research
MS: Governor	to find a cure. Please give so we can find a cure for this dread disease.

CUT TO: Logo

FADE OUT   <u>END</u>

VIDEO	AUDIO

FADE IN: GOV. DOOLITTLE

MS: Governor   I'm Ernest Doolittle.
CG: "Gov. Ernest
Doolittle"   Two-thousand citizens of this

                          state will die next year

CU: Governor   because of euphorbia. We still

                          don't know what causes this

                          disease. It strikes men twice

                          as often as women, and it

                          usually strikes between the

                          ages of 30 and 50. There is

                          no cure, but there is hope.

DISSOLVE TO: In research laboratories,
MS: Research Scientist
                          scientists have found

                          promising new drugs that slow

                          down the onslaught of this

                          terrible disease. It's not a

                          cure yet, but your Euphorbia

                          Foundation is funding research

DISSOLVE TO: to find a cure. Please give
MS: Governor
                          so we can find a cure for this

                          dread disease.

CUT TO: Logo

FADE OUT   <u>END</u>

Less elaborate PSAs can be produced with slides and a script. An organization can distribute PSAs of this sort to stations at very low cost. Again, it is customary to send scripts of varying lengths so that the station can pick the one that fits its schedule best. You can use any of the techniques described in the section on television commercials for television PSAs. However, you will find that the less expensive your techniques, the better chance they have to work as PSAs.

SUMMARY

To review briefly the steps in preparing commercials and public service announcements:

1. Determine clearly what the goal of the campaign is.
2. Carefully study the strong and weak points of the product and its competitors.
3. Decide what the most effective appeals will be in reaching your audience and achieving your goals. Among the most commonly used appeals are appeals involving security, sex, self-esteem, variety, and play.
4. Design your campaign to cope with the problems of selective attention, selective perception, and selective retention.
5. Prepare a storyboard to help coordinate words and pictures.
6. Pick a production technique which will match your goals, budget, and available facilities. Major techniques include
    a. Slides with voice over
    b. Direct pitch with announcer on camera
    c. Announcer with studio set
    d. Announcer filmed or videotaped on location
    e. Dramatized commercials with limited production facilities
    f. Dramatized commercials with full production facilities
    g. Animation
    h. "Documentary"

Public service announcements should be prepared with the same basic considerations as regular commercials. Research is particularly important. You must know the audience and its attitudes toward your organization. You may find that people in charitable organizations, although they have the best of motives, are out of touch with what the audience really thinks or is willing to view on television.

Carefully analyze the basic appeals you will use. Don't expect to convey too much information to the public via public service announcements. Back them up with other devices such as pamphlets. And do not expect much in the way of changed attitudes or behavior as a result of public service announcements. Getting the audience to empathize with those served by your cause is one very useful technique. Be careful not to frighten your audience off with material that is depressing.

Most PSAs should be prepared in multiple versions, of different time lengths, for the convenience of the stations that use them. PSAs can be less elaborate than regular commercials and still be successful, but never use that as an excuse for sloppy techniques.

Whether your goal is to sell chewing gum or to get people to fight cancer, the techniques are similar. If you know your goal and your audience, you should be able to write effective television commercials and PSAs.

RADIO DRAMA

and
Comedy

Both once popular forms of entertainment, the radio drama and radio comedy have fallen on hard times in commercial radio. Nevertheless, there have been signs of revival for both recently. Of the two, comedy has adapted better to the changing times.

RADIO DRAMA

At the network level, radio drama has been a scarce item in recent years. The most successful of the radio dramatic series is the "CBS Mystery Theater," which has been on the air since 1974. It is carried by about 250 stations at this writing. The success of "Mystery Theater" led to other experiments, notably "Sears Radio Theater," which began on CBS in 1978. It was not as successful as the "CBS Mystery Theater," but was later picked up by the Mutual Broadcasting System where it became the "Mutual Radio Theater." It has since been canceled.

The most adventurous network radio dramatic series to date has been "Earplay" on National Public Radio. While other series tended to make heavy use of adaptations, "Earplay" concentrated on commissioning experimental new works. To guarantee the quality of the programming, "Earplay" has tended to work with established writers such as Edward Albee, David Mamet, and Arthur Kopit. (Kopit's "Wings" was later presented as a stage play.) However, it did also present works of little-known writers.

Somewhat in the vein of "The Columbia Workshop," a distinguished experimental radio series on CBS in the 1930s and '40s, "Earplay" has shown a willingness to try unusual material that has not always won the love of the audience. At its best, however, "Earplay" provides an experimental edge to radio drama and demonstrates the genuine advantages that radio can have over television.

In addition to "Earplay," in 1976 NPR began "Masterpiece Radio Theater." Patterned after public television's "Masterpiece Theater," the series used many dramas produced by the British Broadcasting Corporation, but other segments of the series were produced by WGBH radio in Boston. "Masterpiece Radio Theater" has relied heavily on adaptations of such standard works as *Anna Karenina* and *Moby Dick*.

The most impressive undertaking in radio drama recently has been NPR's adaptation of the film *Star Wars* for radio. Budgeted at $200,000 for the entire series—less than the cost of one half-hour segment of a television series—the program nonetheless was the most ambitious attempt yet to bring back radio drama. However small, the budget was well above that usually available for radio drama, and it had its own musical score, almost unheard of in radio drama since the 1940s. (The music was by John Williams, who did the score for the *Star Wars* film and who is conductor of the Boston Pops.) Many of the original performers in the film played the same roles in the radio series, including Mark Hammill as Luke Skywalker and Anthony Daniels as See Threepio. As is the case with most radio drama today, the performers were paid minimum union scale, at this writing a bit under $200 a day.

It is important to note that the NPR producers did not attempt simply to present radio drama as it had been done in its classic years during the 1930s and '40s. They tried to create radio drama for today, recognizing the differences in the medium and its audience. Every use was made of the high-fidelity and stereo capabilities of modern radio to make the series as exciting and engrossing as possible. Tom Voegeli, radio engineer for the series, called it "probably as complicated a radio production" as has ever been attempted.[1]

As in all adaptations, the writers had to give careful thought to what would work in radio. The visually fascinating scene in the cantina filled with strange space creatures, for instance, did not lend itself to an "ears only" approach. Ironically, one of the things that radio does best is create monsters and alien beings—because it leads the listener to create the creatures in his or her own imagination. But there were too many creatures in the cantina scene—and too many people had seen it—to count on creating new images in the minds of

[1]Robert Lindsey, "Will 'Star Wars' Lure Younger Listeners to Radio?" *New York Times*, March 8, 1981, p. 34 D.

the listeners. Voegeli says, "Radio works very well at the intimate level. The quintessential radio moment is when you're listening to the thoughts in someone's head."[2]

While "Star Wars" is a network program, it *is* possible to produce successful radio drama without a network connection. Two of the oldest and most widely carried radio dramas are not broadcast by a regular network. Both are produced by religious organizations and feature stories which emphasize the viewpoints of those organizations. "Unshackled," produced by the Pacific Garden Mission in Chicago, has been on the air since 1950 and is carried by more than 450 stations, which get it at no charge. It is not an ideal market for an aspiring writer, however, because 1,100 of its more than 1,500 scripts have been written by Jack Odell, who also directs, announces, and narrates the show.

The other program is "Heartbeat Theater," produced by the Salvation Army. "Heartbeat Theater" has been broadcasting since 1956. In a sense it is older than "Unshackled" because the Salvation Army took over and renamed an existing program, "Skippy Hollywood Playhouse," which had been on the air for 24 years before it became "Heartbeat Theater."

Perhaps the most ambitious radio drama undertaking in recent years was again not a product of NPR or the commercial networks. That is the National Radio Theater's $1.5 million, 12-hour production of Homer's *Odyssey*. Writer-producer-director Yuri Rasovsky approaches the project with earthy humor and insight, saying the "Odyssey" is "the first soap opera. The 'Odyssey' is about a man trying to get his ass home. That's an archetypical situation—a soldier having to come home and make a place for himself."

And Rasovsky pays homage to Homer's dramatic construction: "Homer set the pattern for narrative adventure literature, with sequences of problems, catastrophes or violent situations one after another and lighter moments in between."

John Glover, who plays Telemachus in the series, had some words about radio acting that a writer ought to keep in mind: ". . . on the stage . . . I've always had my body to rely on to get a point across. With radio everything has to be in the voice. . . . Any kind of action you want to convey . . . has to be done with the voice. That has been the hardest for me."[3]

Radio drama is also alive and well on local stations. Pacifica Foundation's KPFK in Los Angeles has one of the best-known series, "Theater of the Ear," which has produced avant-garde original works and adaptations of works such as James Joyce's *Ulysses* (not easy to adapt to any medium). In one "Theater of the Ear" production, the author simply tapped away at his typewriter before a microphone, while members of the cast tried to see how many different ways they could say "radio." Understandably, the audience for "Theater of the Ear" has been limited.

Another nonnetwork producer is American Radio Theater in Glendale,

[2]Ibid.
[3]Larry Green, "Homer's Epic Odyssey a Radio Drama, By Jove," *Los Angeles Times,* June 22, 1980, p. 10.

California. ART holds contests for radio scripts, producing the best of them on its syndicated series "ART Presents."

The most satisfying aspect of radio drama is the enormous freedom it gives the writer. Like all artistic freedom, it is a freedom that comes with an accompanying set of limitations. Still, radio is supreme as the theater of the imagination. No other medium offers the writer so many opportunities to cast off the usual restrictions of broadcast writing and let the sky be the limit. If you want to set your scene in Heaven, Hell, or Peoria, Illinois, it makes little difference. The cost factors involved in building sets or shooting on location have no effect on radio productions. Your "budget" is your skill in convincing the audience that they are indeed where you say they are.

Cues

Terminology varies somewhat in broadcast usage, but these are the cues usually used by writers for radio drama:

FADE IN (sometimes FADE UP): The sound gradually rises from nothing to normal level. This is the normal opening for most programs and for most scenes within a program.

FADE OUT: Sound becomes gradually fainter until it is no longer heard. This is the normal ending for a program and for most scenes in a program.

SEGUE (pronounced Seg'way): A simultaneous FADE IN and FADE OUT. A SEGUE is the normal transition from one scene to the next. It also can be used to indicate a shift in time or location or a shift from external to internal dialog, as in a shift from a character speaking to the thoughts in the character's mind. Such a transition needs to be enhanced with other techniques, such as a FILTER (discussed below) for the "thinking" voice and perhaps music under or a sting to help the audience understand what is happening.

FILTER: An electronic effect to make the speaker's voice sound hollow or metallic. Various filters can be used for different effects. Usually they are used to indicate something unusual about the speaker—a voice from the grave, the thoughts of a person, the voice of a robot, or other unusual voices.

STING: A short, usually dissonant musical chord used to emphasize some sudden and unexpected event.

UNDER: Music or some other continuing sound is heard softly along with the main dialog or narrative.

UP: A sound that has been heard UNDER is raised to normal level.

OVER: A sound is heard more loudly than other sounds in the same sequence. Essentially, OVER is the opposite of UNDER. OVER, UP, and UNDER are normally used in combination with cues such as FADE, in directions such as FADE MUSIC UP AND OVER, FADE THEME UNDER AND OUT, or SLOWLY FADE TRAFFIC SOUNDS OUT.

OUT: The sound is no longer heard.

SNEAK: The sound is slowly faded in so that its addition to the sound picture is not noticed at first.

Here is how some of those cues might be used:

FADE THEME UP, THEN UNDER

ANNCR: Campus Mystery Theater! (THEME BRIEFLY UP FULL, THEN UNDER) The Broadcasting Arts Department of Lotus State University brings you Campus Mystery Theater . . . stories of the strange and the occult . . . stories to make you shiver . . . (THEME: CRESCENDO AND OUT) Tonight's story, and original drama by Marcia Milstein . . . Bradstone's Tomb.

STING

THUNDER, RAIN, HOWLING WIND

ANNCR: A raging storm. No time for a caller . . . especially to this lonely New England farmhouse, so far from everything . . . except an old, abandoned graveyard. And yet, there is a caller . . .

POUNDING ON DOOR

LAURA: (Over storm noises) Hello! Isn't anyone home?

POUNDING. FOOTSTEPS APPROACHING FROM INSIDE. SOUND OF LOCK BEING UNFASTENED. CREAK OF OPENING DOOR.

CORA: (Hostile) What is it? Who are you?

LAURA: Mrs. Bradstone?

CORA: I'm Cora Bradstone.

LAURA: You're Oliver Bradstone's wife?

CORA: (Frightened) Who are you?

LAURA: I'm Laura Cole. I wrote to Mr. Bradstone.

CORA: (More frightened) You . . . you must be mistaken.

LAURA: But I told him I'd be here today. His letter said I'd be welcome to stay here at the house until my work was finished. I'm preparing a magazine article about the Salem witch trials, and Mr. Bradstone promised I could see the Bradstone family papers . . . See, here's the letter.

CORA: Letter? A letter? (Screams)

SOUND OF BODY SLUMPING TO FLOOR

LAURA: Mrs. Bradstone! Mrs. Bradstone! Are you all right? Mrs. Bradstone!

MUSIC UP QUICKLY AND OUT. STORM STOUNDS NOW ONLY FAINTLY HEARD UNDER.

CORA: (Moans)

LAURA: Mrs. Bradstone. Are you all right?

CORA: (Weakly) What happened?

LAURA: You fainted. I had to drag you into the parlor here so you'd be warm by the fire. I couldn't find a telephone to call a doctor.

CORA: There is no telephone. I'm all right. (Urgently) But you must go. You must leave at once.

LAURA: But your husband said . . .

CORA: He is <u>not</u> my husband. Oliver Bradstone was my uncle.

LAURA: <u>Was</u> your uncle?

CORA: Oliver Bradstone has been dead for over forty years!

STING

SEGUE TO ANNOUNCER

ANNCR: Well . . . not exactly what Laura Cole had expected. Laura is about to learn more than she bargained for in her research on the Salem witch trials. With a letter from a dead man already, is Laura about to meet Oliver Bradstone himself? We'll see, right after this public service announcement.

The Dramatic Script

The radio writer has an enormous amount of freedom in setting his or her script. The writer's obligation is to see that that freedom never leads to confusion for the listener. Everything has to be made clear with words and sounds. A combination of words and sounds is even better. For example, at the start of the preceding mystery script, the writer used sound and words to tell us there was a storm. Words were used to set the locale—an old New England farmhouse near a graveyard. The sound effect of the creaking door gives further indication that the house is old and probably spooky. We are very quickly given the names of the two main female characters via dialog.

The writer will repeat those names several times in the course of the script so that the listener is reminded which voice is which and so that listeners who tuned in late can get things straightened out.

Dialog tells us more about the heroine, Laura, and introduces a reference to the Salem witchcraft trials—a reference repeated by the announcer at the end of the segment. Dialog and narrative are also used to mention the name of Oliver Bradstone several times. Dialog is used to tell the audience that no telephone is available at the old house. In a relatively brief segment, the audience has been set up for sinister things to come in the old house and the graveyard. The narrator teases the audience with hints and questions about what is to come.

Making It Clear for the Listener

There is at least one potentially weak point in the opening segment: The audience is not given a very clear understanding of what happens to Cora Bradstone after she sees the letter. It is not until the next scene that we are told she has fainted. That information is important. The audience should not be left guessing. The writer is presented with something of a dilemma. A radio writer should try to have two persons in a scene whenever possible. (Of course, one-person programs or scenes are possible. Many outstanding examples, such as "Sorry, Wrong Number," are carried mostly by a single performer. But the absence of a second character in a scene always creates new problems for the writer to deal with.

In the script quoted, the writer has briefly reduced the number of characters to one by having Cora Bradstone faint. Were there still another character on the scene, someone could cry, "Grab her! She's fainted." But without such an additional character, the writer either has to hope the sound effects do the job or call upon somewhat less believable artifices such as having Cora Bradstone say, "I think I'm going to faint," or having Laura cry out to herself, "Oh, she's fainted." Such gimmicks are permissible in radio writing, but they should be avoided whenever possible. Here the writer decided to let the audience wonder for a few moments until the dialog in the next scene clarified what had happened.

Often the radio writer does have to rely on little tricks such as "Look out! She has a gun!" A generation grew up on one of the most improbable cries in dramatic history, "The masked man shot the gun right out of his hand!" If audiences could accept that without quibbling (and they did), then an occasional "Oh, my! She's fainted" may not be too bad.

Part of good radio writing is preparing your audience for each event that requires some explanation. For example, the following—assuming there was nothing earlier in the script to clarify it—is weak radio writing:

PHELPS: Foster, look out!

FOSTER: (Scream fading off mike)

PHELPS: My God! He's fallen off the cliff.

It should be written:

```
PHELPS:    Foster!  You're too close to the edge.  Look
           out!

FOSTER:    (Scream fading off mike)

PHELPS:    My God!  He's fallen off the cliff.
```

In the second version, the writer has prepared the audience for what is to come. The writer should also have planted references to the dangerous cliff earlier in the script so that the audience is willing to accept the accident when it occurs. If Foster falls off a cliff that has never even been mentioned before, the audience can justly feel confused.

The Plot

Use the same basic techniques in constructing the plot of your radio drama that you learned for the television drama. Make your main character face a series of increasingly serious problems while struggling to solve the major problem of the drama. Each obstacle should seem to place the heroine or hero farther from the goal. In radio, the denouement can often be held until almost the last moment of the show. The tension dissipates quickly in radio drama once you have passed the major crisis. It is important to tie up loose ends quickly.

The Cast

Keep your cast small. Remember that each character must be identified by her or his voice. The ability of the human ear to distinguish between voices is not great, so the fewer distinctions that have to be made, the better. The director, of course, should try to cast actors with different-sounding voices and work with the performers to emphasize vocal differences. You can help not only by keeping the cast small but by using differing speech patterns, when reasonable to do so, in order to make voices as easy to distinguish as possible. You should also repeat names of characters frequently—especially if those characters' voices have not been heard for several minutes. But try to keep sentence structure simple, easy to read, and easy to understand. The need to keep characters identifiable is not an excuse for sloppy writing.

Word Hazards

Avoid words that are ambiguous or that are hard to pronounce. Hard-to-pronounce words can trip up your actors. Ambiguous words can trip up both the cast and the audience.

Do not saddle a performer with a line like "The volcanoes Popocatepetl and Ixtacihuatl seemed to smile down on the floating gardens of Xochimilco." Even an innocent looking word like "aluminum" can trick the tongue. Other words can trick the ear of the listener. "Mary wanted me to give her one of the pair. I didn't want two." Or did he say, "I didn't want to"? Sometimes the audience may not have a good grasp of what a word means. "Get out of here, you dastard!" (Gee! I didn't know you could say that on the air.) You should try to hear your script read aloud at least once so that you can spot problems. It is even better if you can have someone who is not familiar with the script listen to it with you. If there is any ambiguity, rewrite that segment.

Narration

It is fairly common to use a narrator in a radio drama. In some programs that is the regular style of the show; a narrator is always used. When the narrator is optional, give some thought to it before you add a narrator to the script. Sometimes a narrator can add a certain flavor to a program. The narrator can provide commentary and know things that are unknown to the characters in the show. Nevertheless, a narrator also interrupts and slows down the action of a show. Consider your plot carefully and see if you really need a narrator. On balance, you will probably find that your show has more dramatic impact if it relies entirely upon dialog and sound effects and does not rely upon a narrator to advance the plot and clarify issues. Too often a narrator simply covers the inability of the writer to deal with the script in a professional manner.

Like all forms of broadcast writing, the radio drama should be written only after the writer has made a careful study of the program for which she or he is writing. You must construct your plot around the usual blocks of time the program uses. Since only one or two programs are currently heard on commercial radio, your problem is not quite as acute as it might be for other forms of writing. Nevertheless, the first discipline a broadcast writer should learn is to fit the material within the specified time slots—and to do so precisely.

Remember that your audience does not have the visual cues it would have in television. Make clear when each segment comes to a close, and make sure that each transition between scenes is clear to the audience. Remember that it is a good plot technique to leave the audience expecting a new crisis to be faced in the next segment.

The Market

In short, radio drama still exists, and although it is admittedly not a large market for the script writer, it is a good field for a young writer to experiment in. Most college radio stations can provide an opportunity for you to get your material produced. This can provide a real training ground for your skills and give you a chance to be heard by a broadcast audience. It also provides you with credits to list on your résumé when you are looking for a job.

RADIO COMEDY

At first thought, you might assign radio comedy to the same fate as radio drama. The great network comedies of the 1930s and '40s are long gone. A few of the stars may now be seen on television, but the great era of radio comedy—Jack Benny, Fred Allen, Bob Hope, Edgar Bergen, Amos and Andy, Fibber McGee and Molly, and similar shows—is past, and there is no reason to believe it will return. But while drama declined with the decline of network radio, radio comedy simply shifted gears and adapted to the new radio formats.

Radio today is primarily *local*, not network. Radio comedy, too, is local. Radio is now mostly music and news. Radio comedy has found ways to fit into that format. Today's radio comedy will likely be found as part of a disc jockey program. In some markets comedy is even appearing in segments of news programs. Instead of the weekly half-hour comedy series, radio comedy is now free-form, coming in packages of varying sizes. It is "filler" material to occupy space between records, news, and—of course—commercials.

Today's radio comedy tends to be satirical. Often it is offbeat and antiestablishment to fit the style of the stations and disc jockeys that use it. And, as will be pointed out in the next chapter, some of the best radio comedy written today is found in the commercials.

Length

Most radio comedy today is brief. Skits rarely run more than five minutes, and most are considerably shorter. Casts are minimal. Most shows will have, at the most, two hosts who must use their vocal skills to portray all the characters on the show. Usually they have the assistance of a good engineer, who can help with sound effects and various electronic tricks to expand the seeming range of characters. Sometimes brief excerpts from news programs or commercials are interjected into the show as "dialog." (This should be done *only* after careful consultation with the station's legal department and, in the case of commercials, sales department.)

Some air personalities prefer to work with monologs. Some develop a set of characters who are heard from daily or with reasonable regularity. Fans of Bob and Ray in New York have learned to expect frequent visits from "award-winning Wally Ballew," along with less frequent visits from old standbys like "Natalie Attired."

Characters

Contemporary radio comedy presents a unique set of problems. A major problem is to introduce a character and a funny situation to the audience within the brief time span of the usual skit. Continuing characters such as Wally Ballew simplify the problem somewhat—but the radio writer can never assume that the audience knows *anything*. After all, if your show is any good, you should be attracting *new* listeners daily. You cannot expect the new listener to know the traits of your continuing characters. This means that you must often be fairly bold in getting across the traits you want the audience to know. You can do this in your introduction:

MARC: We're fortunate to have in our studio again today efficiency expert Rollo Dex, author of the new best-seller, <u>Living Your Life in Half the Time</u>.

          Or, you can interject descriptive material into the dialog:

MARC: By popular request, Rollo Dex is back in our studios. Rollo, as an expert on getting people to organize their lives efficiently, I wonder if you could tell our audience just exactly....

Obviously, a great deal of today's radio humor is parody or satire. You can roughly distinguish these two by saying that parody makes fun of a style—a manner of speech, a way of phrasing things, or some similarly obvious characteristic—while satire pokes fun at the foibles of society. Parody imitates and exaggerates. Satire takes existing situations and ideas to illogical and hilarious extremes. It can be argued that both forms can be subtle, that extremes are not always necessary. This is true, but in the short formats allowed for most radio comedy today, there is regrettably little time for subtle treatment of topics. In most cases, your humor will spring from fairly obvious dialog.

Sound Effects

There is a tendency to treat most material as originating in the radio studio. You have little time to create other scenes in the minds of the listeners, although this element can sometimes greatly add to the humor of a skit. Many radio comics today rely almost exclusively on dialog for humor. That is unfortunate because well-planned sound effects can add enormously to the humor of a script. Those old enough to remember are unlikely ever to forget the sound of a cascade of junk tumbling from Fibber McGee's closet or the clanking of chains and locks in Jack Benny's vault. Or take this example from the "Goon Show," a popular British comedy series last heard on BBC Radio in 1974. (The terms "grams" is British terminology for a recorded sound effect.)

<u>GRAMS:</u>   <u>SHELL DROPPING</u>

BLOODNOK: Duck!

SEAGOON: That's no duck, that's a chicken.

CHINSTRAP: By gad, sir, they're firing hens at us.

BLOODNOK: A <u>foul</u> trick.

CHINSTRAP:	<u>Egg</u>-sactly.
MILLIGAN:	We're being <u>shelled</u>.
SEAGON:	Stop cracking yolks.[4]

"Goon Show" humor—especially a string of puns like that—isn't for everyone, but the use of the sound effects helped provide the illogical transition from gun shells to hens.

Building for Laughs

Just as a drama must build from crisis to crisis, so a comedy should build from joke to joke. Radio comedy must be fast paced. There are no visuals to hold the audience. Before the laughter has stopped for one joke, you must be well on the way to another. How closely should the gags follow one another? Analysis of comedy programs from the 1930s and '40s suggests that gags came four or five to the *minute* when the shows were really moving. Almost never would you find a period as long as one minute without at least one gag. Most contemporary comedy shows are a bit slower paced, but they will usually pack five to ten gags in a three- to five-minute skit. There is plenty of room for more humor in most contemporary comedy shows. Some performers prefer a more relaxed pacing for their shows. But the main reasons for the lessened number of jokes are the lack of time for preparing the material, the relatively large amount of time required in short skits to establish characters and basic premises, the subject matter chosen, and the limited comedic skills of the writers.

Problems with Contemporary Radio Humor

Few people in radio today are "gag writers" in the traditional sense. Instead, we have disc jockeys, newswriters, and advertising copywriters who also write some funny material. As has been said too often, "Comedy isn't funny." Writing funny material is an exacting, full-time job, just like anything else. People who devote only part of their time to being funny usually produce material that is funny only part of the time. This is one of the reasons that many student comedy endeavors fall flat. In most aspects, humor is really harder to write than drama. It is not hard to come up with a couple of funny lines or situations, but it is very hard to sustain humor through the length of a program—even a brief one.

Moreover, most of the people writing radio humor today—with the possible exception of advertising copywriters—have very little time to write their material. Often they have to come up with something funny for a show every day, while in the best days of radio, a team of ten or fifteen writers might toil a week on a single half-hour script. Humor is sometimes spontaneous, but sustained humor has to be carefully developed. It takes time.

[4]Terrance A. (Spike) Milligan, "Shifting Sands," quoted in Roger Wilmut and Jimmy Grafton, *The Goon Show Companion* (New York: St. Martin's Press, 1976), p. 77.

As we have noted, the brevity of modern comedy skits presents a problem. A certain amount of any program *cannot* be funny. Certain situations have to be explained and established. They are no more likely to be funny than the instructions for assembling a child's toy. They are a prerequisite to the fun. There is a certain, irreducible amount of this exposition that is needed in any skit. The shorter the skit, the less time left for the gags after the exposition.

Finally, contemporary radio comedy writers often pick dead-end topics for their humor. Radio humor today is satirical and parodic. It feeds upon the items of daily interest. It does not take great skill to come up with one or two gags or an idea based on this type of material—but very often that's as far as you can go. Either there is nothing more that is funny to say on the topic, or the writer beats the topic to death with endless variations on the same theme.

The lesson, then, is pick your topic carefully and give yourself plenty of time to develop your material on that topic. If the topic "will not hold" but must be dealt with before it ceases to be of interest, you had better examine it carefully to be sure you can come up with enough material.

Writing for the Performer

As a writer, you must also know the performer for whom you are writing. Most radio comedy personalities write much, or all, of their own material today. That is a mixed blessing. Probably, if you are writing for yourself, you will know the things you can do well and the things you can't. For example, if you can't do dialect humor, you simply don't write any for your show. Unfortunately, not every performer understands clearly what works with his or her audience. It is one thing to know whether you can tell jokes in dialect. It is something else to know whether the audience thinks you are *funny* when you are telling jokes in dialect.

There is a great deal to be said for dividing up the roles of writer and comedian. The opportunity for such a division of labor is rarely offered today, however, so you must become a good judge of your own abilities as both writer and performer.

Defining Humor

What's funny? Obviously, for radio, it must be words and sounds. The only pictures you have are those you can conjure up in the minds of the listeners—although those can be the funniest of all, if done properly. Your tools are the malapropism, the put-down, the illogical answer, the sharp retort, and the pun. These are the staples of verbal humor. Along with this goes the invaluable element that the performer must provide—timing. The writer can write "(pause)" but only a skilled comedian knows *how long* to pause. The great stars of the past—Fred Allen, George Burns (happily, still performing at this writing), and Jack Benny—all were past masters at milking a pause, waiting that extra beat longer than it seemed possible to wait before delivering the anticipated punch line. A radio pause is *not* a television pause. The actor's face conveys part of the humor during a television pause, but a radio pause must be 100 percent in the listeners' minds. It's pure anticipation.

Even a brief sketch must have structure. It should build through a series of lesser humorous events to a final funny denouement. The best radio humor has an even more sophisticated structure. The story should run through a series of little gags that build up to bigger ones. Then the process begins all over again, but the second big gag should be bigger than the first. In short, your script is something like a series of waves, each slightly larger than the last, building to the final big laugh. It takes real skill to achieve this sort of form in your script. Obviously, the length of the script determines how many of these "waves" you can fit into the story.

As with any broadcast form, you must study the program you wish to write for. You need to know the usual length of the comedy segments and what kind of material is interspersed between them. You might choose a different approach for comedy in a musical program than you would for comedy in a talk show. You have to determine whether the program usually continues a basic comedy theme from one segment to the next or whether each new segment tends to take off on a new topic. If there are continuing characters, you need to know their characteristics. Be sure you know the manner of speech for such continuing characters. Remember that you have to re-identify and establish the key characteristics of these characters each new time they appear on a show.

Building the Plot

Block out each segment of the show. Try to decide what your funniest lines are and determine where they should go. Usually they will go in the final segments of the show, but some disc jockeys may prefer to concentrate the humor in a show near the start or in the middle of the program, leaving the end of the show to music and one-liners.

Within segments, try to outline a progression of increasingly funny lines. Then go back within each segment and try to think of funny material to go between the lines you have sketched in. Then see how much time at the start of the segment is needed to establish the premise for the humor. Finally, see if you cannot come up with little gags to lead up to the other gags you have already planned.

Go over the material and try to "even it out." See if you cannot transfer some material from very funny segments to parts that lack enough humor. Work toward a goal of four or five funny lines per minute. Try never to let a full minute pass without something funny. Time the material carefully to make sure it will fit in the desired segment. One reason that disc jockeys avoid skits near the end of a program is that simple patter and one-line gags are easier to use to make the program time out correctly. You can lengthen or shorten this material as you wish to make the program come out right.

If possible, go over the script with someone else. See if they think it is as funny as you do. See where it drags.

With any script, it's a good idea to put it aside for a few days before you do any extensive revision. Of course, if you are working for a daily program, you may not have that luxury. And some topical gags must be used without delay. If you do have time to let the script sit for a few days, you can often think of some additional material to add to the script. Always look for a funnier line. Never hesitate to throw out a line if you can come up with a funnier replacement. There is a caution to be observed here, however. Jokes may seem stale to you simply because you have heard them too often. This is when the opinion of someone else is especially helpful. By the time you have rewritten and polished your script a number of times, it is natural to begin to find jokes less amusing than they appeared at first. You may discard funny jokes simply because you have lost perspective. Worse, you may replace a funny joke with a less funny one simply because the newer joke is fresh and seems funnier to you. Keeping your perspective on humorous material when you have been working with it for a long time becomes very difficult. A performer in a nightclub or on stage gets immediate feedback on jokes. Audiences vary, and even a good gag may not work every night, but if it fails with any great frequency, out it goes. You do not have that luxury in radio. You must know as a professional what will work. We repeat, when you are unsure about a joke that seemed funny when you first wrote it, try it out on a couple of people who have not heard it.

It goes without saying that you must have a good idea of the audience you are writing for. You do not write the same gags for teen-agers that you do for adults; you do not use the same material on a rock station that you use on a "beautiful music" station. Some humor is universal, but much humor depends upon the frame of reference of the audience. Keep that in mind when you write.

Limitations

Remember, too, that there are limits to what may be said on radio. There are limits of simple decency and good taste, and there are specific legal limits. If you do not transcend the former, you are not likely to transcend the latter. If you are inclined to think that anything goes these days, think again. Remember, it was a comedy monolog by George Carlin that led to the Supreme Court ruling that specifically affirmed the right of the FCC to prohibit certain material from the air under certain circumstances. For decades now, disc jockeys have trod a narrow line between "blue" material and what can be used on the air. One used to have a Spanish soap opera heroine named Luz Morales. Another used to have a continuing story about people who lived "around the corner and up your street." And there was a supposed tax expert with a book called *Up Your Bracket.* Such borderline cases are not at all new. But the Supreme Court decision in the Carlin case adds new importance to keeping your material clean and socially acceptable. When you get right down to it, the material available to base clean jokes on is far greater than that on which dirty jokes are based, so you are not being placed under a horrendous restriction by being asked to keep your broadcast humor clean.

Working with Performers

A writer can gain a great deal by being present when material he or she has written is being rehearsed. Very often it becomes apparent that lines assigned to one character are not working out. Frequently this can be solved simply by assigning those lines to another character. In the interplay between performers at rehearsals, new ideas for gags almost always arise. At the same time, some ideas that looked good on paper simply don't play when they are heard. Last-minute changes in scripts are common in radio comedy, and much can be gained from working through rehearsal with the performers.

SUMMARY

For both radio drama and radio comedy, be sure that you have studied the script format carefully. Pay careful attention to such matters as sound effects. Determine which information can best be transmitted by narration and which by dialog or sound effects. Prepare your audience for action that is to come. Use the standard techniques of plot development you used in television drama for radio dramas. Keep dialog simple.

Ascertain the basic format of the show. Sketch in the points at which you want to use your best gags. Then fill in lesser gags, trying to lead up to those with several funny lines. Aim for at least four or five gags per minute, and never less than one a minute. Have a friend listen to the copy when you begin to doubt your own ability to determine whether a line is funny. Whenever possible, let your script lie a few days before you start revising it. Always try to work through the rehearsal with the cast so you can make last-minute changes.

RADIO COMMERCIALS 7

and
Public
Service
Announcements

The commercial is possibly the most maligned of writing forms. Anyone can cite examples of tasteless or misleading advertising on the air. But there are also *good* commercials—ones that entertain, inform—and sell. If you accept the premise that radio today is mostly music and news, then the primary creative outlet for the radio writer is the commercial. Certainly it is fair to say that some of the best comedy being written and performed on radio today is found in the commercials. Sponsors have learned that, in the relatively relaxed format of today's radio, humor sells products.

You should not, then, look on the radio commercial as something second-rate. The first thing that comes to most people's minds when they hear the word "commercial" is television. But if you think of the hours that Americans spend with their radios—in their cars, out in the yard, on the beach, or at a park—you suddenly realize that people hear literally hundreds of radio commercials every week. Sponsors are fully aware of this Radio is a less costly medium than television for the advertiser, and the audiences are more clearly defined, so a sponsor can pick the specific groups needed to sell a product. Advertisers spend more than $3 billion on radio every year. That should convince you that radio is no second-rate medium.

Think of radio as a *different* medium, but not as a disadvantaged one.

The first question to be faced, of course, is how to get the message across without pictures. The answer is that you paint the pictures with words and sounds—just as you do with all other forms of radio writing. And just as with those other forms, those mental pictures can sometimes be more powerful than any image generated on the television screen. You have great freedom in choosing the locale of your commercial, and relatively few costs to worry about. If you want to put your commercial in the court of Louis XIV or on the planet Saturn, you can do so simply by pressing the right keys on your typewriter.

Use that freeedom. The mind is a far better stage than any movie lot. Take, for example, one of the classic radio spots done by Dick Orkin and Bert Berdis for *Time* magazine. Frantic for his copy of *Time,* a man wraps himself in his wife's housecoat and goes out in search of a magazine stand. He is stopped by the police. You could make a funny television scene out of that, but the mental image of the man in the housecoat facing the police is probably funnier than any television version could ever be.

Like television commercials, radio commercials come in 10-, 20-, and 30-second, and one-minute lengths. Frequently the same commercial may be made in several lengths. Because radio time is relatively cheap, the one-minute commercial is more likely to be found on radio than on television. The chance to write a slightly longer commercial can be helpful in radio because any dramatized radio commercial needs time to establish the scene. Generally, if you are working with less than a one-minute format, you are better choosing a "straight pitch," that is, a commercial which simply describes the reasons why the listener should buy the product instead of "sneaking" the message into some sort of dramatized format. So, one of the first things you need to know in preparing a radio commercial is what length is to be used.

You must know your product to sell it. Use it if possible. What's good about it? What's bad about it? What research is there to indicate how the public feels about the product? And precisely what audience do you want to reach with your message?

BASIC NEEDS

Like television ads, radio commercials should be pitched to some basic human need. Will your product make the listener feel more secure? Loved? Respected? The product must *do* something for the listener. You do not tell the listener, "Eat Whizzo cereal, and you won't feel hungry." Obviously, people eat because they are hungry, but any food product can meet that need, so you have to stress that Whizzo will make you healthier, stronger, thinner, or whatever you decide will sell the product. You must convince the listener that Whizzo will do the job better than competing products in its general price range.

DISTRIBUTION

You must know at the outset how your commercial is to be distributed. More expensive commercials are prepared by an advertising agency and distributed in disc or tape form to the various stations on which time has been purchased. Usually, several lengths of the same commercial are recorded on the same disc, and sometimes more than one commercial is included.

Normally, these discs or tapes will be accompanied by a script. The script provides the lead-in to be read by the local announcer before playing the recording, and the closing to be read after. Usually the script for the material on the disc is also included for the benefit of the station engineer. If the complete script is not included, the running time and opening and closing words of the recorded material are included with the scripted local introduction and closing so that the announcer and engineer know when the recorded material is completed.

Less expensive commercials are prepared in script form only, to be read by the local announcer. Sometimes the script may be accompanied by recorded background music or sound effects. In addition to being inexpensive, the script-only commercial has the advantage of being presented in the familiar voice of a local announcer or disc jockey. (Commercials are also sometimes read by newscasters, but most newsmen frown on this practice, which they argue tends to confuse news and commercials in the mind of the public.)

On the other hand, the prerecorded commercial can use even better-known voices of nationally famous personalities. Teams of performers have a long history of success on radio. Bob and Ray were among the first radio teams to cash in on the commercial value of their voices. In the 1950s Mike Nichols and Elaine May turned their talents to the production of commercials. In the 1970s it was Stiller and Meara with their ads for Blue Nun wine and later for United Van Lines. Orkin and Berdis, who were mentioned earlier, are not nationally known by name (at this writing), but their voices are known to almost everyone. That kind of recognition is valuable because the sound of the voices alone attracts the interest of the audience. Without familiar voices, the writer must find a quick way to get the audience to pay attention to the ad. The writer also has to establish character traits and situations that may be understood by the audience when well-known voices are used. Clearly it makes a difference to the writer how the commercial is packaged and who is heard in it.

SCRIPT-ONLY OR "READER"

If you are preparing a script-only commercial, you are usually limited to a straight pitch. You cannot expect the local announcer or disc jockey to perform as an actor in your commercial. The best you can hope for is that the material will be read clearly and convincingly. Scripts of this sort are sometimes called "readers." Here's an example:

<u>MAINSTREET SALE</u>   20 Seconds

ANNCR: If it feels a little cold around your ears
           these days, better check your calendar. It's
           September already. And just in time for
           those winter winds, <u>The Mainstreet</u> is having
           a sale of men's virgin wool sweaters by Black
           Sheep. Sweaters that regularly sell for
           fifty to seventy-five dollars have been
           marked way down -- some as low as 38-50.
           Better stock up now -- at the place where
           smart folks in Gardendale always shop -- <u>The</u>
           <u>Mainstreet</u> . . . Located -- where else? . . .
           one-thousand Main Street in downtown
           Gardendale.

The ad does not beat around the bush. It simply says sweaters are on sale and tells you where. The writer looked for some sort of "hook" to attract the listeners' attention, but the basic ad is a straight pitch.

Like any ad, this one has certain functions to perform. It appeals to certain basic needs—security (warmth) and prestige (fashionable clothing). It makes an appeal to self-image through price, too. The buyer is given the feeling he is doing something a bit smarter than ordinary by getting the clothes at less than the presumed regular price. At the same time, the prices are not terribly low, so there is a certain amount of prestige involved in buying and wearing clothes that are not "cheap." This is reinforced by stressing the brand name of the product. Probably the basic appeal is to self-esteem. Certainly there are cheaper ways to meet the need if the need is only to stay warm. Given the brevity of the commercial, the writer has done quite a bit to get the appeal in the pitch.

There is nothing difficult for the reader to deal with in the ad. Any competent announcer should be able to deliver the ad convincingly with one or two read-throughs.

Note that the writer was careful to get both the street address and the *city* into the commercial. Radio travels over great distances. The listener always needs to be reminded *where* the product being advertised is for sale. The street address is not enough. In the example given, there could easily be a dozen towns with a Main Street within the broadcast area of a radio station. If there were any numbers that needed to be remembered, the writer would have repeated them two or three times. The name of the shop is mentioned only twice. Three times would have been better.

PRERECORDED COMMERCIALS

There is not doubt that prerecorded commercials are more fun to write than the script-only variety. They allow the writer far greater freedom in approach, and they often run a minute instead of 20 or 30 seconds. Usually little comedies or dramas, often these series can continue for years, presenting essentially the same characters—or the same voices playing similar roles. Stiller and Meara produced three commercials a year for nine years for Blue Nun wine. The audience came to wait for the newest response from Ms. Meara when Jerry Stiller would inevitably announce that he had brought along "a little Blue Nun." "I don't want a miracle," cried Meara in one of them, "I just want a bottle of wine."

Comedy has been a particularly fertile field for radio commercials. Some of the best humor on radio is, undoubtedly, in the commercials. These can look deceptively simple to the student. They aren't. As was emphasized in the chapter on comedy, it takes hard work to write really funny material. To package it into a one-minute format along with a commercial message takes skill. Remember that some of the national advertising campaigns we have mentioned had the advantage of well-known performers. People know what to expect when they hear the voices of Jerry Stiller and Ann Meara because they usually play similar roles from one commercial to the next. The same may be said of Orkin and Berdis. The audience is ready to laugh when it hears those voices, and the types of characters being portrayed usually need little introduction. But without those expectations the writer must use precious seconds introducing characters and situations. Keep that in mind when you begin to sketch out your commercial. Perhaps you have a splendidly funny idea for a commercial using Sir Lancelot and Queen Guinevere at a jousting match. You are going to have to be clever to establish both the characters and the situation without using up most of your time before you get either to humor or selling the product. Still, Guinevere and Lancelot are at least reasonably well known figures to an audience. You have less of a problem introducing them than you would a completely unknown character.

Opening Lines

You must concentrate very carefully on the first couple of lines of dialog in your script. You have to get everything explained to the audience as quickly as possible. Don't forget to make use of music and sound effects to help out. For example, the jousting match could have sounds of horses' hooves or the clanging of swords. Ocean sounds could help establish a seashore scene, and so on.

Remember that you want to try to mention the product at least three times in your dramatization. Location may also be important. Numbers that should be remembered, such as telephone numbers, should be repeated two or three times, and the audience should be made aware that the numbers are coming so it is prepared to memorize them or write them down.

Dramatization

The brevity of the commercial does not obviate the need for having some structure to your script if it is a comedy or a dramatization. It should present some problem to be solved and show some denouement to the problem—usually through the use of the product. Here's an example of a dramatization:

PICNIC   MOCHA-MAX
One Minute

<u>SOUND OF DOOR SLAMMING</u>

CHILD: Mom! Hurry up! We're late for the picnic.

MOTHER: (Tired) In a minute, Tommy. Momma's feeling tired.

FATHER: Hey. What's the matter with my wonderful wife?

MOTHER: Oh, honey, I'm sorry. I'm just all worn out.

FATHER: I know what you need. A coffee break with MOCHA-MAX.

MOTHER: Hey. You've got something there.

SEGUE TO ANNOUNCER

ANNCR: He sure has! MOCHA-MAX is the coffee with double the caffeine of regular coffee. One cup of MOCHA-MAX gives you double the lift of ordinary coffee. And double the taste too. Rich and full-flavored. The perfect treat when you've only time for "half a cup."

SEGUE TO CHILD

CHILD: Mom! Let's climb that big rock.

MOTHER: Okay, Tommy! I'll race you to the top.

FATHER: Now that's my lively wife again!

MOTHER: Thanks to MOCHA-MAX.

ANNCR: MOCHA-MAX, the rich, fine-tasting coffee with double the lift.

<u>END</u>

Closing Lines

It's even more important to have a conclusion to a humorous commercial. Just like a comedy radio show, it should build to its biggest laugh near the end.

NEIGHBORS   KLEENSHAVE
                             One Minute

<u>SOUND OF POUNDING ON DOOR</u>

HARRY: (Annoyed) Okay . . . Okay . . . (<u>SOUND OF DOOR
            OPENING</u>) Fred! What's the matter?

FRED: Harry, I'm out of KLEENSHAVE!

HARRY: KLEENSHAVE! For Pete's sake, Fred. It's six
            a.m.

FRED: I know. I set the alarm half an hour early
            so I wouldn't waste a second getting to
            shaving. Ever since I started using
            KLEENSHAVE, I just can't wait to shave again.

HARRY: Fred, you got me out of bed.

FRED: (Ignoring him) This morning the can was empty.

HARRY: (Annoyed) Well, you should have bought an
            extra can.

FRED: I did! I bought two cans last Thursday.

HARRY: You used up two cans in less than a week!

FRED: I just can't stop shaving since I started
            using KLEENSHAVE. I shave when I get up. I
            shave again after breakfast. Then I shave at
            lunch, and again when I get home . . .

HARRY: Fred, KLEENSHAVE is terrific, but . . .

FRED: It feels so good! Those warm little bubbles
            just bathing your face in special lotions
            that baby your skin. That, clean, woodsy
            smell . . .

HARRY: But, Fred, KLEENSHAVE's specially lubricated
            foam lets you shave so clean and so close that
            you look good all day. You can get through
            the whole day with your morning shave.

FRED: Appearances! That's all on the outside. It's
            the inner me that needs to shave. The razor
            doesn't tug when you use KLEENSHAVE. It . . .
            it caresses your face. The whiskers just
            float away in those beautiful little bubbles.
            It . . . it's a beautiful experience, Harry.

```
HARRY:      Go home, Fred.

FRED:       Harry, please, lend me your KLEENSHAVE.

HARRY:      No way, Fred.  You still haven't returned my
            lawn mower.

FRED:       I'll bring it back this morning.

SLOW SEGUE TO ANNOUNCER

HARRY:      How about the hedge trimmer?

FRED:       I'll bring it back with the lawn mower.

HARRY:      And my golf clubs, and my slide projector,
            and . . .

ANNCR:      KLEENSHAVE, the lotion-lubricated shaving
            foam . . . makes your face feel so good that
            . . . you may want to shave all day.
```

<u>END</u>

PUBLIC SERVICE ANNOUNCEMENTS

As was emphasized in the section on television public service announcements, there is no difference between a public service announcement and a "commercial." A public service announcement *is* a commercial. Only the product being sold is different. You need to make the same sort of preparation for a public service announcement that you would for any other radio advertisement. Determine what audience you are trying to reach. Decide what message you want to get across to that audience. Decide what appeal will best work with that audience and that message.

Be honest with yourself about the good and bad points of the charity you are promoting. *No* organization is *all* good. There are weak aspects of each charity as well as strong ones.

Remember that you must *appeal* to some basic need of your audience. Do not make your public service announcement a threat. It is true that some research indicates that certain threats, up to a point, *may* be effective in certain appeals. However, no one is exactly certain *how much threatening* works and under exactly *what circumstances.* In general, then, you are best advised to steer clear of ads that try to scare the listener. It is too easy to cause the listener to turn off, figuratively or literally, your message. Instead, remember the basic principal for all commercials: Seek a human need to which you can appeal.

That does not mean that you should take a Pollyanna approach to your commercial. An equally bad approach is to promise the listener too much. One danger is that the listener may cease to feel that there is any real need for his or her contribution. And a problem often faced by some charities is that, in promising a cure for a disease or a solution to a problem year after year, the charity begins to make the listener feel that the problem really is hopeless, that no amount of money or help will ever really achieve the desired end. Probably only one charity in recent history really managed to wipe out most of the disease it wanted to conquer—that was the March of Dimes campaign to eliminate infantile paralysis, made possible by the development of the Salk vaccine.

Charities like the American Cancer Society have had a much tougher time of it. Breakthroughs here and there, plus success in treating certain cancers, primed the public to expect some miracle cure for cancer such as the Salk vaccine had been for infantile paralysis. But that miracle has not come to pass, and the Cancer Society has had to find ways of keeping supporters from losing hope and deciding that the fight against cancer is not worth the time and money. In particular, such organizations have to keep justifying to the public the amounts spent on research when the results so far have been disappointing. What you need to understand when you begin preparing your public service announcement is what kinds of public impressions of this sort you must deal with. In the case of the Cancer Society, one approach has been to emphasize stories of people who have been cured of cancer. The slogan "Cure Cancer in Your Lifetime" is unspecific about when, or how soon, a cure for cancer may be found.

Choosing Voices

Radio has some advantages over television. It was pointed out in the discussion of television public service announcements that you should not show seriously maimed or deformed victims of an illness or social problem. Since in radio you are only dealing with the human voice, a good many people who would not be suitable subjects for television PSAs may still be all right for radio. Try, however, to pick someone who has a fairly "standard" and appealing voice, reasonably devoid of regional accent. An English critic once wrote, "An Englishman only has to open his mouth to offend another Englishman." He was talking about the many accents and dialects spoken in the tiny land area of the British Isles. People *can* be annoyed by regional accents. Americans may not take offense as readily as the British critic claimed Englishmen do, but it is safest to pick speakers who are reasonably free of regional accents.

If you are going to use a layperson who has benefited from your charity instead of an actor, that will not free you, the writer, from preparing a script. Few people can get a message across concisely enough to fit it into the confines of a commercial. Some PSAs are created by interviewing people on tape and then editing the interview down to fit time, but most PSAs are written completely in advance. This is one of the toughest forms of writing because you have to come up with material that fits your time frame, gets your message across, and still sounds natural coming from a person who is not a professional actor. It is not simply for the value of having a famous name that charities often have their commercials read by famous actors. Professionals can get your message across far better than most nonprofessionals can. If you are working with a layperson, you will probably have to spend some time with that person, learning his or her speech patterns. Then you will have to be present while that person reads your lines, and be ready to make changes to make your words suit the person who is reading them.

Finding the Right Emotion

Try to make your appeal to natural human instincts such as familial love. Researchers found long ago that a substantial number of smokers, when urged to quit smoking to save their own lives, paid no attention. In the first place, the listener was clearly still alive and therefore could downplay the probability that she or he would die as a result of smoking. Second, the ethics of our society stress the protection of *others*. It can be considered cowardly to save your own life. It is heroic to save the lives of others. Appeals to smokers often are written *not* as appeals to save their own lives but as appeals not to set a bad example for their children. (Studies show that even confirmed smokers don't want their children to risk their health and lives by smoking.) Or the appeal can be pitched not so much to saving your own life as to the meaning of that loss to others left behind—widows, widowers, and orphans left behind because the smoker was too selfish to give up the pleasure of smoking. The thrust of the ad is shifted from asking someone to be self-serving to asking the person not to harm others through selfishness.

Choosing the Right Station

It is unfortunate that only the largest charities have the money to devote to research into the target audience of your messages. Radio stations have highly differentiated audiences. Moreover, the audience can change if the station changes its basic programming format. You need to give consideration to this and tailor your PSAs to the audiences of the stations you send your PSAs to.

If you do not have this sort of research available to you, you can at least take the time to listen to the stations that you want to use your PSA. In particular listen to the commercials they carry. That should give you a clue to the type of PSA to put together for each station. This way you can ride on the coattails of the big national advertising agencies that place spot ads on these stations. They *do* have the time and money to make sure that the commercial spot is directed to the audience of the station. Do not underestimate this need to fit your PSA to the station's format. One of the major reasons given by stations for declining to use PSAs is the failure of the PSAs to fit station formats.

Notice what kinds of products are advertised on the commercials of the station for which you intend to prepare your PSA. Again, the national advertising should give you a clue to the audience and the type of PSA that should be prepared. If you direct your PSA to the same audience as the national spot advertising on a station, you are reasonably sure of producing something that will be more likely to be used and that will be effective in getting the message across.

There are some cautions to be observed here. Despite the popularity of Top-40 programming, a survey of radio usage of public service announcements came to the surprising conclusion that the use of rock music in your PSA is likely to earn you a rejection from most stations. Why this should be was not explained by the study, but it obviously is something you cannot afford to ignore in creating PSAs.

Production Techniques

Radio public service announcements are prepared in a variety of ways. Sometimes the entire spot, or series of spots, is recorded and distributed on discs or tape. Since this is expensive, the bulk of PSAs are prepared in script form only, for reading by an announcer at each station. Obviously, the writer is extremely limited in this sort of PSA. If you want endorsements by figures of national importance, or if you want to make use of music, sound effects, and dramatization to create your PSA, you must plan on distributing it as a recording. This means you must be working for a fairly large organization which can afford this sort of distribution.

However the PSA is distributed, you have your best chance of getting it on the air if it is prepared in several different lengths. As was pointed out in the television section, radio PSAs may also be prepared from the sound tracks of television PSAs. In any case, PSAs are usually prepared in 10-, 20-, and 30-second lengths. Sometimes they are prepared in one-minute formats as well. On the following pages are three versions of a public service announcement sent out to announce a concert at a university. All three were mailed to a list of stations. The stations then chose which, if any, of the versions best fit their time requirements.

In preparing multiple versions of a PSA, it is usually best to start with the shortest version. That must contain the most important information you have to get across to your audience. Arrange the details you want to tell the public in a list of descending importance, and use that to decide what to add to each progressively longer PSA.

PSA Radio Format

Note the format used in the three examples. All the announcements have important information *not* intended to be read on the air along with the message for the public. The source of the PSA, a mailing address, and a telephone contact are provided. This allows any station to check back for clarification or additional information. Larger organizations may provide a 24-hour number to call.

The PSA gives a date on which the message can first be used—in this case (and with most PSAs) immediately. And it tells when the last day is that the PSA should be run.

OFFICE OF PUBLIC EVENTS
California Institute of Technology
Pasadena, California 91125

Ticket Information: (213) 793-7043

Press Contact: Janis Rafferty
(213) 795-6811, Ext. 1689

MEDIA RELEASE

Start using: IMMEDIATELY

Stop using: May 10, 1980

RADIO SPOT

Reading Time: 10 seconds

ANNOUNCER: The Amadeus (ah-ma-day-us) Quartet

will perform at Caltech on Sunday,

May 11. Phone area code 213, 793-7043.

SCBA File #80180-261 EI

The PSA copy provides a pronunciation guide for the announcer to use on tricky words. The 10-second version gives the most basic information—what is happening, who is doing it, where it is happening, when it is happening, and how to get further information about it. It contains the basic elements of the traditional newspaper lead. It is essentially an informational message, which makes no real attempt to motivate the audience to any sort of action. It would be foolish to try in so short a format.

The 20-second version gives more detail about the location and tells what the program will be. The 30-second script gives some background information about the performers. Only in the 30-second version do we go far enough beyond basic information to have some material that might have

OFFICE OF PUBLIC EVENTS
California Institute of Technology
Pasadena, California 91125

Ticket Information: (213) 793-7043

Press Contact: Janis Rafferty
(213) 795-6811, Ext. 1689

MEDIA RELEASE

Start using: IMMEDIATELY

Stop using: May 10, 1980

RADIO SPOT

Reading Time: 20 seconds

ANNOUNCER:

The Amadeus (ah-ma-day-us) Quartet
will perform in Caltech's Beckman
Auditorium on Sunday, May 11, at
3:30 p.m.   The program for this
Coleman Chamber Music Concert will
include compositions by Mozart,
Britten, and Beethoven (bay-toe-ven).
For information, phone area code
213, 793-7043.

SCBA File #80180-261 EI

some "selling" effect on the listener. What there is, however, is extremely low key.

The PSA may be faulted for failing in its longest version to seek more strongly to motivate listeners to attend the concert. However, 30 seconds is a brief time to do much motivating. It can be assumed that the stations most likely to use the PSA would be those that program classical music, and the listeners interested in the PSA would probably be familiar enough with the quartet and the musical selections to decide whether to attend without further inducement.

There are other minor weaknesses in these examples that should be noted. Foremost is the failure to give the telephone number to be called more

OFFICE OF PUBLIC EVENTS
California Institute of Technology
Pasadena, California 91125

Ticket Information: (213) 793-7043

Press Contact: Janis Rafferty
(213) 795-6811, Ext. 1689

MEDIA RELEASE

Start using: IMMEDIATELY

Stop using: May 10, 1980

RADIO SPOT

Reading Time: 30 seconds

ANNOUNCER: The Amadeus (ah-ma-day-us) Quartet
will perform in Caltech's Beckman
Auditorium on Sunday, May 11, at
3:30 p.m. In its thirty-fourth
year with the same personnel, the
Amadeus Quartet offers the widest
active repertory among the world's
string quartets. Their program for
this Coleman Chamber Music Concert
will include compositions by Mozart,
Britten, and Beethoven (bay-toe-ven).
For information, phone area code 213,
793-7043.

SCBA File #80180-261 EI

than once. Telephone numbers should be given at least twice and preferably three times. Moreover, there should be an indication in the PSA at an early point that a number will be given so that the listener can prepare to take it down. Coming at the end of each of the PSAs with no advance warning, the telephone number is virtually useless.

Pronunciation guides have been provided for Amadeus and Beethoven, but not for Britten and Mozart. It seems fair to guess that any announcer who cannot pronounce "Beethoven" might also have trouble with "Mozart." Moreover, the pronunciation guides give no indication of which syllable to accent. It leaves a not-too-bright announcer with the alternatives of "AH-ma-day-us," "ah-MA-day-us," "ah-ma-DAY-us," and "ah-ma-day-US." You may think it unlikely that a professional announcer would pick the wrong one, but, to paraphrase H. L. Mencken, nobody ever got poor underestimating the intelligence of a radio announcer.

The time is stated as "3:30 p.m." Because "p.m." is sometimes misunderstood, the preferred broadcast style would have been "3:30 in the afternoon" or "at 3:30, the afternoon of May eleventh." Most broadcast style books suggest spelling out "eleven" and "eleventh" because "11" can sometimes be confused with a double "L" or with the roman numeral "II."

The copy also fails to make clear to the audience whether the concert is free or whether there is a charge for it.

Grammatically, the copy slips from treating the collective noun "quartet" in the singular ("offers") to the plural ("their") near the end. Since the two references are not in the same sentence, this is not a serious problem, but it would have been preferable to keep the references to the collective noun consistent.

Such minor problems can be expected to crop up in the pressure of getting out announcements of this sort. More often than not, the same person will be responsible for putting out both print and broadcast announcements. Not infrequently, the person preparing the material will have a background in print rather than broadcasting. Nevertheless, the three scripts provide a good example of preparing multiple versions of the same announcement. Since the writer prepared the script in television rather than radio format, it may also be inferred that the same announcements were sent out to television stations, probably accompanied by a slide.

The student may wonder if the announcements are not a bit short. By line count, that would seem true. But if you read them aloud (as you should always try to do with your own PSAs), you will see that they are only a second or two short of the specified time—which is a wise precaution. You should not expect all readers to read at the same speed, so it is best to keep your copy a second or two short of the specified length of the PSA. Moreover, in this case, there are several numbers in the copy. Numbers always take longer to read aloud than line count indicates.

While the scripts shown here deviate considerably from the style specified in our style book, we recommend that the student stick with the rules of style set out in this book. While this actual PSA is perfectly readable, it should be clear from our critique of it that adherence to the rules of style in this book would have strengthened the PSA in many respects.

SUMMARY

Analyze your product. Study the audience you need to reach. Give consideration to the stations on which the commercial will be placed. Determine what essential information must be in the commercial and what particular features of the product are to be emphasized. Decide what form of distribution will be used for the commercial. Sketch out your basic script. Check it for time. Then cut or fill as needed to create the entire message. If you use dramatized or humorous forms be sure that they contain the basic structure required of these forms, that they set out characters and situations quickly at the outset and that they build to a satisfactory conclusion.

Study the public image of the organization for which you are preparing a PSA. If possible, prepare different versions of the PSA for the different audiences of the stations you want to use. Within the limitations of time, try to make the PSA entertaining as well as informative. Pay very careful attention to the timing of your PSAs. Prepare multiple versions of the script for different time lengths.

Be sure that the script, when it goes out, contains information needed by the station as well as that which is intended to be read over the air.

Remember, the station is *giving* you time for your PSA. That is the same as giving your organization money. If you want to get a station to make that contribution to your organization, you must do everything you can to make it easy for the station to use your PSA.

Writing

Of all the forms of broadcast writing, news writing may be the most vexing. Broadcast news writing has grown up over the years in its own way. At first it borrowed from the newspapers and the wire services; it was common for a station to simply read a newspaper story on the air. Newspapers and wire services, of course, took a dim view of this practice. Copyright suits soon established that it was illegal to "pirate" material in this manner. Even had it been legal, it still would have been a poor way to present news on the air, as broadcast newsmen soon came to realize. The human mind simply cannot cope with spoken information in the same way it deals with written material. It can accept, understand, and remember only small quantities of spoken information at one time.

BROADCAST VERSUS PRINT JOURNALISM

The advent of television changed the situation only slightly. Television news is pictures, not words written on a screen. Certain information can be reinforced by adding some written material to the television picture, but the basic differences between broadcast and print news writing remain. The listener or viewer cannot go back to earlier material at will. The material must be absorbed during the short time span that the viewer sees it or the listener hears it. The amount of information presented and the manner in which it is presented must both be such that the audience is not overwhelmed.

It is not surprising, then, that people often describe broadcast news as "shallow" or "superficial." The essence of good broadcast writing is simplifying everything to its most basic elements. Moreover, the information must be compressed into the time frame of the broadcast. The average radio newscast today is a five-minute program; when time is deducted for commercials and opening and closing material, this means the newscast runs about three and a half minutes. In that brief time, the most important of the day's events—international, national, and local—must be presented. It calls to mind Dr. Johnson's analogy of a dog walking on its hind legs: It is not done well, but one is surprised to see it done at all.

In truth, that is an unfair analogy. Given its limitations, radio news is presented surprisingly well. But it is pointless to compare it to newspaper coverage. It is a different medium. No one who really expects to understand the news of the day should expect to get that information from radio—or television. These media give us the main facts of the most important stories of the day. Only the newspaper can provide the details.

THE ROLE OF THE WRITER

A newspaper writer may have the luxury of working on a story for weeks. At worst, the newspaper writer has a deadline once a day. The broadcast writer may have a deadline every hour. What broadcast news lacks in detail it compensates for with timeliness. This morning's newspaper is yesterday's news. Radio news and, to a lesser degree, television news, are the news of the moment.

This means that the broadcast news writer must be an excellent judge of news, must be able to make decisions about news stories in seconds, and must be extremely bright and broadly read. If not, terrible mistakes will occur under the pressures of getting out the news. There is too little time to check things out. The broadcast news writer must sense when something about a story is suspicious. The news writer learns early that no source is reliable all the time, and that even the wire services make mistakes occasionally.

Too many broadcast journalists overlook this crucial point. It is no secret that most radio news today is "rip and read." The copy is taken off the wire machine and read on the air. For some stations, this is enough. But that is a foolish, and even dangerous, approach. The owner of a station is responsible to the Federal Communications Commission for anything that is broadcast on that station. Moreover, anyone involved—from the copyboy to the station owner—can be sued if a station broadcasts material that is libelous or that invades someone's privacy. It is the newsman's job to see that nothing in the news gets the station into trouble.

It isn't enough to "rip and read." Wire stories may be wrong. Sources may be incorrect. Material may be written in such a way that it sounds wrong on the air even though it looks all right in print. A good news department relies upon rip-and-read material only for stories that are of lesser importance and for which there is insufficient time to do a rewrite. A news department should write its own news because that is the only way it can control the material for which it is held responsible. Writing your own news is usually the only way you can provide good local news, and local news is the only news your station can ordinarily provide that is different from and superior to that of your competitors. And writing your own news is the only way you can adapt the news you provide to the needs of your listeners and the style of your station.

The 20-Second Story

In writing for broadcast news, you will have to learn a great many new rules. If you have learned in other writing courses to count copy as so many words, forget it. You are now concerned with how many seconds a story takes to read. You will count lines—and count them very carefully—but only because they are an indicator of how long it takes to read a story. And no story will be very long. Twenty seconds is plenty for most of the day's news stories. If you find that hard to believe, take a stopwatch and time a five-minute newscast. Broadcast news must be tight.

How can you do it in that time? You strip it to the bone—and then strip it some more. You write only the barest essentials, but that does not mean that you write in a telegraphic style. Indeed, despite the pressure to condense everything for the air, you must often add a few words to make the copy easier to understand for the listener. So you begin by cutting out facts. You edit out words only after you have written your basic story. Then you can tell what words should be dropped—and where they need to be added.

Working against time, you must produce scripts that are timed exactly. In spite of the limited show time, you must cram in all the important facts—often dealing in 20 seconds with an event which a newspaper covers in 20 column inches.

The Quick Lead

You will also have to learn how to write a "lead" for a broadcast news story. If you have taken print journalism courses, you have learned to write the traditional "Who? What? Why? When? Where? How?" lead. You do not ignore those vital questions now, but not all of them need be in a broadcast lead. The function of the lead is not to summarize the story, as is the case in newspaper wiriting; rather, it is to give the audience a warning of what the story is going to be about. Remember, the broadcast audience does not have the luxury of going back and listening to material it missed. So you use the lead not to impart important information—since the audience may not be prepared to listen to it—but instead to give the audience enough information for it to decide if it wants to listen carefully to the story.

RADIO FORMAT

You will have to learn an entirely new format for preparing your script. There is one format for radio and another for television. As you learned in chapter 2, each medium has its unique demands, and the formats have been developed to serve those needs. Because these formats differ so much from other broadcast formats, we'll start by reviewing what you learned in chapter 2. So let's begin by looking at a radio news script.

Formats vary from station to station. We have provided you with examples which follow generally accepted principles in broadcast writing —although you may find the format used at any given station is considerably different. Let's look at the radio format first. Examine the radio news format example carefully.

37 Lines

1. TITLE -- PROGRAM -- DATE -- WRITER'S NAME

Set margins at 10 and 80. (Other margins may be

specified.) Double or triple space. Use down style

(unless instructed to use all capital letters). Skip

an extra line instead of indenting for paragraphs.

Type the slug (story title, etc.) about one-and-one-half

inches from the top of the page. Start your story about

one inch below that.

Write only one story to a page. If the story can . . .

not . . . be completed on one page, do . . . not . . .

split a paragraph or a sentence between two pages.

With at least one inch left at the bottom of the page,

complete the paragraph, type "MORE" at the center of the

bottom of the page, and circle it, as is done here.

1. TITLE -- PROGRAM -- DATE -- WRITER'S NAME -- FIRST ADD

The second page slug is identical to the one on the

first page except that it ends in "FIRST ADD." If

there is a third page, it is slugged "SECOND ADD," and

so on. (At some stations, the slug for radio stories

is written as a block in the upper left-hand corner

instead of a single line as we have shown here.)

Type in a pronunciation (pro-nun-see-AY-shun) guide for

(PEN-sil)

any difficult words or pencil it above the word later.

Pencil a wavy line under any tough words.

All words must be completed on the line on which they

are begun. It is never permissible to split a word be-

tween two lines as was just done. If you begin a word

and do not have room to complete it, cross it out and

begin it fresh on the next line.

MORE

1 b TITLE -- PROGRAM -- DATE -- WRITER'S NAME -- SECOND ADD

<u>Underline</u> any words that need special emphasis. Pencil

a circle around anything on the script not meant to be

read aloud.

Pencil the total number of lines (or running time if

so instructed) for your story in the upper right-hand

corner of the first page. Number stories instead of

pages, putting the number to the left of the slug.

When a story runs more than one page, make the second

page "1-a," the third "1-b," and so on.

Set off the word . . . not . . . with a string of dots

so the newscaster can . . . not . . . miss it.

Use the symbol "#" to indicate the end of the story.

Page Numbers

Note in the format example that the page number is written in the upper-left-hand corner in pencil. Pages are not numbered in broadcasting scripts until the show has been assembled in its final form. This allows additions, deletions, and changes with no problems. Not all stations use the upper-left-hand corner, but it is a convenient location where the page number is not likely to be confused with other material. The page number has been circled, as have a number of other items on the page. Anything that is not intended to be read aloud by the newscaster is usually circled as a precaution. If a radio script is to be read by more than one person, the name of the reader for this story is sometimes written after the page number.

Slug

The *slug*, or the name of and information about the story, goes about an inch and a half from the top of the page. The slug lists a name for the story, the program on which it is to be used, the date, and the name of the writer. The single-line, all-capital-letter style we show here is not the most commonly used one. We recommend its use because it is quicker to type, easier to read, and takes up less space. The traditional radio slug is written in a block in the upper-left-hand corner of the page, like this:

> Title
> Program
> Date
> Name

Margins, Timing and Line Count

We recommend that you set your margins at 10 and 80 for a four-second line. Some stations prefer 10 and 75, estimating 16 lines to a minute. We feel that it is easier to work with 15 lines to the minute—an even four-second line.

The line count is made only after the story has been edited. It is written in the upper right-hand corner, and it is circled. It may be changed later if material is added or cut. Many stations prefer to use the actual running time of a story instead of the line count. Line count is usually easier to keep track of than minutes and seconds, but you should familiarize yourself with both systems. The lines are simply estimators of reading time. Each line is supposed to take about four seconds to read. Three and a half minutes of copy for a five-minute newscast should run about 53 lines. Line count must include the running time of any audio material in the story. A 20-second audio cut in a story should be counted as an additional five lines for the line count.

All line counts, of course, are estimates. They are usually based on a reading speed of 150 words per minute. This works pretty well for students, although reading speed for many professional newscasters is 170 words per minute or more. You will have to adjust either your line lengths or your estimated reading time per line to fit the reading speed of the person who will be reading the copy.

Line Spacing and Capitalization

Copy should be double-spaced—triple-spaced if your typewriter will allow. Many writers insist on preparing all copy in capital letters. They argue that it is "easier to read." Dozens of tests have been conducted, and the results are always the same. Copy is easier to read if you use normal lower-case letters and capitalization as you would for any other kind of writing. This is the style we recommend. You will have to conform to the preferred style of the station at which you work, however, and many still insist on all capitals for news copy. Wire-service copy, of course, is all in capitals, but this is simply because teleprinters have no lower-case letters.

Broadcast stories are so brief that they rarely run more than one paragraph. Since indenting the first line of a paragraph and ending the last one short throws the line lengths off when you estimate reading time, we advise against indenting for paragraphs—although many stations use a five-space indentation. You can indicate a new paragraph (if one is really needed) either by skipping an extra line or simply with four or five spaced periods to indicate a break in the reading.

Pronunciation Guides and Copy Preparation

Be sure that you provide a pronunciation guide for any difficult words. Type the guide in parentheses after the word or print the guide above the word in pencil. Any word that may cause the reader difficulty should be underlined with a wavy line.

One Story to a Page

Write only one story to a page. This allows you to make changes and rearrange the order of stories in a script without having to retype several stories. As stations switch to computerized copy preparation, this rule will no doubt disappear because copy will be rearranged at the press of a button and the "page" may only be a video screen.

Words are not split between two lines with a hyphen as they are in printed copy. If you cannot finish a word on the line on which it began, cross it out and start it over on the next line. Split words can confuse someone trying to read them aloud on the air. It goes without saying that the same rule applies to splitting sentences and paragraphs between pages. Sentences and paragraphs must end on the page on which they began. Be sure you let the reader know that there is more of the story on the next page by typing "MORE" at the bottom of the page. At the end of a story, type the symbol "#."

Multipage Stories

The second page of a multipage story begins with the same slug used on the first page. At the end of it, following wire-service style, type FIRST ADD for the second page of the story, and so on. At some stations, the style is simply to end the slug with "2nd page."

GENERAL RULES

Here are some rules to help you in writing broadcast news:

1. Write more informally for broadcast news than for print, remembering that the words are to be spoken.
2. Read your stories aloud. Listen for awkward sounds. Be sparing in the use of "s," "th," and "ing" sounds. Avoid words like *thrusts, risked, wrists,* and *frisked,* all of which are difficult to pronounce.
3. Clever writing signified by alliteration and similar devices is much more meaningful in print than on the air. Puns and tongue twisters tend to confuse many newscasters and may cause the listener to focus so strongly on the words that the sense of them is lost. Simplicity is the keynote.
4. The personal nature of radio and television stories gives them more emotional impact than the same material in print would have. Be sparing with gruesome details of crimes and accidents.
5. Make qualifying statements at the beginning of a sentence, not at the end. That way, the listener is more likely to hear the qualifier.
6. Newspaper and magazine writers often use transitional words in the middle of a sentence (e.g., using *however* after an introductory clause rather than at the beginning of the sentence is usually smoother in print). Broadcast writing calls for using transitions at the beginning. The listener should always be aware of the direction of a statement.
7. The attention span of the broadcast audience is short. Without audio cuts, radio news stories usually run 15 to 20 seconds. Television news stories without visuals rarely run more than 30 seconds. With videotape or film, television news stories usually run 40 seconds to one minute. Radio news with audio cuts usually runs 30 to 50 seconds.
8. Avoid long lists—especially of names or numbers.
9. Round off figures whenever you can. Don't use "9,999,991.85"; write "about 10 (M) million."
10. Never use *a* for *one*, as in "a million." It could sound like "8 million." Always write "one (M) million" or "one hundred." Insert an M in parentheses before "million" and a B in parentheses before "billion" to avoid reading and typing errors.
11. Do not refer to organizations by abbreviations or acronyms—except for very well known organizations such as the FBI or NATO. Note that when each letter of the abbreviation is to be spoken, the letters should be separated by hyphens. F-B-I. Try to use titles of individuals or organizations in full in the first mention in a story. You can shorten the title or use an abbreviation (when well known) on subsequent mentions in a story.
12. Use no symbols (e.g., "$10" for "ten dollars), and use no abbrevia-

tions except for Mrs., Ms., Mr., and Dr. For example, it is correct to write "Dr. Jones," but make it "Father Kelly" and not "Fr. Kelly," and write "Wilshire Boulevard" and not "Wilshire Blvd." Abbreviations commonly used in place names are an exception. It is all right to write "St. Louis" or "Ft. Collins."

These rules are some of the most commonly used in broadcast newswriting. Most broadcast newsrooms will have a deskbook that provides a fairly complete list of the rules used by that station. The following style guide is a deskbook you can use for your exercises in this course. It is designed to be used for both radio and television newswriting.

RADIO-TELEVISION NEWS STYLEBOOK

I. Format
  A. Paper
    1. Use standard 8½ x 11-inch paper.
    2. Use soft paper that will not rattle.
    3. Use white paper for radio, pastels for television.

  B. Typing
    1. Use one side of the page only.
    2. Type only one story to a page.
    3. Always make a carbon copy. Television scripts are normally typed on "books" of paper interleaved with carbon sheets. Each page is a different color. Scripts are collated according to color, each color designating the recipient of the script (e.g., green to anchorperson, pink to director, and so on).
    4. Margins
      a. Radio: 10 and 80
      b. Television: 40 and 75*
    5. Triple-space copy. Double-space copy if the typewriter has no triple-space setting. "Fill" material may be single-spaced.
    6. Use down style, normal capitalization.
    7. Skip an extra line rather than indent for paragraphs.
    8. Never split a word between two lines.
    9. Avoid starting two successive lines with the same word.
    10. Indicate the end of a story by triple spacing and typing "#" in the center of the page.

  C. Numbering
    1. Do not number pages until just before air time.
    2. Number in the upper-left-hand corner.
    3. Number stories, not pages. Make the second page of story number 6, "6*a*," and so on.

  D. Use paper clips to hold the script together. Never staple a script. (After it's been used, the script can be stapled for filing.)

  E. Story Format
    1. Slug
      a. The slug is the information at the top of the page that gives the name of the story, the program for which it was written, the date, and the name of the writer.
      b. This is the television slug:
        FACTORY FIRE—NOON NEWS—7/12/85—MARTIN
      c. The same slug can be used for radio, although some stations prefer typing this in the upper-left-hand corner:

---

*Oversized type requires different margins and different estimates of the reading time per line.

Factory Fire
Noon News
Martin

If this slug is used, the page number goes below the slug.

  d. For second-page slugs, see *2d* below.

 2. Multipage Stories

  a. If a story looks like it will run on to a second page, start looking for a place to split it after the tenth line.

  b. Never split a sentence or a paragraph between two pages.

  c. Centered, near the bottom of the first page, type "MORE," and with a pencil circle it and draw an arrow to the right edge of the page.

(MORE) ——————————⟶

  d. The second page begins with the same slug as used on the first page, followed by the words "FIRST ADD." A third page uses the slug with "SECOND ADD," and so on.

FACTORY FIRE—NOON NEWS—7/12/85—MARTIN—FIRST ADD

or

Factory Fire—First Add
Noon News
7/12/85
Martin

II. Editing

 A. Do not use copyediting symbols.

 B. Use a copy pencil to *completely* mark out any words that are to be deleted or corrected.

 C. Type or print the correction above the material crossed out.

 D. Retype any copy that is difficult to read.

 E. Circle anything not meant to be read aloud.

 F. Underline words to be <u>emphasized</u>.

 G. Mark a wavy line under any words that may cause difficulty for the reader, either with meaning or with pronunciation.

III. Timing

 A. Time permitting, check running time of each story with a stopwatch.

 B. If you cannot time the story with a stopwatch, estimate the running time from the number of lines of copy. Using the margins given in section IB (4), a line of radio copy takes about four seconds and a line of television copy about two seconds.

 C. Record the running time of each story in the upper-right-hand corner of the story's first page.

  1. Running time includes the running time of any audio or video material included in a story. A television story with a 12-second introduction followed by 40 seconds of video tape should have "52 sec." written in the upper-right-hand corner.

2. Many news departments prefer to use the story's line count rather than actual running time in the upper-right-hand corner. This is usually easier to keep track of. Remember to convert the running time of any audio or video material to line count in this case. For example, a television story with a four-line introduction and 20 seconds of videotape would have "14 lines" written in the upper-right-hand corner. A radio story with a 10-line lead-in followed by a 20-second audio cut would have "15 lines" written in the upper-right-hand corner.

3. For times greater than 59 seconds, use minutes and seconds. Write, for example, "2:08," *not* "128 sec." Do *not* write "2:08 min." or "2 min. 8 sec."

D. Back-time material from the start of commercials, the end of the program, or other fixed-time program elements. With a red grease pencil, mark the time at which you must begin reading that material to come out on time. Arrange the script when reading it so you can see these marked times and know when to hit them.

E. Every script should contain "pad" material. This consists of brief items that can be used to fill in before back-timed material so that the back-timed material can be read starting at exactly the specified time.

IV. Writing Style

A. Use *a* or *an* instead of *per* in expressions such as "miles an hour." Do *not* use *a* in expressions such as "a hundred" or "a thousand," where it can be confused with "eight." Always write "one hundred," and so on.

B. Abbreviations

1. The only abbreviations you should use are Mr., Mrs., Ms., and Dr. *Write everything else out.* you may use "Ft." (Fort) and "St." (Saint) when they are commonly used in a place name such at "Ft. Hood" or "St. Louis."

2. *Very* well known organizations may be referred to by their initials. If each letter is to be pronounced, use hyphens, not periods, to separate the initials. For example: F-B-I. An exception to the rule is "AFL-CIO," which would be confusing if written with hyphens between all letters.

3. Well-known acronyms should be written without hyphens. For example: NATO. Do not use an acronym that is not known almost universally.

4. Use a period after initials when the initial is a regularly used part of a person's name. Write "Senator S. I. Hayakawa," *not* "Senator S-I Hayakawa."

C. Addresses

1. Omit addresses except when essential to the story.

2. Group numbers in addresses in normal speech patterns by using hyphens: 18-0-2 South Main Street.

3. If the street name is a number, separate it from the house number by a direction or some other written material: Write "128 *South* 135th Street" or "number 825 on 35th Street."

4. If it is awkward or impractical to separate the house number and the street number, write out the shorter of the two. For example: "seventy-five 185th Street," *but* "12-82 Tenth Street."

5. Always write out "First Street and "Eleventh Street" because "1st" and "11th" can be confusing to read.

D. Ages

1. Omit ages unless essential to your story.

2. Instead of newspaper style ("Mary Jones, 25"), write "Mary Jones, who is 25," or "25-year-old Mary Jones."

3. Ages are customarily used in obituaries and when a person is expected to die soon.

E. Contractions

1. Use contractions only when they are easy for the reader to say and when there is no chance of misunderstanding them.

2. Avoid the use of *n't* contractions except for the few that differ clearly from their positive form, such as "won't," which cannot be confused with "will." Do not use a word such as "hasn't," which can easily be misunderstood as "has." (See section on writing of negatives.)

F. Dates

1. Write all dates as ordinals: "May 10th, 1938," "October 2nd, 1987."

2. Write out "first" and "eleventh."

3. Many writers break the year with a hyphen to indicate the normal way of speaking: "June first, 19-82."

4. "A.D." and "B.C" are easily misunderstood. It is preferable to make it "before the birth of Christ," or "after the birth of Christ." Any date before the birth of Christ must be specified as such. Dates through the year 1000 are usually specified as "after the birth of Christ." Later dates need no such reference except when they are being used in a story that also involves dates before the birth of Christ.

G. Election returns should be simplified for the listener. Don't write: "With 53 percent of the precincts reporting, Lubitch has 3,007,593 and Winslow has 3,000,079." Make it: "With more than half the precincts reporting, Lubitch leads Winslow by 75-hundred votes."

H. License plate numbers are rarely given out in broadcast writing. If needed for a story, give the state of registration and follow it with the numbers and letters separated by hyphens: "California license plate number 4-9-8-R-Z-T." Group long numbers into groups of three, using dots: "Nevada license plate number 8-0

. . . 5-7-5." If you expect the listeners to remember or write down the number, it should be mentioned at least twice, preferably three times.

I. Write out "dollars" and "cents" for all sums of money. Write "2 dollars and 28 cents," not "$2.28." Round off sums whenever possible. Make it "almost 2-thousand dollars," not "$1,963.48."

J. Names
   1. Never lead with an unfamiliar name.
   2. Drop middle initials except when the person is regularly known by the name with the initial included. For example, write "Clifford Alexander," *not* "Clifford L. Alexander," but *do* write "George C. Scott." On occasion, a middle initial may be retained to help distinguish an individual from others with the same first and last names: "The man arrested was Charles J. Smith, but the warrant had been issued for Charles K. Smith."
   3. Nicknames
      a. Put nicknames in parentheses. This indicates that the reader may use the nickname or ignore it. Example: "Ron (the Penguin) Cey (SAY).
      b. Use a nickname without the real name *only* if the nickname is very well-known and is unique. For example, it is safe to say "the Fighting Irish" for the Notre Dame football team, but "the Wildcats" could be one of several teams.

K. Negatives must always be stressed in broadcast writing. Make it "Feldman had <u>not</u> seen the warning" or "Feldman had . . . not . . . seen the warning."

L. Numbers
   1. Avoid using numbers as much as possible. Where they must be used, simplify them and round them off. Try to analogize sums to things the audience is familiar with. For example, instead of saying a boat is "300 feet long," you can say it is "as long as a football field."
   2. Keep numbers out of the leads to stories and out of the first parts of sentences when possible.
   3. If you must use a number as the first word of a sentence, write it out. For example: "Twenty-eight men arrived," *but,* "There were 28 men."
   4. Always write out the numbers "one" and "eleven."
   5. Whole numbers
      a. Use digits from 2 to 999 (except for eleven).
      b. Combine written numbers and digits for all higher numbers. For example: "one-thousand-12."
      c. Write numbers between 1,100 and 9,900 as hundreds. For example: "Eleven-hundred-2," or "95-hundred-24."

(However, write years as specified in the section on dates.)

    d. Write millions and billions like this: "8 (M) million dollars" or "10 (B) billion pounds."

6. Fractions

    a. Write out all fractions: "one-fifth," not "1/5."

    b. Write one-place decimals as tenths: "2-and-three-tenths," not "2.3."

    c. Convert decimals to regular fraction equivalents if they have them. For example, write "three-fourths," not ".75."

    d. Avoid decimals of more than one place. If they must be used, use digits and write out "point" like this: "8-point-32 ounces."

M. Write percentages as digits and write out the word "percent." For example: "130 percent" or "82-point-35 percent." Use "point" with one-place decimals as well as longer ones: "82-point-6 percent."

N. Use pronouns sparingly. Repeat nouns freely to avoid ambiguity. Words such as "former" and "latter" should not be used for the same reason. They create ambiguity.

O. Pronunciation

1. Provide a pronunciation guide for any word that has the *slightest chance* of confusing the reader. Underline the word with a wavy line. Either write the guide in parentheses after the word, like this: "Cholmondeley (CHUM-lee)," or print
   (AH-vee-lah)
   it above the word, like this: "Avila."

2. Use the phonetic guide on this and the next page. Do not use diacritical markings such as are used in dictionaries: "Peruzzi (puh-ROOT-see)," not "(pe-'rüt-sē)."

3. Indicate accented syllables with upper-case letters. Wire copy has no lower-case letters, so accent is shown with an apostrophe at the end of the accented syllable. Some news departments use this system too. Using capitals to show accent, your copy would look like this: "Cordoba (KOHR-doh-bah)." Wire copy would show it "(KOHR' DOH-BAH)."

4. Phonetic spelling

    a. Use the chart on phonetic spelling for vowels.

    b. Use consonants as they are written *except* for the following:

C: Use *K* for words like "cat," and *S* for words like "center."

G: Use *G* for words like "go," use *J* for words like "genius," and use *ZH* for words like "rouge."

Q: Use *KW* for words like "quick" and *K* for words like "croquet."

T: Use *TH* for words like "thin" and *THH* for words like "lather."

    c. Omit silent letters. Do not substitute an apostrophe for the omitted letter. It may be confused with an indication of a stressed syllable.

PHONETIC SPELLING

	A	E	I	O	U	Y
A	apple draught					
AH	arm			opera		
AI*	aisle	eye	I island pi pie sight write paradigm			my
AO				cow bough		
AW	awe paw audition caught			ought		
AY	ale mail mate may	epee eight				
EE		ease seem we	libertine			city
EH		enter				
EW		new		root routine	tune	
I		pretty forfeit	it			
OH		sew tableau		oh so open roe tow		
OO				cook	put	
UH	about	erstwhile		rough thorough	up	
YOO		ewe beauty			unit	

NOTE: If there is any chance of confusing the reader with the pronunciation guide, use some other method, such as providing a rhyme. For example: *Home* (HYOOM, rhymes with room).
*Because this is easily confused with AY, some prefer to write it EYE.

5. Don't expect to be letter perfect in the pronunciation of foreign words. Do your best to approximate them phonetically. Wherever possible, save your newscaster some work and try to find ways to write the story *without* the tough-to-pronounce words. Remember, too, that many foreign words, especially place names, have been anglicized. Don't try to show off your knowledge of foreign languages by providing pronunciation guides for words that already have accepted English pronunciations. Paris is PAYR-iss, not pah-REE. Give some thought to whether your audience is likely to have seen the word you are using in print. You may need to make some reference to unusually spelled words to keep your audience from being confused. For example: "Lord Home (HYOOM) . . . that name, by the way, is spelled H-O-M-E, just like the word "home" . . . Lord Home (HYOOM) urged the President to postpone. . . ."

6. The radio wires of both major wire services provide pronunciation guides for most difficult words in their stories. They also run a daily list of names, places, and words in the news with a phonetic guide for pronouncing them. Another good source for pronunciations is the NBC *Handbook of Pronunciation,* although, at this writing, the last edition is badly out of date. A check with your state capitol or state university library will usually turn up a book that provides pronunciations for communities and locations in your state. Any good, up-to-date dictionary will provide you with correct pronunciation of most words you are likely to encounter, and most dictionaries either incorporate in the main section or provide separate sections with pronouncing gazetteers and pronouncing biographical information. A good atlas, gazetteer, and biographical dictionary are three books that *should* be found in any good newsroom.

   It is a very good rule *never to guess at a pronunciation.* If you have made every effort to find a pronunciation and have failed, however, make up one that seems likely to be correct. That way there will at least be consistency in the pronunciation used until you can find the correct one.

7. Avoid words like *read, lead,* and *bow,* which can be pronounced in more than one way according to meaning.

P. Punctuation
1. Do not use
   a. Semicolons (;)
   b. Exclamation points (!)
   c. Brackets ([ ])
2. Three punctuation marks serve the function usually served by the comma. Each indicates a pause in reading:

a. The comma indicates a short pause. In a few places, it serves more to make reading easier than to indicate a pause, as when it separates a state or country from a city. For example: "In Phoenix, Arizona, today . . ." Writers sometimes omit commas where no pause is desired in the reading, as in "Sammy Davis Junior" rather than "Sammy Davis, Junior."

b. The dash (--) indicates a more complete break in thought, a longer pause in reading, than the comma. Use dashes for parenthetical clauses and wherever they make the reading easier. Be sure you understand the difference between a dash and a hyphen. When written on a type-writer, the hyphen is a single line, with no spacing before or after it, as in "co-operation." The dash is two lines, preceded and followed by a space, as in, "The men - - still angry - - decided to. . . ." Never use dashes to string together groups of words that should be a complete sentence. Don't overuse dashes.

c. The ellipsis, which is three periods (. . .), indicates an even longer and more complete break than a dash. "The contestants were . . . well . . . stark naked." Also use three periods to draw attention to negative words: "He did . . . not . . . say."

3. Use hyphens freely to make combination words easier to read. For example, "multi-talented" or "co-operation." Use them also to link words in multiword titles like "Attorney-General."

Q. Quotations

1. Broadcasters get their quotes on film or tape. Never write a quotation into a script unless it is absolutely essential to the story. Paraphrase every statement you can. Quotes that must be read by a newscaster may confuse the listener.

2. There is no point in using the ellipsis to indicate deletions. The listener cannot hear any indication of the missing words. For example, if you wrote "President Reagan said today, 'We'll get there . . . provided Congress will agree,' " the listeners would have no way of knowing words had been deleted between "there" and "provided." In the same sense, the listener or viewer may not realize when material has been edited out of a video or audiotape or film. If the deletion is not obvious, you should indicate it to the audience with phrases like "Later, the President added."

3. If you must use a quotation, do not rely upon the quotation marks in your copy to clarify things for the audience. Even though the reader is skillful in using inflection in his or her voice to indicate the start and end of the quote, the audience

can still be confused. Take this example: "The soon-to-be released prisoner said that, if he gets out tomorrow, he'll go 'where I always go.' " Hearing that, the listener won't know whether "I" refers to the prisoner or the newscaster.

4. Although you may have heard a newscaster beginning a quotation with the word "quote," then ending with "unquote," it is not necessary. The inflection of the newscaster's voice will help the listeners to understand that he or she is quoting. To make certain that the listeners understand when the quotation begins, you should use one of these forms:

She said - - *and we quote her* - - "That man is a sham." (Never use "unquote" at the end.)

The governor was, *in her words,* "a sham."

She praised the conference, *calling it* "not a boondoggle, the best conference we have ever had."

The best reason to quote these statements directly is because of the use of the words "boondoggle" and "sham." That makes the words distinctive. If, in the third example above, she had said only, "This is the best conference we have ever had," there's nothing distinctive about the words. Thus you shouldn't quote her directly; paraphrase.

5. When you're quoting someone, make it short. Always avoid quoting someone in four or five sentences. If you use long quotations, the listener won't understand when the person being quoted stops speaking and the newscaster begins to speak in his or her own words.

R. Sports
1. Use digits for all scores and statistics.
2. Don't use "82-79." It is better to write "82 to 79." Since "to" can sometimes be confused with "2," however, the best solution is to specify each team with its score: "Texas 82 over 79 for Missouri."
3. Don't waste time looking for substitutes for the words "won" and "lost."

S. Statistics
1. Avoid statistics and other lists of numbers.
2. Where statistics must be used, follow the regular rules for writing numbers.
3. Try to convert statistics into terms the audience can understand. Round off figures whenever possible.

T. Use telephone numbers only when absolutely essential. Use hyphens between the numbers and set off the prefix with dots: "4-9-8 . . . 4-9-8-1." Set the area code in a separate phrase if it is used: "The area code is 2-1-3, and the number is 4-9-8 . . . 4-9-8-1."

U. Time

1. Write times in the regular way: "2 o'clock" or "3:15."
2. Don't say "10 *past*" or "a quarter *to.*"
3. Minimize use of the word "today." The assumption is that broadcast news *is* today's news.
4. Do not use "a.m." or "p.m." Make it "this morning," "last night," or some similar expression.
5. Specific times are rarely needed. "Early this morning" is usually better than "5:27 this morning."
6. Use present and present perfect tenses as much as possible to reduce need to specify times.
7. Do not use "This just in" or "We have just learned" unless the information is less than five minutes old. Don't describe an event as happening "just a few minutes ago" unless it happened less than one half hour previously.
8. For times more than one hour, don't use terms like "90 minutes." Make it "one and one-half hours."

V. Titles

1. Most titles of individuals and names of organizations should be stated in full the first time they are used. Subsequent references can shorten the name or title. For example: "The Federal Bureau of Investigation is . . . An F-B-I spokesman said . . ." or, "Secretary of Health and Human Services Sandra Fein has . . . Secretary Fein told . . ."
2. *Very* long titles may be shortened. For example, instead of "The Joint House-Senate Subcommittee on Tariffs and Import Duties is . . ." make it: "A congressional committee wants to increase taxes on foreign-made automobiles. The subcommittee on Tariffs and Import Duties is recommending that import taxes be doubled on most foreign cars. The joint committee of House and Senate conferees voted to. . . ." The same information is provided, but it is spread out in easy-to-follow segments.
3. Avoid combinations such as the "House-Senate" adjective used in the previous section. Make it "a conference committee of the Senate and House" or "the joint congressional agriculture committee."
4. Don't make place names into adjectives in titles. Say "Premier Adoula of the Congo," not "Congolese Premier Adoula." Be particularly careful not to use such adjectives at the start of a story.
5. Use "Mr." for three purposes only:
   a. The President of the United States is customarily referred to either as "President Jones" or "Mr. Jones." While many stations have taken to just saying "Jones," traditionalists still insist on "Mr."

     b. The correct title for a male Protestant minister after he has been first mentioned, is "Mr." This is widely ignored, however. Check with the minister himself and see what he wishes to be called. (See section on religious titles.)

     c. Use "Mr." when a story concerns both a husband and wife.

     d. All other references to men with no special title should be "John Jones" on the first reference and simply "Jones" thereafter.

6. Traditionalists refer to women on the first mention as "Mrs.," "Miss," or "Ms." followed by the first name and the last name, then subsequently just as "Ms. Jones" or "Miss Smith." Today, many stations omit the title and make it "Mary Jones" at first mention, then "Mrs. Jones." And a growing number of stations follow the same rule for women as for men, simply "Mary Jones" at first mention and "Jones" thereafter. It may be necessary, of course, to use Miss, Ms., or Mrs. when more than one person in the story has the same last name.

7. Religious titles are extremely tricky, and your safest bet at all times is to check with the person whose name is being used or someone who is an official of the religious organization involved. Generally, rabbis should be called "Rabbi John Levin" and subsequently, "Rabbi Levin." Most Christian clergymen and clergywomen should first be referred to with the title "the Reverend," followed by first and last name. It is not proper to omit "the" or the first name. On subsequent mention, Roman Catholic, Greek Orthodox, and Anglican members of the clergy are usually referred to as "Father Jones." According to the rulebook, Protestant ministers should subsequently be referred to as "Mr. Jones" or "Mrs. Jones." Usage varies widely, however, so check to make sure what the correct form is.

8. For most other titles, use the title with the first and last name on first mention. Subsequently, use last name only or, optionally, the title and the last name. For example, after first reference to "Congressman Chip O'Veal," you could subsequently write either "Congressman O'Veal" or just "O'Veal." It is usually wise to repeat the title if it has any bearing on the story.

9. A few *very* well known persons, such as the President or the Governor, may be mentioned the first time by title and last name only.

10. Technically, you should use the title "junior" only if there is a "senior" living. For news purposes, however, use the terms any time there may be confusion about the person being

referred to. Don't bother with them otherwise. Some writers omit the commas around these words because there is no pause in speech where the commas fall.

W. "To" is sometimes a confusing word. It is preferable to say a score was "10 to 6" rather than "10-6," and it is better to write that one candidate beat the other by "32-hundred to 28-hundred" rather than "31,987-28,169," and that a bill passed "271 to 118," rather than "271-118." Because the word "to" itself can be confused with "2," the safest course is to find a way of stating these figures without using the hypen *or* "to." Don't go out of your way to find a substitute if there is little danger of the word being misunderstood.

X. Words to watch out for
1. Strings of sibilants such as "Commissioner Strauss's suggestions."
2. Alliteration—repetition of words beginning with similar vowels or consonants. For example: "In an unenviable spot."
3. Words that sound alike but have different meanings. For example, "great" and "grate," "bear" and "bare." Check word combinations for the same problem. For example, "a tax on" and "attacks on," or "and effects" and "and defects."
4. Pronouns—he, she, it, they— may be ambiguous. Check all pronouns carefully. Repeat nouns wherever possible.
5. Avoid words like "former" and "latter," which may confuse your audience.

V. Transitions
A. Do not write transitions as part of a story. This makes it too difficult to rearrange stories if you have to. First arrange script as it is to be used on the air, then write transitions on separate sheets and insert them in the proper places. Brief transitions may be penciled in at the top of the page of a story, provided material is easy to read.
B. Make each story in the script logically lead to the next one. This minimizes the need for transitions. A carefully arranged script may need no transitions at all.

SPECIAL NEWS PROGRAM

The rules we have cited apply to all news writing. However, not all radio news programs are alike. For example, in many cities there are stations that broadcast only news, 24 hours a day. They must present their news in a different way from those stations that provide only five-minute newscasts with an occasional longer program. Unusual approaches to news call for different formats.

One notable exception to the usual radio news format is National Public Radio's "All Things Considered." This program should be of special interest to students because it is one place where a student may have a chance to get a story heard nationally.

"All Things Considered" has no commercials, of course, and it runs for a full hour and a half. Faithful to its title, it presents stories on almost anything of interest. In addition to stories provided by its own small staff, it buys stories from reporters at various NPR affiliates. This means that if you have entrée to an NPR affiliate, you have a chance to sell stories to "All Things Considered." It is a good way for a young news writer to get some national exposure and gain some items to put on a job résumé.

Listen to "All Things Considered" carefully before you attempt to sell them a story. The stories tend to be longer than those used on commercial stations, but that is not an excuse for being long-winded. As with any broadcast news story, you should have a reason for everything you use in the story. Moreover, given the choice of longer audio cut or more short audio cuts, you will usually find that the latter approach makes for a more interesting news story.

We suggest that you approach "All Things Considered" with an eye for the things it does well, those it does poorly, and simply those it does differently. Be critical, and learn from all of them. Always keep in mind that "All Things Considered" is not, and was never intended to be, a typical news program.

NEWS COMMENTARY

Most broadcast news is what we call "straight news." It contains a factual account of an event and does not attempt to provide any interpretation of that event. Given the short time format available for radio, it is not often that we are even tempted to try to do more than present the facts. Yet, historically, commentary has been an important part of American radio news.

Throughout the 1930s and '40s, radio abounded in commentators. In fairness, the reason for this was not wholly a passion for interpreting the news. During the 1930s the wire services, to please their newspaper owners and customers, forced radio to limit its news programming to two 15-minute programs a day. One way to stay within the letter of the agreement and still have more news programs was to throw in a few words of comment and call a newscast a commentary. Nevertheless, a host of well-known commentators on the air did more than dress up news commentary. Only a few well-known commentators, such as Paul Harvey, are still on radio. As you read along you will find that Harvey does not strictly fit our definition of a commentator, but represents a specific, conservative political and religious viewpoint. He appeals to an audience that sympathizes with that viewpoint. (Although, to be fair, Harvey's appeal also stems from his broadcast style, which even his enemies concede is almost without equal.) However, we do not think broadcasters who present news from a particular viewpoint should be classified as commentators. We take the view of the major networks that commentary does not imply taking sides in issues.

It is a mistake students often make to think they can intermix straight news and opinions. These are very different things. Facts are facts. We may not like all of them, but we accept them because we must deal with them. Opinions are something else again. In short, we think there is much more to be said for the front page than for the editorial page. Most important, opinions must be clearly labeled as such and kept distinct from straight news.

Commentary should not be confused with editorializing. It is important for a student to understand from the outset that, under the laws as they exist as this book is being written, noncommercial stations may not editorialize. You may have commentary or opinions expressed by *individuals*, but no editorial viewpoint may be expressed *in the name of the station itself*.

It is important at this point to clarify the differences between straight news, commentary, analysis, and editorials. Straight news is the factual accounting of events without interpretation. Editorials, on the other hand, represent the official viewpoint of the station and are usually presented by the manager or a representative of management. They take a position on specific issues of public concern and they usually advocate some course of action.

Commentary and analysis may mean different things at some stations, but in general usage they describe the same type of material. For example, since 1974, CBS has reserved the word "analysis" for analytical material presented immediately following a speech by the President or following other speeches. All other analytical material on CBS is called "commentary." The *CBS News Standards Manual* notes that "the distinction is one of nomenclature only—not of substance."[1] The function of commentary is to explain the news so that the audience can understand it better. The purpose is not to influence the audience to any particular point of view. Rather, it is to make the material more understandable so that the audience members can reach their own decisions. The commentator tries to discover causes of events and to discuss possible consequences of them. Both sides of issues should be presented fairly. In the words of Paul White, who set up CBS News: "The function . . . is to . . . inform . . . listeners rather than persuade them. . . . Ideally, . . . the audience should be left with no impression as to which side the analyst himself actually favors."[2]

The job of the commentator begins with research, and this is where many student commentators fall down on the job. They see an article in a magazine, hear a speech, or otherwise acquire a viewpoint about an issue, and presto, they are ready to present that viewpoint as commentary. Anyone who acquires an opinion on a topic with no more thought or research than that has no business even being a voter, much less a commentator. Moreover, if you simply regurgitate what you have heard or read somewhere else, you are simply a conduit for someone else's ideas. You should be examining all sides of the issue you are commenting on.

[1] Columbia Broadcasting System, *CBS News Standards* (CBS: New York, 1976), p. 3.
[2] Ibid.

Such an examination should begin by marshaling all the facts you can obtain on the issue first. Turn to the varying opinions on the issue only after you are sure you have mastered all the facts. Be sure the opinions are those of people who have some background that entitles them to discuss the subject. Evaluate the opinions in view of the facts. Approach each opinion as an adversary, doing all you can to knock it down. Then see what, if anything, is left of it. Finally, see what you can synthesize from the facts and the opinions. Are there points on which everyone agrees? What are the major points of disagreement? How do the facts support or conflict with the various points of view?

The process of analyzing an issue for commentary is really no different from the logical procedure any intelligent individual should follow in formulating an opinion on any topic. But few of us have the time or inclination to accept that sort of discipline. So you, the commentator, can do some of the work for your audience.

Undoubtedly, in analyzing the issue, you will reach some decisions on it yourself. Fine. But remember that your job is not to tell the audience what to think. If you think you are particularly partial to one point of view on an issue, go out of your way to be particularly hard on that viewpoint in your commentary so that any unrecognized bias on your part is balanced out.

In writing your commentary, remember that the audience cannot absorb or retain many details. You must find ways of making the factual material in the matter understandable to the audience. You must repeat facts or numbers that are important to keep in mind. Of course, as in all broadcast writing, you must fit your material into a specific time frame. Commentary can be more procrustean than regular news because commentary is often scheduled for a specific time slot, meaning that you must lengthen or shorten all your commentaries to make them run the same length of time.

Traditionally, commentary is all talk by the commentator. There is, however, no reason the tradition cannot be violated from time to time. The inclusion of interview material or other audio cuts into radio commentary should add to the interest and authenticity of the commentary. Use all the production techniques you can to make your commentary interesting without making it hokey.

SUMMARY

To recapitulate, boil all your stories down to the essential facts, but do not hesitate to add words where they make the story easier to read or understand. Use the lead to attract the interest of the listener, not to carry important facts. Always write your script in the proper radio format. Unless instructed otherwise, use standard upper- and lower-case letters. Keep your writing simple and low key. Qualifying statements go at the start of sentences, and the source of a statement is always given before the statement itself. Always provide a pronunciation guide for difficult words, and mark tricky parts of the script. Don't split words between lines or sentences between pages. Avoid numbers and lists. Do not use abbreviations except for the few specified in the stylebook. Learn to think of your story in terms of reading time, not words. Use correct margin settings so that you can estimate reading time from line count. Remember to include the running time of any audio inserts in the reading time. Always mark your script with the correct running time or line count. Use an easily identified slug on each story. Read your story aloud to check for problems with the spoken copy. Teach yourself to write under a deadline, rapidly turning out copy that requires minimal editing. Always rewrite wire copy when possible.

News writing presents a great many rules for you to learn. It requires a very different approach to writing from what you have learned for other broadcast writing. Don't be discouraged if you have trouble learning all the rules at first. It will come with practice; and once you learn the rules, you will find that most of them can also be used when you write for television.

As for commentary, it is not easy to write. It is not something you do "off the top of your head." It must be well researched, well thought out, and carefully written. Nevertheless, well-done commentary can be interesting to the audience and satisfying to the writer. Just remember, your job is to help the audience make up its own mind, not to tell it what to think.

Writing

Most of the rules for television news format are the same as those applicable to radio news. The major differences are the margin settings and the cues used. Typewriter margins for television are set at 40 and 75, giving you a two-second line. Television copy is frequently written on typewriters that produce oversized type. With such machines, you may get six or fewer characters per inch. On such machines, the 40 setting is on the extreme right side of the page. Instead of 40 and 75, you may have to use 20 and 37 or some such setting, producing only a one-second line. Some stations also have the rule that copy to be read over videotape or film should be further indented, resulting in a still shorter line. These are variations that you need worry about only when you work where they are used. As with audio inserts in radio scripts, videotape or film segments of a story which have their own sound must be counted as additional lines in the total line count. A 20-second sound-on-video-tape segment of a story would add 10 lines to the line count.

The rule about not splitting sentences between lines may also be disregarded at stations with certain types of teleprompters. On some models, the script is taped together in one long strip. In such cases, a sentence may be continued from one page to the next because the newscaster does not see the individual pages, only the long strip of stories.

CUES

The most important change in format between radio and television scripts is in the cues that appear on the left side of the television page. These pages tell everyone involved in the production of the story what must be done technically to get the story to come out right. The writer must understand the visual and technical aspects of the story as well as its writing. You must "write" the pictures and sound as well as the words. Here is a list of some of the most commonly used cues. Again, you will find that these terms vary greatly from station to station—and sometimes even within the same script at the same station.

MOC.	Microphone on camera—newscaster is seen on camera reading copy.
OC.	Outcue—the last three or four words of a radio cart story or a sound on videotape segment for television news. Also sometimes used to mean "on camera," usually preceded by the name of the person reading the copy, as in "JOHN OC."
LIVE.	Same as on camera.
SI VT.	Silent videotape; picture shown without sound.
SI FILM.	Silent film.
SOVT.	Sound on videotape; source of sound is sound track of videotape.
SOF.	Sound on film; film sound track is source of sound.
SOMT.	Sound on magnetic track; used at some stations to designate film with a magnetic-stripe sound track as opposed to an optical sound track.
SLIDE.	35-mm slide.
FULL SCREEN.	Slide or other visual to occupy entire screen.
RP.	Rear Projection; material shown on a rear projection screen.
KEY.	Chromakey; material to be matted electronically into the picture using Chromakey.
VIZMO.	Material to be projected on a screen on the set using Vizmo.
SUPER.	Superimposition; one picture to be superimposed over another.
CG.	Character Generator; written material to appear on the screen via an electronic character generator.
VF.	Videfont, brand of character generator.
FONT.	Character generator.
A ROLL; B ROLL.	Film shown simultaneously on two film chain projectors.
VO.	Voice Over; newscaster's voice to be heard as silent picture is seen on screen or over sound on film or videotape.
UNDER.	Sound to be heard under other sounds.

RULES FOR WRITING TELEVISION NEWS

Words: many for the newscaster, few for videotape. When the television camera is focused on the newscaster, words dominate. Although the newscaster should not orate, she or he is on the screen not so much to be seen as to speak. There is nothing difficult about matching sight and sound while the newscaster is on camera; the picture is simple—the newscaster and perhaps some background visual—and the viewers can give their full attention to the words. But when film or videotape appears on the screen, the viewers must cope with words and pictures in a different perspective. The pictures draw attention; words must be subordinated. "Rich" writing is almost certain to conflict with the stark facts presented by the pictures. Keep your writing simple.

Writing for the Picture

First, see the videotape or film. Occasionally a writer must write a story "blind," without having had the chance to see the tape or film for which a story is to be written. This should be done only when there is no other way to get the story ready for the air in time. Ideally, the writer should also be on hand when the tape or film is edited. This gives the writer a chance to be sure that the pictures she or he had in mind are those that are used. If you have not seen the material before you write a story about it, you have no idea whether the visuals will fit your words.

Let the picture describe the action. No competent professional will attempt to compete with the graphic impact of film or videotape. Moments of silence are welcome on television news; overwriting is the mark of a novice. Nothing is more likely to irritate viewers than hearing extravagantly detailed descriptions of scenes that they can clearly see for themselves.

Writing for the Audience

Throw a few words away. Borrowing from the techniques of radio news writing, television writers learned long ago that viewers must be allowed a few seconds of orientation before they are prepared to absorb a series of hard facts. The involved, five-W newspaper lead is clearly impossible for television. Here are some examples of television leads:

"Hopes for those 3 new city schools suffered a jolt today. The city budget manager said . . ."

"In Washington, still another hat in the political ring. Senator Bart Blatt announced that he is available . . ."

"The French are at it again. For the 37th time since World War II, the French government has fallen . . ."

Even though the listener was not paying attention to what was being said at the beginning of each story, the listener could get the facts because they are delayed to the second sentence of the story.

The television news writer has to pay attention to "visual rhetoric." Pictures in a videotape or film story cannot be arranged randomly. Films and television have accustomed us to seeing things in a certain way—with shots arranged in a predictable sequence. These rules are often violated in other forms of production for artistic purposes, but in news there is little time to be "arty." The material must get the message across as concisely as possible, with no ambiguity. This means that most videotape or film edited for use in news work must conform to the basic rules of visual rhetoric. For the writer, this means that you must not write copy that makes it difficult to edit the visuals in conformity with the rules. This is too involved a matter to deal with in detail in this brief chapter, but we can give one or two examples in the sections that follow.

Suiting the Word to the Action

Time is needed to see what the newscaster is talking about. This is a perfectly good sentence for newpaper writing: "Guests of honor at the banquet were Sen. Bart Blatt, Gov. Ernest Doolittle, and Sec. of State May Sing Tew." For broadcast writing, we would begin, of course, by writing out the abbreviated titles in full. But the main problem with the sentence is that it does not allow time to see the people being talked about. The best the videotape editor could provide would be a wide shot showing all three. On the television screen, that would make the three guests of honor very small and hard to see. It is preferable to allow time for a close-up of each person.

That means that the writer must provide four or five seconds of copy for each person in turn. That allows a close-up of each person to remain on the screen long enough to be seen while that person is being talked about. The writer must "fill," that is, write enough extra lines about each person to fill the time that person's picture is on the screen. This technique seems to violate the basic rule of writing tightly, but it is necessary here to obey the rules of visual rhetoric. The copy might read something like this:

```
          Guests of honor at the dinner

          included Senator Bart Blatt,

          who flew back from Washington

          so that he could receive the

          award . . . Governor Ernest

          Doolittle, who is seeking the

          group's endorsement in his
```

```
        re-election campaign . . .


        and Secretary of State....
```

Keeping Sequence

A second problem might be encountered when dealing with the sequence of events in a story. A newspaper story might read: "There was a full house at the evening session of the conference. That was in sharp contrast to the afternoon meeting, which drew an audience of less than a hundred. Most of those at the evening meeting. . . ." This skipping about in time works well in print, but if you decide that you want to show both the afternoon and evening meetings on film or videotape, you will have to present all the material for one meeting and then all the material for the other—preferably in chronological order. Skipping back and forth between the two events will confuse the audience.

These are only a few of the problems of visual rhetoric. The crucial point, of course, is that the television news writer must always think of both words and pictures. If you cannot think the story out visually, it will do you little good to be able to write the words well. The words and pictures must go together—and that can only happen when the writer understands visual writing as well as verbal writing.

DOCUMENTARIES

The documentary is a widely used technique for examining issues in greater depth than would be allowed by a regular news story. Documentaries are sometimes produced by independent producers, but more frequently they are produced by the news or the public affairs division of a station or network. Script format may be either television film format or television news format, depending upon the desires of the producer.

It is important to realize that the term "documentary" does not describe any single type of program. Rather, it covers a number of different program types that have in common the use of factual material as their basis. We have discussed the "docudrama" elsewhere in this book, and we pointed out there that the distinction between the two forms can become blurred.

There are three documentary techniques, and those three techinques can each be used in one of two ways. That makes six basic types of documentary (although other writers might come up with different numbers, using different systems of categorization). The most common form of documentary is the "actuality" documentary, which is constructed of actual film or videotape of events and persons and uses no dramatization. Most documentaries you see on television are of this type.

Less common is the dramatized documentary, which should be distinguished from historical dramas and "docudramas." The dramatized documentary uses actors to re-create events, but uses no action or dialog that is not recorded in reliable documents. The old CBS series, "CBS Is There" (also known as "You Are There"), is the best example of this technique.

The least used of the documentary techniques at present is the fact-based drama, which uses fictional characters and situations to present factual material to the audience. Almost never used today, this form was common on radio during and before World War II, and is exemplified by such programs as Norman Corwin's "On a Note of Triumph" or some of the "March of Time" series programs and films. It's fair to point out that many purists would eliminate the last category entirely from the definition of "documentary" and would have reservations about the second category. We think they deserve inclusion simply because they were generally accepted as documentaries by the audience and the broadcast industry at the time they were most frequently used. Strict followers of the teachings of such documentary gurus as John Grierson insist that only actuality should be called documentary. Perhaps so—just as the bison should probably not be called a "buffalo"—but if most Americans think of a bison when they hear the word "buffalo," then it becomes very difficult to talk about bison without making some reference to the buffalo too.

Each of the three documentary types we have mentioned can be prepared either from newly gathered material or from material in existing archives, which gives us the six categories we have specified. There can also be a mixture of the techniques within a given program.

Content and Purpose

Whichever technique is used, the documentary places peculiar restrictions on the writer. You cannot write whatever comes into your head. What you write is determined by the existing material relating to the documentary. In the dramatized documentary, the writer's job is to edit existing material and link it together with narrative or other connective material. In the fact-based drama, the writer must create characters and situations that clearly present specific facts to the audience—it is essentially an audiovisual lesson in some topic.

In the actuality documentary your content is dictated by available material if you are creating an archive documentary. If you are working from new material, you can specify what visuals you want—but you may not be able to get all the visuals you want. In the end, the available visuals dictate what you write.

The first thing you must determine in planning a documentary is what its purpose is. A documentary may either be a simple, unbiased study of an issue or it may take sides and become an editorial—or less elegantly, propaganda. American journalistic practice favors the former, but there are many examples of documentaries that by intent or through lack of caution became editorials. In the first place, the decision to make a documentary on a topic usually is made because someone in authority has an opinion on the topic. Moreover, it is difficult for a writer to examine a topic in detail without developing some opinions on the topic. These can slip into the script if the writer is not very careful.

A documentary can be designed primarily to entertain, but this is not frequently selected as its purpose. We tend to think of documentaries as dealing with serious matters. Nevertheless, all documentaries must "entertain" to the extent that they hold the audience. The writer's task is to find interesting and entertaining ways of presenting sometimes unappealing facts.

When the purpose is determined, then the writer must learn what the budget for the program is, what facilities are available for its production, and how much time has been allotted for production. You also need to know whether the medium is to be film or videotape—although the nature of the topic may dictate that. Many archive actuality documentaries, for example, will have to be on film because videotape dates only from 1956. (Ironically, videotape and color have proved to be tragedies for the archive documentary. Videotape tends to deteriorate in quality with age, especially if not carefully stored. The color film that replaced Technicolor for film production after World War II fades markedly in seven to ten years, so much of the history that television and the films have recorded since World War II has already been lost.)

The documentaries that you are most likely to remember are those that had high budgets and a full range of production facilities with plenty of production time to make use of them. Classic documentary series of this sort, such as Jacob Bronowski's "The Ascent of Man" and Sir Kenneth Clark's "Civilisation," are available in many school audiovisual libraries and are still rerun on television. But money and time do not always make the difference. Carl Sagan's "Cosmos" series, which went both over budget and over time in production, received only lukewarm reaction from the critics—despite a dazzling array of special effects.

The point is that, as a beginning writer, you are likely to have to confine your thinking to fairly modest goals. You should study the more elaborate documentaries, of course. "Nova" is probably one of the most consistently well produced documentary series on the air at this writing. While not all agree that they really constitute documentaries, the segments on "60 Minutes," "20-20," and "NBC Journal" are all good examples of documentary production. You should pay close attention to all of them. However, when you start your career, you will probably have to start by writing shows that are much less expensive to produce.

Typically, documentaries are handled as a sort of sideline for station news departments. When a decision is made to do a documentary, it usually begins by checking what film or videotape on the topic is available in the station archives. The next step is to assign camera crews to shoot additional material. Usually the assignment editor will try to combine this with the regular shooting schedule of the news crews—picking up extra footage for the documentaries along with shooting the regular news. A camera crew may be assigned for some exclusive shooting for the documentary, but usually this time is strictly limited.

Production budget may also be simply the people and facilities of the news department that can be borrowed from their regular tasks. Clearly you cannot send crews around the world, as does "Nova," and you cannot use specially built models, sets, and special effects, as "Cosmos" did. You must content yourself with what the station can provide.

Research

Once you have gotten the basic information about the production of the documentary, the next step is research. That means time spent in the library, checking on the background of the issue. You need to consult books, periodicals, and newspapers. You begin compiling a list of people who are spokespersons for various points of view on the issue. You also need to consult your station's archives to see what film or videotape you have on the topic. If you have the budget for it, you may hire a professional researcher who is familiar with film and videotape archives in New York, Los Angeles, Washington, and other places where important material is stored. This is costly, but it is virtually impossible for a novice to make use of most of the major archives.

You must, of course, view all the relevant film and videotape. You begin keeping a card file of the various reels of tape and film, indicating where key material is. Indicate what is said, who says it, and about how long it runs. Note any visual problems with the material on the card. Time permitting (and it usually doesn't), cross-index your cards. You can indicate locations on specific tapes or reels of film by time (e.g., "12 minutes in"), footage count (for film), or by the numbers on the counter on the videotape machine. Reels of film and tape must be carefully marked and shelved in a way that makes it easy to get desired material quickly.

Now you can begin collecting any new material that is to be shot for the program. Usually it is a good idea to do the interviews first. They often provide clues to additional material you may need, and they will dictate many of the visuals that you use in the final production. The person assigned to conduct the interview (whether it's you or someone else) must be well prepared for the interview. Know the interviewee's name, how the name is pronounced, what he or she does, what the interviewee's position is on the topic, and what the interviewee's biases and qualifications to comment are. As far as possible, the interviewer should know pretty much what the interviewee is going to say. Of course, the interviewer should be ready to pick up on the material if the interviewee says something different than expected or introduces unexpected topics. As long as the interview is kept on the main topics of discussion, the interviewer should not try to force the interviewee into making specific statements just because they are expected. It is wise for the interviewer to try to keep statements by the interviewee clear and concise. The interviewer can always ask the interviewee to clarify a statement or to sum up a long one.

While the interviewer should be fully briefed on the person being interviewed and the subject of the interview, the interviewer must never let that knowledge get in the way of making the material simple for the audience.

While the interviewer should be well informed, he or she must ask the questions that the average viewer would want answered. They should be designed to elicit a detailed response from the interviewee, and not as dissertations on the topic in themselves.

The interviews must be seen and cataloged just as the other material was. Once this is done, you can usually begin sketching out your script. We say "usually" because some documentaries may depend heavily upon visual material rather than interviews. The Cousteau films are a good example. With that type of documentary, you do not want to start your writing until you have most or all of the visual material shot.

In the documentary, your writing is usually secondary to the visual and interview material—but that's not an excuse for sloppy writing. In some ways, documentary writing is more difficult than other forms. But the core of the documentary—at least of the actuality documentary, which is the most common form—is the actuality material, not the narrative. Indeed, a perfectly viable approach to many documentaries is to use *no* narration, to adopt the cinema vérité technique. The pictures and interviews in such documentaries tell the entire story. This is a difficult and demanding way to make a documentary, but it can be extremely effective.

Whatever technique you choose, you begin as you would with any television program by checking out the time blocks to be used. You must know where the breaks come in the program. Then consult your notes and decide which issues should be dealt with in each section of the program.

It is fairly common to open a documentary with a "teaser," a short scene that indicates what is to come. Ideally, it should be something strong enough to "hook" your audience. A documentary has dramatic structure, just like any other program. You want to build to a climax within each segment, and you want the entire program to build to a high point near the end. Try to have each segment end with the introduction of a new set of problems to be dealt with in the next segment. This will help hold the audience.

Obviously, climaxes in actuality material cannot be tailor-made as are climaxes in a drama. You have to settle for what you have, but you should strive for dramatic structure. It is very unlikely, for example, that you will be able to end the program on its high point, because most documentaries end in some sort of summing up—either a reprise of the key scenes or a summation by the narrator. But you can place your most dramatic moments very close to the end and keep the summation brief.

When you have sketched out the material you want in each section, you begin deciding on the specific segments to use and carefully checking the timing. Probably you will have to eliminate some of your favorite choices because time is too short. You may decide to eliminate some of the less important topics under discussion. You must check over each statement time after time to decide how it can be shortened. Here you will have to be conscious not only of the words but of the visual aspects as well. Not every cut in the audio track will also work as a cut in the picture.

The Script

When you have pretty well decided on the segments you are going to use, you can begin making a list of the additional visuals you will need to go with those segments. While the camera crews are getting this material, you can finally begin to write your script. Remember that your job is to bring the various segments together in a unified whole. There must be a logical progression from one segment to the next. Your narrative must lay out the basic issues for the viewer and must explain the qualifications of those who present opinions in the program. So explain your speakers' qualifications and biases in concrete terms that make sense and are easy to understand.

It is best to keep writing to a minimum in a documentary. Use most of your words for setting out the problems and for summing up. Otherwise, let the actualities tell as much of the story as possible and use words only to link them together and to provide needed explanations.

The final script is prepared after all the visuals are available. Consideration must be given to time for credits, and to music if music is to be used. Timing must be checked carefully. If possible, a read-through with the narrator should be arranged to check timing and see if any phrases give the narrator problems. One decision that must be made at the outset is whether the narrator is to be seen on screen or simply be an off-screen voice. Both techniques are used. The on-screen narrator is probably a bit more common. Use of an on-screen narrator requires additional time in the script to introduce the narrator to the audience at the start of the script.

Last-minute changes in script are fairly common for documentaries. The writer is usually involved right up to air time. You have to be flexible and inventive.

As we've noted earlier, the documentary can be used to give a specific point of view, but it is more common to use it to examine all sides of an issue. That means that, even if you come to some editorial viewpoint at the conclusion, you should be sure that you have given fair treatment to all the major viewpoints on the issue. This can be difficult. Oddly, partisans are not always the best spokespersons for their points of view. There may be times when the narrator can present their case better than any of the actualities you have. If you use this approach, it is wise to explain it to the speakers beforehand so you are not accused of distorting what they have said.

While some speakers are fascinating to watch, most are not. Usually you will want to introduce the speaker visually, then dissolve into B-Roll visuals that illustrate what the speaker is talking about. "Talking heads" are the curse of documentary television.

You are not free to use interview material in any sequence you wish. Ethical considerations, often spelled out in company rules, require that all interview material be used in the sequence in which it was shot. You may edit out material, but you should not transpose sequences. Also, the questions asked by an interviewer are frequently reshot after an interview, so the camera can get a head-on reverse angle shot of the interviewer. These "reverses" should be shot while the interviewee is present. If you intercut statements from different interviewees on issues, you should make it clear to the audience that this is not a "debate," that the speakers were not responding to each other but to questions by the interviewers.

Obviously if you write nonactuality documentaries, you have far more freedom in your script. You can control the dramatic development much better—but you must still keep to the factual material that is the basis of the script. If the documentary does not rely heavily upon interviews, you can sometimes sketch much of it out before it is actually shot. But most of the time, the documentary writing comes after the assembling of the visuals and is subordinate to those visuals.

Documentaries tend to be expensive to make and attract small audiences. (Although the success of "60 Minutes" suggests that some types of documentaries can draw huge audiences.) Your chances to write documentaries may be limited. Nevertheless, the documentary is a powerful and satisfying form of writing. It places many demands upon the writer, and its discipline is a stimulating challenge.

SUMMARY

Be sure you understand the special rules for television news. Make sure you can use the format and the cues. (In teaching students television news, we have found that students tend to be particularly weak in learning the cues. That's a serious problem because, without the correct cue, nothing you have written will ever get on the air.) Remember that you are "writing" pictures as well as words. Let the pictures tell the story, and learn to make your words conform to the visual rhetoric. See your visuals before you attempt to write. Tight writing is desirable, although there are also times when you must throw away a few words.

For the documentary, you must usually assemble the visual aspects of the story before you begin to write the narrative. Make sure that your writing is geared to the comprehension of your viewers. Be certain you have decided upon the purpose of your documentary before you start to write, and attempt to assemble your material so that it has appropriate dramatic structure. And be sure that you are aware of all the ethical considerations involved in the writing of documentaries.

Music, Talk, and
Interview Shows

To some degree, every program on the air must have a script. Programs do not just go on and off the air by magic. There are always scripted openings, closings, and lead-ins to commercials; no show could operate without them. And, depending on the program, a substantial amount of any program may have been scripted in advance. The scripted material linking the unscripted portions of programs is usually called *continuity*.

Many forms of broadcast program require only a partial script. These are programs in which much of the material is spontaneous and unrehearsed. The degree of "spontaneity" varies greatly. For example, on many television panel programs, panelists are told of the topics to be discussed well in advance of the program. This permits them to prepare material which can be "ad-libbed" at the proper time. The panelists do not have a script as such, but they do have well-thought-out comments in their minds before the program begins.

DISC JOCKEY SHOWS

Probably the most widely used form of semiscripted show is the radio disc jockey program. The amount of scripting depends very much on the individual disc jockey. A great many use scripts only for openings, closings, and commercial lead-ins. A relatively small number have almost completely scripted shows. While it is true that in most cases there is not a great deal of writing to be done, we have included this section on disc jockey programs because so many students these days seem to have an interest in being disc jockeys.

The disc jockey must plan each show carefully in advance. The first thing to check is how many commercials have been sold for the show, what times they are to run, and how long each commercial is. This information can be found in the station's daily program log. Some latitude may be allowed in disc jockey programs, but the commercials usually must run at the times specified. The script—or outline—for the program is built around these preset commercial breaks.

Selecting the Music

The disc jockey undoubtedly is already familiar with the lists of top records in his field. These are published in such trade magazines as *Billboard, Cash Box,* and *Record World*. (Since different systems are used by these magazines for drawing up their lists, there can be great differences in the rankings of various records. One example, in late July, 1980, the single "Funkytown" was ranked Number 3 in *Record World,* Number 36 in *Cash Box,* and Number 45 in *Billboard*.)

The disc jockey probably already has drawn up a list of the numbers he or she wants to play. The selections, of course, must conform to the format of the station and the program, be it acid rock, soul, country and western, easy listening, rhythm and blues, middle of the road, or any of the other formats in use. The list will usually include a few numbers not on the Top-40 list, simply to provide variety and to try out new releases.

Most stations receive large numbers of free recordings from record companies. The disc jockey needs to find time to listen to at least some of these. He or she also needs to keep a list of recordings that are not in the station record library that might be useful for the program. Some of these may be bought by the station, or some may be solicited from record promoters.

The key to success for a disc jockey—and for almost anyone else in the mass media—is understanding the audience. Even in the homogeneous, mass media society we live in today, a record that is a smash in Seattle may bomb in Boston, and vice versa. Choosing the right selections for a program is an art.

The disc jockey lists the amount of time available in each segment between commercials, then checks the playing time of each selection he or she wants to use. For each block of time, the disc jockey writes in the specific selections to be played and adds up the total playing time to make sure there is adequate time for introductions and other material between selections.

The disc jockey tries to arrange the records so that they form logical groupings—songs on similar themes, performed by the same artists, or written by the same composer. Care must be taken that music adjacent to commercials does not have themes that conflict with the commercial message. A lament for someone killed in an auto wreck is not a good lead into a used car commercial. When the sequence of the musical selections has been decided, the disc jockey begins to sketch out what he or she will say in the time between records.

Writing the Copy

There are actually several companies that will provide disc jockeys with prewritten material such as jokes, lead-ins to popular songs, and patter on topics of current interest. Nevertheless, here is one place where your skills as a broadcast writer can stand you in good stead. Remember, in most cases, the disc jockey is already playing the same music that can be heard on other stations. If you also use the same spoken material that any other disc jockey in town can have for a price, there is almost nothing to distinguish your show from the rest. No one ever got to the top that way. If you have the skill to write your own material, you are well ahead of the game.

Most disc jockeys are quite informal about the material between songs. Light chatter comes easily to them, and they simply ad-lib as they go along. Some disc jockeys do prepare fairly elaborate scripts. This is especially true of those who incorporate special effects and prerecorded skits into their shows.

Other Aspects of the Job

Most disc jockeys "combo," that is, they not only talk between records but they also operate the audio control board. If the disc jockey is lucky enough to have an engineer to operate the board, the scripting of parts of the show becomes more important, since the engineer needs to know what is coming and what the cues are. Disc jockeys who do have engineers are often those who make more use of skits, sound effects, and other techniques to liven up the program. This may call for several hours a day of working with the engineer, planning the material to be used.

The script or outline should have a tentative playing time marked for each musical selection. Usually these are marked NLT, meaning "not later than." The disc jockey must play the recordings at more or less preset times, or some of them will not get played. It will cause no problem to play a record a bit early, but if a record is played late, time must be made up for it in the nonmusical sections of the program or some of the musical selections must be scratched.

The script must contain an ample supply of "pad" or disaster" material—that is, stories, informational items, or notes on things to talk about in case problems arise in the course of the show. Suppose, for example, a cart jams and a commercial is not played on schedule. The disc jockey must be able to explain the problem to the audience quickly, and there must be extra material to read or ad-lib to fill in the time left over by the deletion of the commercial. Or, if a five-minute musical selection has to be cut because the program is running three minutes over scheduled time, the disc jockey needs two minutes worth of material to fill in.

Restrictions

When you write material for a disc jockey program, you must, of course, be conscious of all the restrictions on what may be said over the air. When substantial parts of the program are to be ad-libbed, it is even more important that the disc jockey be well acquainted with the laws of broadcasting. For protection, it is wise, even in a program that is mostly ad-libs, to briefly outline the material to be used in the show in advance. That way, it should be possible to spot potential trouble spots.

Here are just a few points you must keep in mind when preparing material for the air—be it fully scripted or semiscripted:

- Profane or obscene material is forbidden.
- Lotteries are forbidden, as is, with certain exceptions, information about lotteries.
- False or misleading claims are illegal.
- Statements that defame a person or group, bringing them into hatred, contempt, or ridicule, may result in libel or slander suits. (Public figures have a somewhat more difficult burden of legal proof in such cases than do private individuals.)
- You may not invade a person's privacy nor make use of a person's name for commercial purposes without written consent.
- Interviewees must be notified in advance that interview material—live or recorded—is intended for broadcast use. They must give their consent to its use.
- You cannot interview candidates for political office without your station being required to provide equal time for all candidates for the same position.
- You cannot attack individuals or groups without providing them a transcript of the attack and making time available for response.
- You cannot raise issues of substantial public interest without obligating your station to deal fairly with all sides of the issue.
- If you are broadcasting on a noncommercial station, you may not editorialize.
- You may not broadcast material that causes breaches of the peace. (Stations have lost their licenses for broadcasting material that led to rioting.)

Those are just a few of the hundreds of rules, laws, and regulations that may affect you. As you can see, any broadcaster must be on the alert at all times. One who deals with much unscripted material is walking through a minefield of legal threats.

Music Rights

An area of legal restriction that is of particular concern to anyone playing records is copyright. Music is copyrighted for the life of the composer plus 50 years. The composer normally assigns his copyright to one of the major licensing agencies—the American Society of Composers, Authors, and Publishers (ASCAP) or Broadcast Music, Incorporated (BMI). Both the record jacket and the record label normally list the licensing agency for each cut on a record. Not all the cuts on a record are necessarily licensed by the same agency. You must check each selection you intend to play.

Radio and television stations normally sign a contract with ASCAP, BMI, or both, which authorizes use of all material licensed by that agency for a set fee. (In 1979, the U.S. Supreme Court rejected a broadcast industry challenge to these blanket fees. However, the court did not rule out legal challenges on other bases. So, at this writing, the issue is still subject to litigation.) ASCAP and BMI used to grant licenses to noncommercial stations without charge. Today, noncommercial stations are charged a small fee.

You may not use any music on your program unless your station has a licensing agreement covering it. Even with a contract, certain uses of recordings may be prohibited, so you should check over your licensing agreement carefully. If you encounter a song that is licensed by some other organization, you must obtain permission from the copyright holder before using it. A few songs are "in public domain," meaning that any copyright on them has expired. However, that is meaningless if there are any new lyrics or a new arrangement of the music. Those would come under another copyright. Where television is concerned, it is sometimes necessary to obtain "synchronization rights," but that is not something we need be concerned with here.

The question of music rights for programs rebroadcast on cable television is still being litigated at this writing. A new issue that may affect disc jockey programs in the future is the matter of playing entire albums on the air in one time block. Record manufacturers argue that this is an open invitation to tape-record the album instead of buying it. (Many of these programs are sponsored by recording tape manufacturers.) New restrictions on the music available for record programs may grow out of this dispute.

It is essential for students to realize the importance of the various legal issues that affect programming such as disc jockey shows. Many students get their first broadcast experience on university stations. These stations usually have small audiences and are not likely to be the target of many legal threats. It is too easy, in that atmosphere, to become careless. Learn the legal limits of broadcasting well, or your career will be short.

Formats

The formats used for disc jockey scripts are probably as numerous as the people who prepare them. Here is one possible format:

MUSIC: THEME UP AND UNDER

JULIE: Hey out there, all you Romans. Time to stop
roamin'. It's four o'clock and time for the
Julie Caesar Show.

MUSIC: THEME UP AND OUT

JULIE: Well, look at that, will you? Here it is
Friday. The whole week just kind of snuck by.
Hey, don't start packing up for the weekend
yet. Big Julie's got some heavy music to lay
on you this afternoon. So, just hang in there
for the next two hours. Your ears are in for
a real Roman treat . . . Hey, well, let's
start it right off with the big number five
this week. You got it. It's Grushenka and
the Brothers with "How Come You Said You Did
It?"

NLT 4:02
MUSIC: "How Come You Said You Did It?"
RUNS 4:18

JULIE: OKAY! How's that start you off for a Friday
afternoon? Man, that Grushenka is really
something, isn't she? That's four platinum
platters for her just this year. The lady's
got a lot of class -- and a whole lot of
platinum.

I read somewhere that her real name is Sally
Brown. You believe that? Nah . . . Would

```
          you believe Grushenka Brown? . . . Ah, well

          . . . You don't believe ol' Julie?  Whatsa

          matta you? . . . Look, here's a name you can

          believe -- Kelly's, the best name in jeans.

          Just listen up to this . . .

NLT 9:00

COMMCL:   Kelly Jeans #827-3

          RUNS: 1:00

          OUTCUE:  ". . . when you buy Kelly's."
```

```
JULIE:    You can buy those smooth-fitting Kelly Jeans

          at The Pants Place, 7-55 South Broadway, here

          in luscious Lotusville.  You got that?  Seven-

          five-five South Broadway, in good ol'

          Lotusville . . . OKAY!  Friends, Romans, and

          paisanos, let's keep the show moving with....
```

OTHER MUSIC PROGRAMS

Other forms of musical programs for radio can follow a similar pattern, but those outside the popular music field are usually fully scripted. The material dealt with is usually more formal, and often requires considerable research. Because you are usually dealing with an audience that is well educated and knows a great deal about music, it is essential that the writer know the subject matter well.

When preparing scripts for classical music programs, it is important to make use of the news-writing technique of putting wavy lines under difficult words and providing pronunciation guides. The announcers for such programs are usually well trained, and normally take some time checking over the script before air time. Nevertheless, it is only fair for the writer to offer a warning and a pronunciation guide before writing names like Mstislav Rostropovich into a script.

The preparation of musical programs for television can vary from a simple program with a single performer to elaborate sound-stage productions with orchestra, dancers, and chorus. The key here is for the writer to work with the directors and producers through the entire preparation of the program. Timing is a headache with programs of this sort, and frequent revisions of the script are called for to pad out this segment or shorten that one. Where possible, production numbers are pretaped so that the exact running time can be known. Whether pretaped or not, musical numbers that require dancing or much movement by a singer usually have a prerecorded sound track to which the performer mimes, or "lip-synchs" the vocal. This kind of prerecording also provides an exact running time for musical numbers and allows the director more security in planning out camera movements.

The writer is not usually involved in the selection of shots for musical numbers. That is handled by the director, sometimes in collaboration with a choreographer. The writer's job is to provide the continuity that links the musical numbers together.

Both the television film format and the live television format are used for scripting musical programs. The choice usually depends upon the preference of the director. Prepare the script just as you would for any other program, but make note of each musical number and its running time in the script. It might look like this:

```
     VIDEO                              AUDIO


MS: Joan                                JOAN

                             Six weeks ago, a new show

                             opened on Broadway, and

                             overnight everyone was talking

                             about a new star.  She's here

                             with us tonight to sing her

                             hit number from that show.

                             Let's have a big hand for Miss

                             Anna Bolena and "I Lost My

                             Head."

                             (APPLAUSE)


DISSOLVE TO:                  MUSIC:  Bolena
  Bolena                      RUNS:   5:25

DISSOLVE TO:                           JOAN
  2 Shot:
  Joan & Anna                 Anna Bolena!  Anna, that was
```

```
fantastic.  They tell me that

you almost turned down the

part that....
```

TALK SHOWS, INTERVIEW PROGRAMS, AND CALL-IN SHOWS

There is a great deal of similarity among these three types of programs, and many programs contain elements of all three. The terms "talk show" and "interview program" are often used interchangeably. For convenience here, we'll describe a talk show as one in which a host brings in several guests to discuss one or several topics. The subject matter is often fairly lightweight. We'll use the term "interview program" to designate those shows in which a host devotes the entire program to discussing a few related issues with only one or two guests. Call-in shows are those in which the broadcast audience telephones in to speak with the host or with special guests. All three forms of program are found in both radio and television, but the call-in show is more likely to be a radio program. Talk shows with large numbers of guests can present problems on radio because it is difficult to keep track of who is talking.

For all three kinds of show, the major scripted portions are the openings, closings, and the commercial lead-ins. However, the host may have some carefully scripted material to introduce guests or to introduce the topic of discussion. If it is sufficiently predictable, the host may also script a few concluding remarks for the program. Formats used are the standard radio script format and the live television format.

The writer's job here is to do careful research so that the introductions of guests or topics are both interesting and factual. It is helpful if the writer can spend some time with the guests prior to preparing the script, but often this is not possible. The writer needs to keep a file of clippings and information on potential guests and issues and should know where to get additional information either from experts or via library research. A high-budget show may have a researcher or even a research staff to do this work for the writer, but usually the writer must do the work alone.

The introduction should provide an opening question, which begins the discussion. The script must contain the times at which commercials are to run and the times at which different guests are to be introduced. This information is vital for the engineers and director. However flexible the rest of the program may be, these times must be met and lead-in material must be read exactly as written. The reason should be fairly obvious, but let's take just one example. Suppose the engineer had to decide when to start a prerecorded commercial, and no script had been provided. The engineer would know from the log that the Fizzo commercial was set for a specific time, so he would be ready when the host began to ad-lib a lead-in. But exactly when should the engineer push the button? Each slash in the lead-in below marks a point that might seem to end the lead-in if there were no script:

```
ANNCR:    And now, let's pause/ for this message/ from

          Fizzos/ -- Fizzos,/ those wonderful pink

          tablets/ that make your stomach say ahhhh!/
```

You can see why there has to be a script and why it has to be followed.

Avoiding Risky Topics

A heavy burden is placed on the host and the director to see that nothing said on the program creates legal problems. The writer's role here is to try to pick topics and prepare questions that will be interesting and provocative without having the potential for getting the program sued or thrown off the air. It's not easy.

A clear example is the "topless radio" talk shows that popped up in the early 1970s. Some talk show hosts began encouraging guests to call in and discuss their sex lives. For obvious reasons, the shows attracted large audiences—but it should have been easy to see that they were headed for disaster. The trend died very quickly after the FCC levied a $2,000 fine against an Illinois station. The FCC indicated that a discussion of the use of peanut butter, whipped cream, and marshmallow topping as adjuncts to oral sex did not particularly meet the criteria of serving the public interest, convenience, and necessity.

Researching the Program

The writer should also try to see to it that the program does not violate the FCC's Fairness Doctrine. Call-in shows in particular have been used by special-interest groups from time to time as a means of promoting their own ends. Essentially, this is a problem for the program's producer and the host. Moreover, Fairness is really a problem for the station, since it involves overall balance in programming, not balance within a specific program. Nevertheless, the writer has some obligation to see to it that the questions and guests used do not give the program a particular slant—unless that is the intent of the producer or the host. Some programs do, of course, represent some specific viewpoint. William F. Buckley's "Firing Line" is an obvious example. Some talk show hosts have made a career of taking controversial stands. And some simply attack anyone who calls in, regardless of viewpoint. You must clearly understand the concept of the program before you begin to prepare material for it.

It may be the writer's job on programs of this sort to provide lists of questions for the host to use. If so, it is essential that they be many and varied.

Nothing is so harmful to a program of this sort as dead air. If a topic is launched and nothing happens—no one calls in, the guests say little or nothing—it is imperative that there be another topic to turn to at once to get the show moving.

Service Shows

One variant of the talk show usually found only in smaller towns is the trading post. On these shows people write or call in to offer services or items for sale or for trade. It is important in scripting this type of show that the writer learn to keep the descriptive material brief and yet accurate and clear. Beyond that, it is important to check to see that the goods offered are not stolen and that services offered are legal.

SUMMARY

The various programs discussed in this chapter are just a few of the many forms of semiscripted programs. It may seem strange to contemplate writing a script for a program that, essentially, has no script, but many writers make a good living doing just that.

Disc jockey shows require careful planning of the introduction and close, the introduction to each record, and the lead-in to each commercial. It is also wise to script a good deal of the "patter" that goes between the records and commercials. The script should indicate times for various records and commercials. When preparing such programs, it is very important to know the laws affecting broadcasting and music rights. You must, of course, be sure you have legal right to use specific recordings on the air.

In preparing a script for other music programs, it is usually important to have a pronunciation guide for difficult names.

Television "host" programs probably will have a script for the opening, closing, and introduction of guests plus some well-planned questions to ask guests. Commercial introductions are always scripted. Introductions and closings of musical numbers are usually scripted too.

Similar rules apply to radio talk shows. Good research by the writer is important. Topics must be carefully chosen so that they will be interesting without running the risk of getting the program in trouble.

It should be obvious by now that there is a great deal to the writing of a show that "has no script." Keep in mind the point with which we began this chapter: Every program needs some sort of script to get on the air.

Programming

It isn't possible in a book of this length to cover all the many forms of broadcast writing. We have tried to include the most important ones. But there are probably ten left out for every one we have included here. Most of the other forms of programming for both radio and television are ones for which you can use the styles of writing we have already described and adapt them to the special requirements of the program for which you are writing.

A great many of these kinds of programming are defined by the groups they serve. Thus there are programs to serve minorities in the community, programs for those with particular handicaps, programs for specific age groups, and so on. In almost all of these cases, more than one of the kinds of programming we have written about earlier can be used. Suppose, for example, you wanted to write programs to serve the needs of some minority in your community. You might prepare a call-in program, a panel discussion, a drama or comedy, or even a news program that emphasized the special interests of that group. And any of those programs could be prepared either for radio or for television.

CHILDREN'S TELEVISION PROGRAMS

Many students, for example, are interested in writing "children's programs." But before you can write this kind of show, you must know what kind of children's program you mean. So you should begin by defining what you intend to do. One of the writers of this book has a former student whose job is the preparation of instructional television programs for mentally retarded children. And within that specialized area, the former student has turned out some marvelously creative and interesting programs. Not every writer could work within the confines of a program of that nature.

Generally, when we think of children's programming, we think only of television, and that's a pity. With the wonderful capacity children have for imagination, radio can be a marvelous form of programming for the young. In years gone by, such children's shows as "Let's Pretend" made charming radio dramatizations of children's stories. The Canadian Broadcasting System still provides some wonderful material for children, as do a few stations in the United States. But, for the most part, children's programming today means television programming, and we shall limit this discussion to television, although some of the considerations for television are equally applicable to radio.

Most people assume that children's television should, in some sense, be "educational." In fact, much children's television does nothing but keep children occupied and out of their parents' hair while providing sponsors with a vehicle for selling goods. Since the average American adult spends 30 hours and 25 minutes a week viewing television—most of it material that has no educational value and serves only to occupy time and sell products—there is a certain amount of hypocrisy in insisting that the average American child age two to five should be edified in the 31 hours and 23 minutes he or she spends watching television. Nevertheless, most writers would prefer to write material that helps make the child a better person.

The Entertainment Factor

There is really nothing sinful about writing good material simply to entertain, and some of the great classics of literature were written as, or have become, children's entertainment. Writers of the caliber of E. B. White have turned their hand to children's books with delightful results. Probably one of the true hallmarks of good children's writing is that it can be appreciated by people of all ages. The problem is, of course, that few writers are talented enough to write that well. The mistake in undertaking children's writing is to assume that somehow it is "easier" than other forms. It isn't. Not good children's writing, at least. It is among the most difficult genres of writing there are.

Even if your stated goal is not simply to entertain, you cannot hope to succeed in writing children's programs unless they do just that. Children are not interested in a good, solid evening of intellectual meat to gnaw on. If they are not entertained, they find something else to do. Says Bob Keeshan, CBS's Captain Kangaroo, "I think a child is entitled to pure entertainment, as long as it is constructive in nature."[1]

There is more than one problem for the writer here. Television has been criticized for contributing to the restlessness of children. Because children demand to be entertained, television programs strive to entertain them—resulting, some say, in simply more demand to be entertained and less willingness to pay attention to anything that does not entertain. Generally praised programs, such as "Sesame Street," have been criticized on this very point—that children become accustomed to having all their learning sugar-coated with entertainment. We may be spawning a generation that expects college professors to explain particle physics with hand puppets and cartoons. The British Broadcasting Corporation turned down "Sesame Street" on the basis that it left children too passive.[2]

Be that as it may, as a writer you have little choice but to make your material entertaining if you hope to hold an audience of children. What entertains depends very much on the kind and age of child you are writing for.

Comedy is one useful instructional device. "Sesame Street" 's Cookie Monster is a good example of a comic character used to impart information.

Defining the Audience

You have to define your audience specifically when writing material for children, and age is one crucial factor. Children's interests and capabilities change radically with age. Age groupings, of course, are never perfect indicators, but they can tell us much about most of the children in the age group we are seeking to reach. So you must define the age of your intended audience precisely.

Sex can be a factor, but is usually less important for young children. This is increasingly true as parents move away from the stereotyped sex roles assigned to children in the past. It's a good idea to look over your material to see if you have unconsciously carried over some of these stereotypes into your writing.

You must also understand the vocabulary and general level of knowledge of the age gruop for which you are writing. What the preschool child learns is pretty much limited to what she or he learns from the family or from television. But that is an astounding amount. Recognizing that a child starts with virtually zero knowledge, it is likely that more is learned in the first five or six years of life than in any later period. Yet that knowledge is limited. There is much that we take for granted in everyday life that has to be learned as a child. A high school student would probably know what a carburetor is, a grammar school child might not. A grammar school child might know what a triangle is, a preschool child might not. A grammar school child might understand the

[1]Tom Jorry, "From Captain Kangaroo's Pouch," *Los Angeles Times,* July 13, 1978, sec. 4, p. 24.
[2]"Sesame Street Making Debut on Italian TV," *Los Angeles Times,* January 23, 1978, sec. 1, p. 5.

idea of people voting to elect an official, a preschool child might not. What you can talk about and how you can talk about it depends upon the age of your audience.

On the other hand, if you make your material too simple, you may lose your audience too. A 12-year-old child will not be interested in a program whose dialog runs: "See the house. The house is green. It has a brown roof." Says Bob Keeshan, "I think respect is the basic element in all television, and if you respect the child's intelligence and good taste, then the specifics of production will lead to good programming."[3]

Deciding on Techniques

Once you have identified your goal, and specified the age group of your audience, you must decide what techniques you intend to use. In some cases, this may already be decided for you, especially if you are writing for a program that is already on the air. Essentially the same techniques are available to you for children's programs as would be available for any other type of programming. The BBC, for example, has an evening news program geared to children of about age 11. However, the technique must be tailored to the needs and abilities of the target audience. A panel discussion is not going to hold the interest of children under 12 for very long, and a half-hour dramatization will probably not hold many children under five.

Attention span, of course, is one of the key factors in determining your approach. In general, the younger the child, the shorter the attention span. The child simply cannot concentrate on the same thing for very long. Note how brief most of the segments in "Sesame Street" are. Again, television has been faulted for keying material to short attention spans—thus, perhaps, keeping those attention spans from increasing. But there is little a writer can do except write for the known attention span of the audience age group. Otherwise, most of the young audience will be lost.

Writing for the attention span of very young children is great discipline for a writer. The first reaction is almost always, "You can't do anything good in that little time." But you can. And forcing yourself to pare material down to these tiny time spans will make you much more aware of how much you really can accomplish in a short amount of time. Just as there is room in art for the room-sized canvases of Monet's water lilies and for tiny Persian miniatures, so in writing there is room for *War and Peace* and for a polished epigram of only a few words. You can work within the time limits of children's programming, but you must work at it.

Repetition

Younger children—especially preschoolers—enjoy repetition. Songs or rhymes that repeat the same words over and over seem to please youngsters,

[3]Jorry, "From Captain Kangaroo's Pouch."

and they also are a useful tool in helping the child to memorize new material. Information that you want to be remembered needs to be repeated several times for any age group; however, for the very young, it is not only useful but also seems to be entertaining.

Again, the use of much repetition in children's programming has drawn some criticism. It is obvious that most of today's popular music follows the same pattern—continual repetition of one or two simple verbal and musical phrases. Critics argue that by catering to the child's love of repetition, we are training a generation incapable of learning or enjoying anything that does not involve the same endless infantile repetition. Be that as it may, successful children's programs such as "Sesame Street" make heavy use of repetition, and it is probably a necessary element of writing for preschool children.

The problem for the writer, of course, is to present this repetition in some logical context. You need to use your imagination to develop reasons for the amount of repetition used in children's writing. (That may be an adult view imposed on this form of writing. It does not appear that children feel any need for there to be a reason for repetition. In view of the criticism that endless use of repetition prevents children from growing out of the need for repetition, however, it seems wise to see that there is some valid reason for repetition whenever it is used in your script.)

You must, of course, pay close attention to the age of your intended audience. Fewer repetitions are needed for older children, and the entertainment value of repetition may decline somewhat with older age groups.

Violence

No matter what age group you write for, there are limitations on the material you can use. It is generally agreed today that viewing violent material on television may make some children more violent. Even though most are probably not affected, you do not want to contribute to making society violent by using violence in programs for children. That rules out a much larger area of writing than most people would like to admit. Joseph Barbera, who with William Hanna created the famous "Tom and Jerry" cartoons (now condemned as too violent), has summed up the simplicity of writing before violence and educational content became major concerns: "When a cat chases a mouse, he doesn't have to stop and teach him how to blow glass or weave a basket."[4]

There is no doubt that many children (and adults) enjoy violence in their entertainment. The great literature of almost all societies contains large doses of violence. One of the first, and most difficult, jobs for the writer is to come up with a clear idea of what she or he means by "violence."

It is obvious, of course, that people shooting, stabbing, or hitting each other is violent, but what about a Punch and Judy show, in which the puppets traditionally clobber each other time after time? What about a hunter shooting

[4]Lee Margulies, "Pressure Groups Faulted for TV Kid Fare," *Los Angeles Times,* December 15, 1977, sec. 4, p. 37.

an animal? Is that violent? What about a boxing match? A football game? Is it violent when a cartoon character flattens another character with a steamroller and the flattened character goes back to normal shape in a few seconds? Is it violent to show self-defense against an attacking animal or person? Is George Washington violent? His troops killed thousands of people. How about Abraham Lincoln? How about Jesus driving the money-changers from the Temple—or the Crucifixion? Is the *Star Wars* film series less violent because the action takes place in another galaxy?

It's clear that you can lose your mind simply trying to decide what is violent and what isn't. You will have to make some general decisions—or they may already have been made for you by the producers of the program—and stick with them. Don't hope to cover every eventuality. You will have to satisfy your own conscience and that of your producers. Beyond that, you will have to face the fact that it is possible to define almost anything as violent if you want to.

Violence is not the only taboo for children's programs. In general, you should not depict any activities you would not wish a child to imitate. "Sesame Street" makes a practice of observing sample groups of children as they watch the show. Those observations have clearly demonstrated the extent to which children imitate what they see on the show:

> Our early observations of children watching television contained innumerable instances of specific modeling. It became obvious that children frequently imitate the physical motions of televised characters. When "Sesame Street" cast members count on their fingers or use their fingers or other parts of the body to shape letters or forms, many children copy them. In particular, one device used on "Sesame Street" has evoked a remarkable amount of physical imitation: all the viewer sees on the screen is a hand trying in various ways to make a noise. As the hand tries snapping its fingers and making other movements, children often imitate these actions. When the hand delightedly discovers that, with the cooperation of the other hand, it can make a clapping sound, the hands of young viewers tend to share in this gratifying experience. Giggling, washing, scratching, hopping, rubbing, and various comical actions also evoke considerable imitation. If a character on television does something absurd, such as stepping in a bucket, children will get up and pretend to walk around with buckets on their feet, too.[5]

These findings agree with the findings of researchers such as Paul Bandura at Stanford, who examined the more serious question of children viewing violent behavior on television. Such findings raise some very difficult questions about the proper way to warn children of the consequences of doing things they should not do. The research is far from clear in this area. In some circumstances children may comprehend and benefit from the basic warning: If you do this, this is what will happen to you. But in other cases, the child may only be stimulated to try out the forbidden activity.

You can write, of course, without demonstrating the consequences of indulging in prohibited activities—but again, you have cut out an enormous

[5]Gerald S. Lesser, "Growing up on Sesame Street," *Harvard Today*, July 1974, pp. 7 and 8.

area of literature, starting with the story of Adam and Eve in the Garden of Eden. Not surprisingly, large numbers of traditional stories deal with the consequences of breaking rules—Lot's wife, Samson, Daedalus and Icarus, Cupid and Psyche, Beauty and the Beast, Hansel and Gretel, and so on. This has been the traditional way societies impressed upon the young the importance of obeying the rules.

The extent to which you rule out this material will depend partly on your audience. An older child might benefit from a warning about consuming poisonous plants or poisonous items around the house, while a younger child might be stimulated to try some of the forbidden materials. A warning about careless driving might work with some young people old enough to drive, but might encourage others to show off while driving. You will have to make your own decisions about what activities you show. In a real sense, there is almost nothing you can mention that might not lead some youngsters into trouble. You must weigh in your own mind the probable effects on your target audience.

Can you find material, given all these restrictions? Of course. Writes Gerald Lesser of "Sesame Street": ". . . 'myths' need not be modern resurrections of valor in combat, romantic love or religious zeal. Myths for children can be simple presentations of a simple goodness."[6]

Language

A difficult question to decide in writing for children's programs is what sort of dialog to use. Obviously, you must keep your dialog simple, at the level of the intended audience. But how far should you deviate from standard English in trying to make your characters seem realistic? Probably not very far. Children are learning the language, and they should not be confused with non-standard English. You should neither have your characters talk "baby talk" nor should you have them indulge in dialects. Standard English is the language of our mass media. We must all learn it if we are to make use of mass media. Certainly there are many regional and ethnic dialects, and they should not be treated as inferior. But the mass media cannot remain mass media if they do not communicate in a mass language. Regional and ethnic dialects have their place within the groups that use them. But every broadcast writer has a vested interest in seeing that children learn standard English well. That requires that you write for children's programs in good standard English.

Other Things to Watch For

Much of the criticism that has been directed at children's programming is aimed at the commercials. Since we have included commercial writing in this book, it seems fair to mention a few of these criticisms.

One accusation is that commercials encourage children to develop poor dietary habits. Children sometimes are encouraged to buy food products

---

[6]Ibid., p. 9.

because of prizes or other enticements in the box that have nothing to do with food value or getting good value for money. Much of the cereal advertised on children's programs has relatively little food value and is heavily dosed with sugar. (Try reading the labels on cereal packages sometime. The authors have been able to find only two nationally sold cold cereals that do not list sugar as a major ingredient.) Sadly, studies show that the children most likely to be fooled by ads encouraging them to eat junk foods are those from poor and minority backgrounds.

If you are paid to write commercials, of course you must write material that sells the product. We hope that in time sufficient concern about food advertising will grow up in the advertising industry that major firms will become selective about what they will try to sell to children—just as some major advertising agencies in the past have refused to accept cigarette advertising. But even if you are not writing commercials, it is easy enough to slip material into your script that will suggest bad food habits to children. Does your writing picture kids slurping soda pop, wolfing down ice cream, and begging for candy? Clichés like these become self-perpetuating. You owe it to the children in your audience to get rid of material that encourages bad habits—especially those that have to do with eating and hygiene.

A related criticism is that children's programs make children improperly trained consumers. Again, the primary target is commercials—those that encourage children to buy products for the wrong reasons or those which delude the child about the nature of the product being sold. In 1978, the nation's largest toymaker, the General Mills Fun Group, agreed to change ads that the Federal Trade Commission said showed toys doing things they could not really do. (Since then, Congress has stripped the FTC of virtually all its authority to investigate advertising—a signal victory for manufacturers who didn't like this sort of examination of their ads.)

And again, you may unintentionally introduce material into programming other than commercials which might encourage children to be poor consumers. Keep an eye on your copy. Does that mean *Jack and the Beanstalk* is out? Probably not, but it should be made clear in the script that trading cows for beans is not the kind of economic behavior children should copy.

OTHER SPECIAL INTERESTS

Children are only the most obvious of the many groups in society for whom special programming can be written. We noted that there are dozens of types of radio and television programs that can serve the ethnic and religious minorities of our society. You can bring a group specialized news, you can present discussions of relevant issues, you can take religious ceremonies into the home, you can provide material in foreign languages or local dialects.

For most purposes, you can plan your general approach in a way similar to the one we described for children's programming. You must first define the audience. It is not enough to decide you will have a program for the blind, or for women, or for Asian Americans. These groups are too diverse. You must pin it down to specific subgroups within those groups. Only then can you isolate the special needs and particular problems that need to be dealt with. Then, when you have determined what well-defined groups you wish you reach, you can decide upon the approach.

Radio for the Blind

Some groups have needs uniquely adapted to one specific medium. Radio, for example, is obviously better suited than television to serving the blind. Still, some of the best-intended programming goes astray. For example, several radio stations have programs that read the daily newspaper for the blind. The basic idea is good, but it ignores the fact that most people with good eyesight can read silently much faster than they can read aloud. Thus it takes much more time to read the newspaper on the radio than it would to read it with your own eyes. The assumption becomes that the blind person has nothing better to do than sit at home all morning and listen to the newspaper. (Of course, the blind person could tape-record the program, as some do.)

Such programs also assume that the listener is capable of absorbing huge amounts of spoken information. It is true that most sightless people can recall more spoken information than can the average person with normal sight, but it would take a mental marvel to recall all the news in a large metropolitan daily. Nor do such programs take into account the specific interests of the audience. Many news stories might be skipped over if the sightless person had the chance to skip them.

Obviously, what is needed is a program that takes more of the approach of radio news, but attempts to provide more stories and a bit more detail than the usual radio news program. Such programs need to be backed up with research to determine what kinds of news the members of the audience want to hear.

Often the most obvious things that could be done for a specific group are overlooked until they appear in research. For example, one survey of blind listeners to a "radio newspaper" indicated that many blind listeners wanted to have advertisements from the newspaper read to them. Unable to read the newspaper, they were missing a major daily source of information about the prices and locations of items they wanted to purchase. Unfortunately, most commercial stations would not want to have someone read ads from the newspaper on the air free, and noncommercial stations are not allowed to carry advertising, so the idea could not be implemented. The point is, however, that until the research was conducted, no one associated with the program had given any thought to newspaper ads being something a blind person would be interested in. Despite the fact that 60 to 70 percent of most newspapers is advertising, no one had ever thought that it might have a place in a "radio newspaper" for the blind.

Radio can provide many other services for the blind. Readings from books or magazine articles can be helpful. An alternative to reading such material is providing dramatized versions. Obviously, from the radio writer's standpoint, this is more of a challenge. If your audience is blind, however, you must give some thought to substituting dramatization for readings. You will probably want to make greater use of narration that directly quotes from the book than you would otherwise. This gives the listener an idea of the style and texture of the writing. Often, where stories in print are concerned, the style of writing can be of more importance than the plot. For example, the novel *True Grit* translated very successfully into a motion picture. The film could not convey much of the charm of the writer's style, however. To convey this to a blind audience by radio, you would have to have your narrator quote heavily from the narrative portions of the book. A well thought out adaptation of a novel or a story for the blind can provide the best of both straight reading and regular radio dramatization.

It is a mistake, of course, ever to think of all the people in a group as having the same interests and needs. Not all blind people want to know what is in the newspapers or the latest books and magazines. With some research and thought, you might be able to come up with new services for the blind. Perhaps there are areas of sports that ought to have special treatment for the blind. Maybe there are subjects such as music that could be better handled for blind listeners than is now the case. Might some blind people like to hear readings from *Opera News*—or from *Rolling Stone?* Research could tell you. Or, since the blind must learn to play instruments primarily by ear, would it be feasible to teach classes in different types of instruments for the blind via radio? Imagination and research can indicate hundreds of new approaches you might follow.

Women's Programming

"Women's programming" is another category that is too broad in concept. It used to be assumed that "women's programs," either on radio or television, were cooking shows, gossip programs, household hint shows, and similar material. This kind of thinking won't do for today. Many women would just as soon watch a program about sports, many men are interested in cooking, and everybody loves gossip. You will have to decide what specific groups of women you are trying to reach. The woman who works has different needs from the woman who is a housewife. The woman who is a housewife and works as well has different needs from those in the other two groups. Programs that have as their goal only to be "women's programs" often fail simply because the writers don't really know the audience for which they are writing.

Two forms of programming that we have already discussed draw large audiences of women—television soap operas and daytime talk shows on both radio and television. Talk shows run the gamut from seriously oriented programs such as the Phil Donahue Show (which tackles tough social and political issues—but also tosses in a dash of sex from time to time) to programs like the Richard Simmons Show, which deals primarily with exercise and diet. There is no clear pattern in the preferences of the audience. Donahue projects a tough, masculine image; Simmons sometimes does skits in drag. Both draw fanatical followings. It is interesting to note, however, that with the exception of the Donahue segments in the "Today Show," the networks have not taken much interest in talk shows, and most talk shows are syndicated. That may change. At this writing, NBC is reported to be considering setting up a radio network that would aim all of its programming at women. This seems to follow the line of WOMN in Hamden, Connecticut, which announced in 1978 that it would direct its programming to women.

Radio call-in programs are another form of programming that draws audiences which are predominantly made up of women. Again, these programs vary in subject matter from politics to cooking. They serve as a sounding board for opinions, and, sadly, for many they simply provide someone to talk to.

Instructional Programs

One specialized form of writing you may be called upon to provide is instructional material. Teaching goes on in many places beside the classroom. Writers are often asked to develop mass media presentations that can be used for specific educational purposes. One of the writers of this book was asked to prepare a training film for a branch of the American Cancer Society. After thinking the problem over, he decided to avoid the formal lecture approach and use humor. The admittedly not very original idea of the script was to have the main character, Fred, botch everything he did. Then an off-camera narrator would patiently explain to Fred the right way to do it. Each step was also presented in a short printed summary that appeared on the screen after each section of the film. All the material was reprised in spoken and printed words at the end. The material was further backed up with a pamphlet that stressed the main points again. It was assumed from the outset that the viewer would not really be able to remember all the key points in the presentation, so it was important that a printed version be available. The film material would get the viewer interested and give the viewer the main points, then the printed material would provide the necessary details and means of rechecking what the viewer remembered from the program.

Be sure that you have the goal of your instructional program clearly in mind. Keep goals simple and limited in number. Define your audience carefully, and study the research available on that audience. Make sure you understand the limitations of your medium. Most instructional use of the media calls for considerable repetition and for a backup of some sort of printed material. You must also allow time in your programming for the students to take notes. Radio and television *can* be excellent teaching tools, but only if the material is carefully planned to match the medium and the audience.

Ethnic Programs

Ethnic programming in many ways replicates the material available on nonethnic radio and television shows. In many large cities today, you can see on television soap operas, comedies, game shows, and movies in Spanish, Japanese, or Korean. However, ethnic radio and television stations also provide specialized news coverage and reports of local events that concentrate on the minority community. Often they also provide foreign news coverage that focuses on areas ignored in regular news coverage, and they emphasize local news of interest to the minority community that might not be carried by nonethnic programs.

One thing you can do as a writer is to look for new areas that can contribute to the well-being of specific ethnic groups. Black stations, for example, might provide special programming to keep their audiences aware of health problems, such as sickle-cell anemia or hypertension, that are of particular concern to blacks. The Spanish International Networks has broadcast documentaries dealing with problems of illegal immigrants and, in 1981, began a regular half-hour daily network news program in Spanish. (It is worth noting that there are some 90 Spanish-language television stations in the United States now. The Los Angeles area alone has more than two million people with Spanish surnames and also boasts the largest Korean population outside of Korea.)

To write for most ethnic stations, you must be proficient in the language of the station, even though an increasing number of ethnic stations are providing some English-language programs for members of that ethnic group who are no longer proficient in the group's language or who wish to improve their English. For example, a Los Angeles television station that programs primarily in Japanese has recently introduced several English-language programs aimed at non-first-generation Japanese Americans.

Ethnic programs do tend to be similar to English language programs. When it comes to entertainment, the same things are often popular in many different cultures. Ethnic stations tend to stick with known winners such as soap operas and comedies. However, as a writer, you have a chance to look for new and innovative programming in this field. Give it some thought. What are the unique needs of a particular group, and how can you meet those needs through radio or television? Ethnic programming is a growing area. If you have contacts with some ethnic group, you may be able to come up with successful new program ideas that may both serve the ethnic community and launch your career as a writer.

RADIO AS A SPECIAL-INTEREST MEDIUM

You should pay special attention to radio if you want to write programs for specialized audiences. At this writing, there are about 9,000 radio stations in the United States. The competition among them is fierce, and at present about 40 percent of them are losing money. Television has won most of the national advertising that is aimed at a mass audience, and newspapers get most of the local advertising which is aimed at the mass audience. Two-thirds of radio's income comes from local advertising. To attract advertisers and survive, radio stations have had to imitate magazines and try to draw audiences of specifiable compositions. For example, an advertiser trying to sell country and western records could reach a huge audience by advertising on a television comedy program, but only a small portion of that audience would be interested in country and western music. The advertiser would do better to place ads on radio stations that specialize in country and western music, because virtually everyone who hears the ads is a potential customer for his records.

The high cost of television advertising and the need for specialized audiences has given radio a new appeal for advertisers. The advent of satellite technology has also made it quicker, easier, and cheaper to link stations together into networks. All this is bringing about a revival of network radio—but the new networks are designed for specialized audiences, not general ones.

At this writing, there are 19 radio networks, nearly all aiming for some specialized audience. They should provide a young writer with plenty of ideas for special markets for which you could write. The *Wall Street Journal* operates a financial radio network. Two radio networks program primarily for black audiences. Another provides medical information for doctors. Yet another broadcasts only sports programming, including a 13-hour daily talk show. New radio networks provide disc jockey programs that may replace the local and syndicated record music programs carried by many stations. NBC's "The Source" programs news, features, and music for the 18- to 34-year-old group. ABC operates four networks—FM, Contemporary, Entertainment, and Information.[7] A spokesperson for the Mutual Network is quoted in the *New York Times* as saying, "Eventually, local stations will receive a vast cornucopia of quality programming from the networks."

THE AUDIENCE AND THE MEDIUM

We have stressed throughout that research plays an important role in writing for specialized audiences. If you know what people use radio and television for, you can write more efficiently. We know, for example, that four groups use television more heavily than the average—women, blacks, those with the least education, and the elderly. Thus, these are groups that can be particularly well served by special-interest programs. However, simple categories like that are rarely enough. For example, adult women are greater users than men of television, but significantly so only during the daytime hours. Thus, to reach women as a special group, you should aim for daytime pro-

---

[7]In 1981, ABC announced plans for two additional radio networks.

gramming—something the television stations and networks have obviously already figured out.

Young blacks, according to studies, tend to use television for information on appropriate ways to behave. Older blacks, on the other hand, usually turn to television simply for entertainment—thus you should consider the age as well as the race of your audience in preparing specialized programs. Blacks as a group rely much more heavily than whites on television as a source of news. This suggests that there may be a place for more informational programming aimed at the black audience. However, do not assume television is the only medium to use in speaking to the black community. Blacks also are much heavier users of radio than are whites. About 14 percent of the radio stations in the United States program primarily for blacks.

Television consumes most of the leisure hours of people over 65. Studies show that older people have a greater interest in public affairs programs and less in entertainment programs than the public as a whole. Oddly, there are only a few television programs, such as "Over Easy" and "Prime of Your Life," which are directed at older age groups.

Teen-aged girls watch the least television, with men 18 to 34 a close second. Teen-aged boys rank third. These are groups that will be toughest to program for on television—although it could be argued that appropriate programming might draw more of this audience. These might be groups you could consider for special radio programming. It would be illusory to say you would reach more people in these groups with radio. Television consumes so much of our time that even though these groups are "low" users of television, they still devote more time to television than to radio. (All three groups view more than 21 hours of television a week.) However, given the great number of radio stations and relatively low costs of radio programming, it may be useful to consider these groups as special targets for radio programs. Teen-agers constitute the largest group of listeners to FM stations, which now make up about half of all the stations in the United States. One study indicated that over one-third of the population listens to radio more than four hours a day. However, listening patterns are almost the reverse of those for television. The peak listening time for radio is about 8:00 a.m. There is a second peak at around 6:00 p.m. The hours from 7:00 p.m. to 11:00 p.m. belong to television. A great deal of listening is done in automobiles, which should also suggest some specialized programming to you. Some 95 percent of U.S. automobiles have radios, and nearly half of them can receive FM as well as AM.

Statistics—the "demographics" of the media—may not appeal to you as a writer, but it is very important that you understand them. Only by knowing the existing audiences for radio and television can you plan specialized programming efficiently.

SUMMARY

Whatever the specialized form of broadcast writing you are interested in—religious, ethnic, instructional, or something else—your approach should be the same. You must know what your audience wants and needs. As we said at the start of this chapter, we cannot discuss all the many types of programs for which you may wish to write. But you should find that the same basic rules apply for nearly all types. You must clearly define your audience and your goals, then choose the technique you think can best reach that audience and achieve those goals in the medium for which you are writing.

Writing does not begin at the typewriter. It begins with your clearly deciding what you want to do with your writing. If you know your audience and have clearly defined goals, the writing will follow with minimal effort on your part.

A closing note: Be sure that your goals are realistic. One of the authors of this book was once engaged in the preparation of a documentary about a public health clinic in a black urban ghetto. The executive producer preferred to deal only in "concepts." One was, "I want the film to project warmth." People who are poor, sick, and discriminated against do not look or act very "warm." Housing projects and medical clinics do not photograph "warmly." Candidly, the treatment of the patients was not particularly "warm." The staff, mostly recruited from the same ghetto, had learned long ago that the best way to be understood by some of their barely literate patients was simply to issue orders. In short, the concept of showing "warmth" was not a realistic goal. Be sure that you pick goals that can be achieved. The microphone and camera are not magic wands. They can inform and they can entertain, but they cannot remake the real world. Keep your goals within the capabilities of the broadcast media.

THE JOB 12

At a villa in the south of France, the writer slides reluctantly from the clear, warm waters of the pool. A butler comes forward with a bathsheet and robe, then hastens to the poolside bar to fetch a perfectly chilled glass of champagne. Glancing pensively down from the hillside villa, across the red-tiled roofs to the azure arc of the Mediterranean, the writer takes a sip of champagne and then begins dictating the next scene of the script to a waiting secretary.

Ah, would that it were so!

The truth of the matter is that writing is a job—an occupation like accounting or bricklaying. It happens to be a wonderful job for those who enjoy writing. Young people beginning a career of writing sometimes feel that they are almost stealing because they are being paid for doing something that is so much fun. But that euphoria passes. You have a valuable skill, and people are willing to pay you for it. The fact that it is often fun is irrelevant. And, like any job, it isn't always fun. There are deadlines to be met, compromises that must be made, and times when things do not go right.

Writers are unique in their ability to make their private feelings public matters, and the images the public has of the writer stem from the things that writers have written about writers. The villa at Cap d'Antibes, the dashing war correspondent, the burned-out writer hocking the trusty portable typewriter for a fifth of cheap muscatel—all these are images that may have some basis in truth but have usually been elaborated from ordinary events that the writer's imagination has elevated to adventure or tragedy.

What's it really like?

Most writers do not write in a villa on the Côte d'Azur, but in an office. A few writers do work in their own homes—but not very many. You need a place free from distractions. A not-too-comfortable place with a typewriter, sharp pencils, and lots of paper—or, as we move into the microchip age, a room with a computerized word processor on which you can compose your work. For most writers, it is preferable to have an office to go to each day and a regular routine not much different from any other office worker. We know, of course, some writers who claim that they can work only in the silence of the night between midnight and dawn. But the vast majority of writers like to lead normal lives with normal hours. And many, being a bit lazy, need the discipline of knowing they must be at the office at nine and start working.

Writers tend to write alone, but some writers find they work better with a partner. They may do sections of the script by themselves and then work them over together or they may write the whole script together, one typing and both adding lines. Whether you work better with a partner or by yourself is something you will have to learn from experience. Comedy writers in particular seem to work best in teams, sometimes with several writers working together in the same room, tossing off funny lines. To some writers this might seem to be pure chaos, but for others it obviously works. It should be noted, however, that successful comedy teams have usually worked together for many years. Just throwing four people together in a room guarantees nothing except that you have enough to play bridge.

THE TELEVISION SERIES WRITER

Most of the scripts for the dramas and comedies you see on television are written by members of the Writers Guild of America, East, Inc., which is headquartered in New York, and the Writers Guild of America, West, Inc., which is headquartered in Los Angeles. There are about 8,000 members of the Writers Guild, and the average income of members in 1981 was between $18,000 and $20,000 a year. That means that a few very successful writers are making a great deal more than $20,000, and a far larger group is making well under that amount.

Some of these writers work at home, but the great bulk of them work in offices in or near the studios for which they produce their scripts. A television script, whether done live, on film, or on videotape, is never finished until the program is on the air. It is important for the writer to be available to the producers, directors, and performers so that revisions can be made quickly when needed.

Writers who regularly contribute to a program may be under contract to write for that program. Probably more often today, the regular writer holds some position in the production company such as associate producer. This means that the writer receives a regular salary from the show in addition to the fee paid for the scripts the writer writes. This is a preferable situation for most writers to the uncertainty of living from script to script. The writer is involved in all aspects of the production of the program, which helps the writer to know what kind of material is needed. Typically, a weekly series may take four or five scripts a season from outside sources. The rest are usually done by those connected with the show.

Generally a writer is given the assignment of writing a story for the program by the producers. Usually the producer will have some basic story in mind. The writer produces a treatment of ten pages or so for the producer. Whether it is used or not, the writer will be paid for the treatment. If the producer is happy with the treatment, the writer then is given a deadline for turning in the complete script. For a 30-minute show, the writer has about ten days to turn in a 36- to 40-page script. If the producer is not satisfied, he or she may request a rewrite from the writer. Beyond that, if the writer is not under contract to the show, the writer has no further obligation. The writer will be paid for the script, and if it is used, will be entitled to residual payments for reruns.

The script then goes to the story editors for almost certain changes. Sometimes it may go through an almost total rewrite. Whether it is the original writer or someone on the staff of the program, a writer will be involved in the revisions of the script, which will continue until the show is "in the can."

Episodes of most weekly television series are produced over a five-day period. The script goes to the cast on the morning of the first day for a read-through with the director. Numerous changes will be made. That afternoon the script will be rewritten in the version that will be used for shooting. The third day will be the first rehearsal. This will usually be followed by another rewrite. The writer may be up late on this because the script will have to be ready for a full day of rehearsal the next morning. At the end of the fourth day's rehearsal, the program is viewed on the screen to see how it "plays." There will be changes for timing and to improve the dialog. It could be another late night for the writer. On the fifth day, the program is taped. Even then, in some cases, there may be additional revisions and a second taping.

As you can see, writers are involved in every step of the production of the show. Whether it is the same writer or different ones, a writer must be there.

Obviously, this can be a demanding life. A writer has to decide whether to take the risks of freelancing where the obligations usually end with the first rewrite of the script or to hope for the greater security—but more demanding work—of being a member of the staff of a show. Either way, it is exciting. You are involved with famous people and your credits appear on the screen at the start of an episode of a (we hope) successful series. You are around the hustle and bustle of studio production, and that is exciting.

But every good writer knows it's a job, not play. You have your deadlines to meet. You have the script requirements of the producer and the performers to satisfy. You may have to make changes you do not like. And for all the excitement, there is also a great deal of "hurry up and wait" in television production.

What are the chances of landing a job writing for a television series? For a beginning writer, virtually nil. You need to establish your reputation first. You need to gain experience perhaps by writing advertising copy or as a news writer. Of course, you must have an agent. With a number of well-written scripts and some good story ideas from you, your agent may be able to sell a few scripts to shows. You will begin to be known by producers in the field, and eventually they may begin to assign stories to you for scripting. If the producers of a show are sufficiently impressed with your ability to produce the kind of material they need, you may wind up with a job on the staff of the show.

If you want to make writing for television series your career, you will have to move to New York or Los Angeles sooner or later. That doesn't mean that you should chuck your job in Seattle today and grab the next bus for Los Angeles. Get your experience and build up your store of scripts and stories first. If you can find an agent who will handle your material, you may be able to sell some of your scripts without having to move. (However, you will find it harder to get an agent if you do not live in or near one of those cities.)

Another way to work your way into the business is to get an entry-level job with one of the networks or production companies. If you start in the mailroom or as a production assistant somewhere, you can eventually work your way up to a position where people with good contacts in the industry know you and recognize your abilities. If you have put together a good portfolio of scripts and story ideas, eventually you will probably find someone who will read them.

It is important to recognize that you must have scripts to show. Chances are that you may never sell your early scripts, but they will serve to show producers that you have the kind of talent they are looking for. Producers are swamped with people who "have an idea" for a show or a series. That's too vague, and almost no producer will bother with it. You must provide scripts.

Because the television market changes, being a writer of scripts for television series can be a chancy way to make a living. However, good writers are in steady demand by producers, and they make a very good living in a very pleasant way. If you have the talent and the ambition, you could be one of those writers.

THE NEWS WRITER

News writing for radio or television is a demanding job that takes training and skill. For those who choose it as a career, it can also be enormously satisfying. It deals with important events. It always involves the latest happenings. It presents a continual challenge to be met under tough time limitations. Every day brings something new. It is unlike any of the other forms of television writing. Yet it has been the training field for many who went on to other forms of television writing. As a television news writer, you learn to sit down at your typewriter (or computer terminal) and write. There is no time for pencil sharpening and pondering the application of the Aristotelian dramatic unities to your script. You discover that you can write a lot of copy in a short time and do it well. Not all good writing can be done at top speed, of course, but many young writers spend far more time than is needed to do good work. The discipline of news writing forces the writer to get rid of these self-indulgent habits and get right down to work.

You cannot be a good broadcast news writer if you are not interested in news. You must devour daily newspapers and news magazines from cover to cover. You must listen constantly to radio news and watch television news regularly. You can no more learn to write television news without watching television news than you can learn to write television drama without watching television dramas. Watch television news programs analytically. Ask yourself why a story was handled the way it was and how certain effects were accomplished. Visit a local radio or television station if you can and watch the production of a news show first hand. See if you can obtain a copy of a news script. Keep your stopwatch handy when you are watching or listening to a news show. Pay attention to the selection and placement of stories. Compare the content of a news program with that of a newspaper. Ask yourself why certain stories were used by one but not the other. Compare the differences in local and network newscasts, and compare the news on independent stations to that of network affiliates.

If you are going to be a broadcast newsperson, you must "live" news 24 hours a day. That's not for everyone. But if you like it, few careers provide more excitement and satisfaction.

There are probably some 20,000 people working in radio news production and another 20,000 working in television news. That covers everything from 10-watt radio stations to network news operations, and includes news staffs as small as one person and as large as several hundred. Salaries are extremely varied. Small stations may offer salaries as low as $8,000 a year. Network news writers are usually paid around $30,000 a year. Reporters, anchors, and other on-the-air personalities usually make considerably more. A few top personalities with the networks and in the largest markets make in excess of $200,000 a year—but keep in mind, that is a very few people, and their jobs often last for only a few years.

A small number of young writers do start out at large stations or network stations, but most young writers must spend time developing their skills at small stations in remote areas. As you accumulate examples of your work, you begin looking for jobs in larger markets, working your way up to the major markets.

The way news writers work varies from station to station. At radio stations, the writer is often also a reporter, gathering news with a tape recorder and telephone, writing the stories to contain the material gathered. The same is true at smaller television stations. At larger stations, particularly in television stations, work is more compartmentalized. The writer's job may be simply to stay in the newsroom and write stories from material brought in by news wire, reporters, and camera crews.

News writers have to be ready to work odd hours. There are early morning shifts, overnight, afternoon shifts, and so on—almost everything but nine-to-five shifts. A radio news writer may have to be in early in the morning to prepare news for the morning "drive time" shows. Often that is a 4:00 a.m. to noon shift. Television news writers may work from 10:00 a.m. to 7:00 p.m. or 2:00 p.m. to midnight. Reporters usually have to be on the job by 7:00 or 8:00 in the morning. Above all, anyone working in news has to be ready to come in to work or stay overtime on the job whenever a big story is breaking. It can be hard on family and social life. But it is rarely dull. It isn't the life for everyone, but most news writers wouldn't trade it for anything.

THE ADVERTISING COPYWRITER

The advertising copywriter may work for an advertising agency, for the advertising department of a corporation or charity, or may prepare copy for advertisers who buy time on the radio or television station for which the writer works. The basic job is the same, but the facilities and support the writer has to work with vary greatly. Advertising agencies themselves may vary from huge international organizations with thousands of employees to small one- or two-person agencies. The major agencies are located in New York and, to a lesser degree, Chicago, Los Angeles, St. Louis, and other major cities —but even relatively small communities may support one or two small agencies.

In a typical agency, the writer is part of the creative staff. The account executive works out the basic details of a campaign with the client. The research department makes a careful analysis of the market and the best techniques for reaching it. The media selection staff decides how to apportion the advertising among the various media. Then it is up to the writers and artists in the creative department to come up with scripts, storyboards, and the general content of the campaign.

Advertising is a well-paid profession and a heavily populated one. Over half a million people work in advertising of one sort or another. Starting salaries are around $12,000 to $15,000, with good chance of doubling that in five to ten years. Usually, at larger agencies, you will have to start at the bottom in the mailroom and work your way into a higher post. A good alternative is to start with a smaller agency, then when you have had some success, look for a job with a larger one.

Your chances for employment and advancement in advertising will be greater if you are skilled in the print media as well as broadcasting. It is unlikely that you will have a chance simply to specialize in writing broadcast copy at most agencies—certainly not at first. However, if you do have skills in broadcast writing, that is an important plus because many people come to agency work with only a print background. You will have more opportunity to work in television copywriting if you work for a national agency because local advertising tends to be mostly newspaper advertising.

The advertising copywriter usually works a standard nine-to-five day in an agency office. However, you may be expected to burn a good deal of midnight oil when working on specific projects or presentations for new campaigns. You also may have to spend considerable time in conferences with clients and with other people at the agency. Much has been made of the "pressures" of the advertising business. No doubt they are there. It is not for everyone. If you do not work well under pressure, advertising is probably not for you—but then writing news or even preparing scripts for series involves a considerable amount of working under pressure, so the problem is not unique to advertising.

You also have to have some perspective about what you are doing. You are there to sell goods. While you should not have to lie to do that, you may well find that you do not always wholly believe or agree with what you are writing. If you cannot live with that, then you may be better suited for some other form of writing. It is the news writer's job to tell what's wrong with things, not the advertising copywriter's.

It is possible to take pride in writing a new jingle or a slogan. Advertising, with its extreme time limitations, is a challenge, and it takes a very good writer to be a good copywriter. Copywriting is a much maligned profession, but even its sharpest critics will usually admit that some of the best writing in America appears in our advertising.

Remember, too, that advertising is not all selling chewing gum. There are dozens of important charities and worthy causes that rely upon good advertising copy to reach the public with their messages. There are many satisfying ways for a writer to make a living in advertising.

AND THE OTHERS

As we have tried to point out, there are many kinds of writing. In addition to the jobs described so far in this chapter, there are writers producing copy for hundreds of specialized types of shows. Most are staff writers, although there are some other areas for freelancing. Most staff writers work at the offices of the production company that produces the show for which they are working. Some work regular nine-to-five hours, others have schedules more like the writers for television series programs. The demands of the jobs are as varied as the programs.

A writer for a talk show must do a great deal of research. The writer must know the backgrounds of the people who will appear on the program and must be familiar with the topics on which they are to speak. Often, the writer on such a show is the host, but some shows have writers whose job is to prepare the copy for the host. Good research is as important as good writing in a job like this. You cannot afford to embarrass the host. You have to know the limits of what can and cannot be discussed on your show. For example, one of the writers of this book once thought it would be amusing for the host of a program to mention his real name on the air. The host did *not* think it was funny. That line was cut.

Very often, the writer for a talk show has the job of figuring out how to introduce and discuss dry or complex topics in a way that is interesting to the audience. You must complement your research with the ability to think in terms of the audience and its ability to understand the material.

Disc jockeys usually prepare their own material. Very few have writers. Some do use material from national services that provide scripted material for disc jockeys. If you are writing for a disc jockey, you probably are the disc jockey. The job calls for a knowledge of the music and artists you program, and an understanding of the audience you are seeking. You have to develop a personality which stands out in a very crowded field.

Disc jockeys sometimes prepare their material at home, but usually they put together what scripts they use in an office at the radio station. Often the script is only notes on a pad of paper. But a well-organized DJ has the program carefully planned out and the material at least partially written out for use on the air.

Most disc jockeys have to start at small stations and work up to larger markets. Wages for those starting out can be near the starvation level, but the most successful disc jockeys can make huge salaries. There is a great deal of uncertainty in the business. You are only as good as your last rating book, and even a successful disc jockey may lose a job when management changes at a station or a new format is adopted. Still, those who enjoy the music and life style can find great satisfaction in the business. Hours can be odd and the workload sometimes heavy, but if you enjoy the work, you probably won't be fazed by that.

Preparing scripts for special-interest programming may vary from writing dramas or documentaries to providing copy for talk shows. Most writers are staff writers, but some shows accept freelance material. Your best bet for getting a writing job with a show of this sort is to become acquainted with the people on the show. Take an entry-level job or volunteer for work with the show. Most programs of this sort are produced by relatively small groups of people. It won't be hard to find out whom you need to know to see if you can interest them in your writing.

INTERNSHIPS AND VOLUNTEER WORK

Many stations accept students as interns while they are in school. Usually this means you work one semester, trimester, or quarter with the station. If may be a full-time job or a part-time one. Some are paid, some are not. The important point of an internship is that it gets you into a station where you can meet people who can help you get a job or sell a script. Students often overestimate what they can expect from an internship. For example, if you are working at a large station—especially one in a major market—you cannot expect to do much real writing or much of anything else at the station. The stations have union contracts that spell out who is permitted to perform certain tasks. Moreover, the station cannot take a chance on work by unknowns. Most of your internship will be spent observing and occasionally helping out in some minor way. If you want a chance to really get involved, you are probably better off to seek a smaller station. But do not overlook the valuable contacts you can make at the large station, plus the advantage of seeing how top professionals work.

Another way to get a foot in the door is to volunteer your time. While most major stations do not take volunteers, noncommercial stations and some smaller commercial stations may accept them. You can also offer your services for special programs, charity fund-raisers and such, for which nearly all stations accept volunteer workers.

Don't overlook campus radio and television stations. There are hundreds of them across the country. They are a place where you can get your first broadcast experience. Even if you are not a student at the school that operates the station, it is sometimes possible to volunteer your services there.

AGENTS

If you plan to sell dramatic or comedy scripts to radio or television, you will need an agent. Most producers will not look at a script that comes in "over the transom." In the first place, the producer simply doesn't have time. The agent knows the type of material a producer needs and filters out scripts that would only waste the producer's time.

Second, the producer takes a legal risk if he or she reads a script not submitted through an agent. There are really only a few basic plot ideas in writing. A producer may encounter dozens of scripts with the same basic idea. Yet, if the producer uses one of those scripts, the writers of the other scripts may think that the producer has "stolen" their idea. No doubt, stories are stolen sometimes, but for the most part such thefts are simply imagined by the writer. If the producer reads every script that anyone sends in, the probability of being sued by someone who thinks an idea has been stolen is greatly increased. So nearly all producers limit the material they will look at to material submitted by an agent. Other material will be returned unread.

Incidentally, any script submitted for reading must be accompanied by a standard release form. This is a simple legal document through which the writer gives the producer the legal right to read the script. Again, no producer will look at a script unless it is accompanied by a release form.

Aside from drama and comedy scripts, most broadcast writing is done by members of the staff of the program, and no agent is needed. Do not sign a contract with an agent unless you know that you will be dealing with the kinds of writing that require an agent for submission. An agent normally collects 10 percent of a writer's earnings. Where the freelance writer is concerned, it is well worth the price. But if you are not aiming for that market, you may find yourself tied to an expensive contract, paying for an agent who really has no services to perform for you. If you do sign with an agent, check the contract to see that the agent's 10 percent comes only from material the agent has sold for you or from jobs the agent has helped you obtain.

If you do need an agent, it is often difficult for a young writer to find an agent willing to handle an "unknown." You simply must be persistent, going from agency to agency until you find someone willing to look at your work. As with producers, it is essential that you have scripts and story ideas with you for the agent to read. It is also important to convince the agent that you are serious about writing and that you intend to write as a career, not as a hobby or part-time job. After all, the agent makes his or her living by selling your scripts. If you are going to turn out only one or two scripts a year, you are hardly worth the agent's time.

It is unwise for a young writer to sign a long-term contract with an agent, as it is possible that the agent you first sign with may not turn out to be the best one to market your scripts. Rightly or wrongly, most writers feel that their agents do not do enough for them. After all, an agent may represent dozens of writers. You cannot really expect your scripts to get special attention. In the long run, it is likely that your agent is doing as much as possible for you, since the agent has to sell scripts to make a living. But you should protect yourself from unpleasant situations with agents by trying to avoid long-term commitments. This may not be too difficult. After all, the agent may not want to be tied to an unknown writer for long either. However, the writer will suffer a great deal more than the agent if the agent is not doing a good job of selling the writer's scripts.

UNIONS

Broadcasting has long been a highly unionized industry, although the degree of unionization varies widely. In small communities, there may be no union members at a station. At other stations, the engineers may be unionized but the rest of the staff not. In the nation's major markets—New York, Chicago, and Los Angeles—most television and a substantial portion of the radio stations are unionized. The networks are all unionized.

Unions present a perplexing issue to the student planning a broadcast career. With some happy exceptions, unions have not welcomed new members with open arms. The reason is that there is a surplus of workers in many fields, and the unions would prefer to see all their present members working before they welcome new ones. Even unions that do not have more members than there are jobs have seen the obvious advantage of keeping it that way. The fewer people with union cards, the more they can demand for their labor—so long as the producers are limited to using union labor.

Students often face the dilemma of a prospective employer who will not hire someone who is not a member of a union and a union that will only admit people to membership who already have jobs in the field. If you are persistent, you will usually be able to get around this problem. Generally, if an employer wants to hire you, an arrangement can be worked out with the union for membership.

Things are changing. Some unions that had reputations for being "father-son" unions—those that you had to be a relative or a friend of a member to get into—have had pressure put on them by the Department of Health and Human Services, and by the Department of Labor or other government agencies, to make membership more accessible, especially to members of minority groups and to women.

A second hurdle to get over is the cost of joining a union. There are fairly stiff initiation fees plus regular dues to be paid. In most cases, initiation fees can be paid over a period of months or years in regular monthly payments. At most places of work, the initiation fee and dues will automatically be deducted from your paycheck each month.

A third hurdle is the long apprenticeship periods required by many unions. An apprenticeship of eight years before you could become a full-fledged (journeyman) member used to be fairly common in the entertainment industry. During apprenticeship, the apprentice is restricted in the work she or he can perform. Expulsion from the union for infraction of rules is always a possibility. Apprentices may be limited to little more than menial tasks during the period of apprenticeship, and many become discouraged and drop out.

Even after obtaining full membership, it is usually necessary to spend several years in various subordinate "assistant" categories of membership before you reach the top category of union membership. However, it is sometimes possible to obtain a "temporary" rating in one of the higher categories in order to perform necessary work. (Usually it is necessary to make some pro forma demonstration that no members in the higher category are available for the job.)

After reading all this, you may feel "turned off" by unions. If you work a few years in some nonunion jobs, however, you may revise your thinking. Whatever the faults and failings of the unions in the broadcasting industry—and there are many—they have won and maintained decent wages and working conditions for the people in the industry. Certainly there are some nonunion shops that provide the same wages and benefits, but you will find too many nonunion shops where employees are sadly overworked and underpaid.

There is little doubt that unions in broadcasting have become progressively weaker vis-à-vis their employers over the past quarter-century. The proliferation of stations has made it difficult for the unions to organize more than a fraction of the stations in the country. Probably the major cause of weakness has been the jurisdictional divisiveness of the unions themselves. Competition among unions to represent broadcast employees has made the labor scene in broadcasting an alphabet soup of competing unions, none very strong because of these divisions. The multiplicity of unions is a headache for management because there are so many entities to deal with, but the major effect has been to weaken the unions. For employees, holding membership in several different unions is common in broadcasting—and often necessary.

There are two basic kinds of union contracts in the industry. A union may either represent members of a specific craft at a station or network or it may have a blanket contract to represent all employees at that institution. For example, writers at CBS News are represented by the Writers Guild. The Guild does not try to represent the interests of nonwriters at CBS News, who are covered by other unions. On the other hand, newswriters at ABC and NBC are members of the National Association of Broadcast Employees and Technicians (NABET), which also represents engineers, secretaries, pages, and a host of other ABC and NBC employes. What union a writer belongs to depends on where the writer works.

The major union for writers is the Writers Guild. The standard Guild contract sets the minimum rates for most forms of broadcast writing, and spells out the rights and obligations of writers and their employers. The actual contract is a booklet something over 125 pages long. It is renegotiated periodically, and copies are sent to Guild members. If extra copies are available, the Guild will usually send one on request. Most writers haven't the time to wade through all the legal phrasing of the contract, but they rely on it to protect their rights and their incomes.

Fortunately for young writers, the Guild is one of the most open of all unions. It allows a writer to sell one script to a producer without being a member. Once you have sold that script, you are a "professional," and if you wish to sell any more scripts, you must join the Guild. No attempt is made to limit the number of members. You are expected to pay initiation charges and dues and abide by the rules of the Guild (mainly, not to sell scripts to producers while the Guild is on strike). In return, the Guild provides certain services such as registering titles and story ideas for writers and supplying them with information about various programs that may be in the market for scripts.

SUMMARY

There are many jobs available in the area of broadcast writing. Most are interesting and provide a comfortable income. But the jobs will not come to you. You must go after them. You must have a plan. You must know what your goals are. And you must be persistent. Do not be discouraged if you get turned down the first time—or the second—or the hundredth. If you want to write and you have the talent for it, you have to keep trying until you have accomplished what you set out to do.

But set realistic goals. Not everyone has to write for the network evening news or the top-rated television series. There are thousands of happy people working in small stations, in advertising agencies, in public relations firms, and at dozens of other jobs for broadcast writers. And remember that you cannot expect to start at the top. You will have to be content with that small-town job until your skills and experience will let you move on to bigger things.

The marvelous thing about writing is that you can do it anywhere. After a day of turning out radio commercials, you can still turn to your typewriter at home and work on that drama. When you finish your daily stint as a disc jockey, you may want to go back to working on a documentary. Even when you are sitting in a bus or riding a bicycle, you can be thinking out the plot or the next scene of your comedy script.

There is probably no other profession that gives you that opportunity. Most people who are writers or aspire to being writers love to write. Sitting down at the typewriter keyboard is as satisfying to them as sitting down to the piano keyboard is to a pianist. And broadcast writing is the writing of this century. It is "state of the art." It's work, or course, but much of the time it is also just plain fun. However, never treat it trivially. You have to work at it. Like a pianist, the more you sit at that keyboard, the better the results will be. Try to write something every day. And follow radio and television closely so that you understand the medium for which you are writing.

And pay attention to the credits when you hear them or they roll by on the screen. Remember, someday your name will be there.

GLOSSARY
of
Special
Terms

ABC.	The American Broadcasting Company.
Above-the-line.	The cost of talent in the production of a show; includes fees for writers, actors, directors, and producers.
AD.	Assistant director or, in some locations, associate director.
Adjacencies.	The program or time periods immediately preceding or following a program.
Ad-libs.	Unscripted remarks.
Air check.	A recording, usually used to see or hear how well a performer sounds or looks on the air; may be used for checking other aspects of a program as well.
Air time.	The time at which a program starts.
AM.	Amplitude Modulation, older of the two systems of radio broadcasting.
Arc.	Camera makes a circular movement in the direction specified.
A Roll.	First of two reels of film (or sometimes vid-

eotape) run in an AB-Roll story. If only one sound track is used, normally it is on the A Roll.

Audio. Sound.

Back-timing. Marking various segments of a script with the times at which they must begin for the program to end on time.

Balop. Balopticon, trademark of Bausch and Lomb opaque projector. Often used to designate any projector that shows opaque graphics instead of transparencies. Not as commonly used as it was in earlier days of television.

Beeper. An outdated term for a telephone call recorded for use on the air. It used to be required by law that such recordings have an electronic beep in them at regular intervals.

Below-the-line. Costs for production other than talent costs; includes studio costs, costs of equipment, and so forth.

BG. Background.

Billboard. The standard opening of a program, with music and identifying material.

Bit part. A minor role, with few or no lines.

Bloop. To edit out.

BMI. Broadcast Music, Inc., a music licensing agency set up by the broadcasting industry. One of the two major music licensing agencies.

Breakdown. A detailed analysis of a script indicating what scenery, equipment, and personnel are needed for each shot.

Bridge. A transitional scene or a musical transition.

B Roll. Second of two rolls of film used simultaneously in a news story. Usually contains silent footage that is run while sound from the A Roll is heard.

Budget. The list of important news stories of the day.

Business. Actions of performers.

Canned. Prerecorded.

CBS. Columbia Broadcasting System.

Chromakey. See *Key*.

Clearance. Obtaining legal permission to use material that has been copyrighted.

C-O. Company owned, term for a network-owned station. See also *O & O.*

Cold. Done without rehearsal.

Crane. Only for high-budget shows. Camera is mounted on a big crane and can be moved in almost any direction as specified.

Crawl. Credits or other written material moving slowly across the screen. Movement may be either vertical or horizontal, but many stations limit the term "crawl" to horizontal movement and use "roll" for vertical movement.

Credits. Names of those involved in producing a program.

Cross-fade. Sometimes used to mean *segue.* Also a film transition in which the first scene fades to gray and the second scene fades up from gray.

CU. Close-up. Anything showing just head and shoulders.

Cushion. Material that can be read to fill time or cut at will to make a program come out on time. Sometimes called *Pad.*

Cutaway. Any shot that briefly switches attention from the main action to some related activity.

Cutback. Returning to the main action after a cutaway or after several scenes of concurrent action.

Cut to. A straight cut from one shot to another, usually used within a scene, but sometimes used as a transition between scenes if change of locale between two shots is clear.

Dailies. Film or videotape sequences viewed the same day or the day after they are shot. Important in film production to allow for retakes of unsatisfactory material. Also called *Rushes.*

Day-for-night. Scenes shot in daylight, using special filters to give the effect of nighttime shooting.

Director. The person responsible for the rehearsing and actual shooting of a television or film production.

Disc (sometimes *Disk*). Phonograph recording.

Dissolve.	First picture grows dimmer as second becomes clearer and replaces first picture. Used to show change of scene, passage of time, or for poetic effects.
Docudrama.	A dramatization, using actors, but based on authenticated documents of the event. See *Documentary*.
Documentary.	Radio, television, or film programs based on actual facts. By most modern definitions, they should be constructed from "actualities," material shot or recorded at an actual event rather than staged in a studio. Early radio "documentaries" often used staged re-creations of events or fictionalized stories based on factual material. Dramatizations of actual events today are usually called *docudramas*.
Dolly.	Camera physically moves toward (IN) or away from (OUT) subject as specified.
Double system.	Synchronous separate recording of sound and picture; it is time-consuming and expensive, but usually produces better results for film. Almost always used for all forms of film production except news.
Double-take.	Stage business for performers in which the actor first shows one reaction to a statement or event, then shows a different reaction as the "real" meaning of the event sinks in.
Dropout.	Loss of sound or video picture because of defects in tape.
Dry rehearsal.	Rehearsal without cameras.
Dry run.	See *Dry rehearsal*.
Dual role.	One actor performing more than one role in the same program.
Dub.	To rerecord something or to add recorded material to existing material.
Easel shot.	Photographs, drawings, or similar material mounted and shot by a studio camera. Sometimes called a *Flip* or a *Stand*.
ECU.	Extreme close-up. Often ETCU or XCU.
Echo.	Audio effect to sound like an echo.
Editing.	Assembling of film or videotape for air use. Revision of copy.
Episode.	One complete program in a continuing story.

Establishing shot. Camera shot that sets the relationships between camera and the elements of the scene.

ET. Electrical transcription.

ETV. Educational television.

Exclusive. A story or interview obtained by a single reporter to the exclusion of competitors.

Extra. A performer with no lines or specific action used simply to provide people in the background of scenes where more than the main characters would normally be seen on camera.

Fade in (sometimes Fade up). 1. The sound gradually rises from nothing to normal level. This is the normal opening for most programs and for most scenes within a program.
2. Picture slowly becomes visible on previously black screen.

Fade out. 1. Sound becomes gradually fainter until it is no longer heard. This is the normal ending for a program and for most scenes in a program.
2. The scene fades to black. Usually the end of a program or scene.

Fax. Facsimile; a system of transmitting pictures or written material via radio or wire transmission.

FCC. Federal Communications Commission, the governmental body responsible for regulating broadcasting.

Feed. Material transmitted to a station by the network, by another station, or from a remote.

Feedback. Noise caused by a microphone picking up its own signal through some amplified source such as a loudspeaker.

FG. Foreground.

Fill. Material written to be used only if there are slow moments in some event. In news, fill is written to be read in case there is a loss of audio or picture in a story using recorded material.

Filter. An electronic effect to make the speaker's voice sound hollow or metallic. Various filters can be used for different effects;

	usually they are used to indicate something unusual about the speaker—a voice from the grave, the thoughts of a person, the voice of a robot, or other unusual voices.
Flip card.	Material prepared for an *Easel* or *Stand* shot.
Fluff.	A minor error by a performer—usually a word missed or mispronounced.
FM.	Frequency Modulation, a system of radio broadcasting that permits better quality audio than the old AM system.
Follow shot or following shot.	Camera moves with performer and stays in same relationship to performer throughout the shot.
Format.	Accepted pattern of arranging material.
Forty-five or 45.	A disc recorded at 45 rpm. Less frequently used than they once were.
Freelance.	Material provided by nonstaff writers. Sometimes used to refer to other noncontract personnel, such as directors.
Freeze frame.	The same picture remains with no change for as long as specified.
From the top.	To redo a performance from the beginning.
Full shot.	See *LS*.
Gaffer.	An electrician.
Glass shot.	Shot taken through glass on which some elements of the set have been painted to reduce costs of set construction. Also describes shot taken through unbreakable glass to protect camera from water, tossed custard pies, and so forth.
Glitch.	Interference in video.
Glossy print.	The usual type of photographic print; not usually suitable for use on television because it is too reflective. See *Matte print*.
Graphics.	Any illustrative material.
Green film.	Freshly processed film. May cause problems in use, but often must be used in news work.
Ground noise.	Sound caused by poor-quality recording material.
Heavy.	The villain.
Helical scan.	A system of video recording originally used

mainly for industrial or home recording purposes; high-quality units are now used for commercial television.

Hertz. One cycle per second.

High angle; Low angle. Normal camera height is about the height of a person's head. *High* and *low* are designated in reference to this and often require some additional description.

High-band recording. Video recording providing superior quality to the older low-band recordings.

High-contrast film. Film from which other films are printed is usually low contrast. Film meant to be shown on the air without reprinting, such as news film, is usually high contrast.

High key. Brightly lit with few shadows.

Hiss. Unwanted sound usually caused by poor-quality recording equipment.

Holdover. Audience from preceding program that remains tuned to the next show.

Hook. A plot device to involve the audience.

Hot. Too bright; overexposed.

Iconoscope. Early form of video camera tube developed by RCA.

Idiot card. A cue card.

Image orthicon. Form of relatively sensitive television camera tube, once the general standard of the industry, now somewhat replaced by newer devices such as Plumbicons.

Inlay. A system of matting material from another source onto videotape.

Insert. A shot, usually a close-up, inserted between two shots of the main action. Also a program item from an outside source included in a program, such as an insert from a remote source into a news program.

Institutional. Designed to promote image rather than product.

Intercut. To switch back and forth between two simultaneous happenings in a plot.

Interior. Any scene with an indoor location.

Interlock. System of showing film with synchronized sound track when double system sound has been used. See *Double system.*

IPS. Inches per second; usually the higher the speed, the better the quality of recording.

Iris. A circular wipe. In *Iris Out,* the picture on the screen shrinks to a dot in the center and disappears. In *Iris In,* the new picture begins as a dot at the center and fills the entire screen.

Item. A news story.

Jump cut. Cut from one shot to the next in which both shots appear identical except for the sudden and disturbing change in one object; often a problem in news film or videotape editing. An example would be a cut between two shots of a speaker in which nothing changes except the position of the speaker's head.

Kaleidoscope. A multiple-image shot, often rotating.

Key (Chromakey). 1. Image matted into colored (usually blue) area on set. Material to be keyed must be specified.
2. Type of light. See *High key* and *Low key.*

Key light. Primary source of light on a set.

Kicker. A light news story, used for humor. A small spotlight, usually mounted on or near the camera, aimed at the head of a performer to make eyes and teeth sparkle. Sometimes called an *Eye light.*

Kill. Eliminate.

Kilocycle. See *KiloHertz.*

KiloHertz. One thousand *Hertz*; formerly *Kilocycle.*

KiloWatt. One thousand watts.

Kine. See *Kinescope.*

Kinescope. A television receiving tube; a film recording made from a television picture tube. Common in the days before videotape.

Lap. A dissolve in which details of both pictures are visible for some length of time; sometimes simply used to mean *Super.*

Lead. First sentence of a news story; sometimes first story of a news program.

Lead-in. Line preceding a cued action of some sort, such as a lead-in to an audio cart story in radio news.

Limbo. Shot before a plain background, usually black. Also sometimes used for *Easel* or *Stand.*

Live. 1. Performed as it is being broadcast.
2. Same as MOC. If more than one newscaster is involved, both cues must be preceded by name of newscaster reading story.

Lip synchronization. Performer mouths lines that have been prerecorded. Also used to refer to any sequence in which sound and action must be perfectly synchronized.

Location. Any shooting location not on studio grounds.

Logo. Symbol used for a program or to designate an organization.

Long shot. Any shot that is taken from sufficient distance to show normal persons from head to toe.

Loop. A short piece of tape or film with one end spliced to the other so that it can produce a continuous shot or sound. Also rerecording previously shot sequences with performers matching words or sounds to the action on the film. Done when it is not possible to obtain satisfactory sound under shooting conditions, or when another performer is to read or sing material for the performer seen on the screen. Sometimes called *dubbing*. Also, the connections between a network and its affiliates by which it can transmit material to them or they can feed material back to the network.

Low key. Darkly lit scenes.

LS. Long shot.

M and E. The music (M) track and sound effects (E) track in productions that use a multitrack mix for sound.

Mag stripe. Magnetically striped film, the type commonly used in television film for single-system recording.

Master. A long shot of the action in a scene; the final version of a script; the official schedule. A film or tape from which copies are made. Potentiometer (pot) controlling the output of a control board.

Match dissolve. Dissolve in which the objects in the two shots appear, at first, similar or identical.

Matte. Any of several systems for combining two images from different sources so that they appear to be part of the same scene. Unlike superimposition, there is no overlap of images; the image matted into the other picture appears to stand in front of or behind objects in the other picture. The most common system of matting in television is Chromakey.

Matte print. A photographic print with a nonglossy finish; preferred for television use because it reflects little glare.

MBS. Mutual Broadcasting System radio network.

MC. Master control; master of ceremonies.

MCU. Medium close-up, usually head and neck shot.

MegaHertz. One million Hertz; formerly *Megacycle*.

MI. Move in (move closer to camera).

Microwave. High-frequency signal used to transmit television material.

Mix. To combine, or the process of combining production elements, as in "sound mix."

MOC. Microphone on camera. Newscaster is seen on camera.

Monitor. 1. Video material shown on a large videoscreen on the news set (usually caps: MONITOR).

2. Any device for viewing or listening to material, usually while the material is being recorded. Also, to view or listen to material.

Monochrome. Black and white.

Montage. Several images appearing in the same shot or in a rapid series of shots.

Mood music. Music keyed to the action of a scene. Also called *background music*.

MS. Medium shot. A shot wide enough to show characters from waist to head.

Multilock. An Ampex of Canada system for double system production with videotape.

Multiple image. Shot with same image repeated at several positions in the frame, done either electronically or optically.

Multiplex. To transmit more than one signal using the same radio frequency or wire. Also, electronic or mechanical systems of feeding pictures from several sources to a single camera as in a telecine.

NAB. National Association of Broadcasters.

NARB. National Advertising Review Board.

NARTB. National Association of Radio and Television Broadcasters.

NBC. National Broadcasting Company, a wholly owned subsidiary of Radio Corporation of America (RCA).

Nemo. A remote.

Network. A number of broadcasting stations linked by wire or microwave so that they can carry the same programs at the same time or at a specified delay time to fit local time needs. Affiliates are paid by the network for commercial time used for the programs carried, but usually at a rate well below the usual time charges for the same time slot.

Noise. Any interference in either the audio or video signal.

O & O. A station owned and operated by a network.

Off-line. Videotape editing done after the actual taping.

On line. Videotape editing done at the control board while the taping is going on.

Off mike. Sound coming from a distance away from the microphone.

On mike. Sound at proper distance from microphone.

Optical recording. Sound for film recorded via one of several systems that prints the sound recording in a strip at the edge of the film. Most film that is to be reproduced in several film copies uses optical sound. Material to be used in its original form, such as news film, is usually *mag stripe* film. Most optical recording is done *double system,* beginning with recordings on magnetic tape that are transferred to optical form later.

OS. Off stage. Out of view of the camera.

OUT. The sound is no longer heard.

Out take. Material edited out and not used in the final version.

Over.	A sound is heard more loudly than other sounds in the same sequence. Essentially, OVER is the opposite of UNDER.
Pad.	Extra material at the end of a script to be read as needed to make the show come out on time. Also, extra film or videotape at the end of a story that can be kept on the screen if the newscaster reads too slowly to complete the story at the proper point.
Pan.	Camera turns in direction specified while remaining in same location. Similar to turning your head.
Passing shot.	Camera is stationary and performer or other subject matter moves past it.
Paste.	Put together a news program by pasting or stapling wire stories in the desired sequence, sometimes including some material prepared by the local news staff.
Patch.	Connecting two sources of sound or video. Technically, it means that they should be connected by plugging a cable in from one to the other; however, electronic connection of various sources is sometimes called patching.
Patch board; Patch panel.	An electrical connection board that allows signals from one source to be connected to another.
PB.	Pull back camera.
PD.	Public domain; material no longer or never covered by copyright.
Pedestal.	Camera physically moves up or down as specified. Effect is similar to looking out of a moving elevator.
Piggyback.	Two or more commercials combined in a single one-minute time slot.
Pick-up.	To speed up; location of program origination; quality of sound being received at a location; the tone arm of a phonograph.
Pixlock.	A system of synchronizing all sources used when recording color on videotape.
Plain lighting.	Lighting at an angle that gives the appearance of morning or afternoon sunlight.
Platter.	Disc.
Playback.	Listening to or viewing recorded material, usually just after it has been recorded.

Plug.
: To insert material promoting a product, person, or program.

Plumbicon.
: A high-quality Phillips television tube that has more or less replaced the image orthicon.

Polarity.
: The polarity determines whether a television picture is seen as positive or negative. This makes it possible to use negative film in some instances in television and still have the picture seen by the audience as positive because the engineer has "reversed polarity."

Postsynchronization.
: Recording and synchronizing sound after the picture has been completed.

Pot.
: See *Potentiometer*.

Potentiometer.
: Device on an audio control board to control the amplitude of a signal from a given source. While not a correct technical definition, it is something like a volume control on a radio receiver.

POV.
: A shot from the point of view of a specified character.

Practical prop.
: A stage prop that actually works as opposed to one that is painted on or is a dummy.

Prerecording.
: Recording a sound track prior to videotaping or filming. The performer then "lip synchs" to the sound track. It simplifies microphone placement, obviates mistakes, and permits performers to dance or engage in other strenuous activities without their having to pant for breath when they "sing." Also permits use of voices other than the performers' for special effects.

Presence.
: Quality of a performer's being close as produced by a microphone.

Presynchronization.
: Prerecording; term is used most commonly in relation to animation.

Print-through.
: Damage to recording caused by the signal from one layer of tape being transferred to surrounding layers on a reel.

Process shot.
: Any of several techniques that permit a performer to appear before a previously shot background.

Producer.
: The person responsible for the overall production of a program or a film.

Punch.   To emphasize in delivery. To prepare a video or audio source for input on a board or to insert it into a program, as in "punch up camera five."

Q.   Cue.

Rack.   To change focus on a lens or to switch to a different turret-mounted lens.

Radio wire.   A wire-service wire written so that the material can be used on the air without rewriting. Provides complete programs written for specified reading times.

Raw stock.   Unexposed film or unrecorded video- or audiotape.

Recap.   A brief news summary.

Release.   A legal form giving permission to use pictures of a person or material produced by that person on the air. Also, a publicity handout.

Remote.   Any broadcast material originating outside the studios at the time of broadcast.

Residual.   Payment for replays of filmed or recorded productions on the air.

Retake.   To do a shot or scene over for the cameras.

Reverb.   An echo effect.

Reversal film.   The film usually used in television news. It is processed to produce a positive image on the original film, obviating the usual steps of making a negative and then making prints from that.

Reverse.   A shot from the opposite angle of the previous shot.

Ride gain.   To manipulate the amplitude of various inputs while on the air, recording, or rerecording material to compensate for material that is too soft or too loud.

Roll.   To start film or video tape. See also *crawl*.

Rough cut.   The first editing of a program.

RPM.   Revolutions per minute.

RP.   Visual seen on rear projection screen. Visual must be specified.

RTNA.   Radio-Television News Association.

RTNDA.   Radio-Television News Directors' Association.

Running shot. Camera and subject both moving and re-maining in same relation to each other.

Runover. Going past the designated end time of a program—the unforgiveable sin in broad-casting.

Run through. A rehearsal without cameras.

Rushes. See *Dailies*.

Safe area; Safety area. The area in a camera viewfinder within which material photographed will be sure to appear uncropped on a television screen. Also called *Cutoff*.

SAG. Screen Actors Guild.

Scenario. Treatment.

Schmaltz. Sickeningly sweet dialog, action, or music.

Score. Original music for a production.

Segue. Pronounced "SEG-way." A simultaneous audio *Fade In* and *Fade Out*. A *Segue* is the normal transition from one scene to the next. It also can be used to indicate a shift in time or location. It may also be used to provide a shift from external to internal dialog, as in a shift from a character speak-ing to the thoughts in the character's mind. Such a transition needs to be enhanced with other techniques as a *Filter* for the "thinking" voice and perhaps music under or a sting to help the audience understand what is happening.

Sets in use. Percentage of homes measured by a rating service in which at least one set is turned on.

Set up. Video levels set by engineers for video re-cording.

Seventy-eights or 78s. Discs recorded at 78 rpm. No longer pro-duced.

SI FILM. Silent film.

Signature. Musical theme.

Simulcast. To carry the same program on radio and television at the same time.

Single-system. Recording sound on the same film that the picture is recorded on, recording both simultaneously. Television news is the most common use for single-system sound.

SI VT. Silent videotape.

SI VT/VO. Silent videotape; newscaster's voice heard over pictures.

Slide. A 35-mm slide seen full screen. Slide must be further identified.

SMPTE. Society of Motion Picture and Television Engineers.

SNEAK. The sound is slowly faded in so that its addition to the sound picture is not noticed at first.

Snow. Television interference.

SOF. Sound on film.

Sound truck. Stand, mounted on rollers, containing turntables and other sound-effects gear.

SOVTR. Same as VTR.

Split screen. Screen divided to show more than one picture.

Stab. A sharp musical passage of only a few notes or of just one note. Also called a *Sting.*

Stand. Material on easel or stand in studio to be shot.

Stand-by. A program prepared to be used in case something goes wrong with scheduled material.

Stand-in. A performer who takes the place of major performers during dangerous or tedious parts of making a program.

Sting. A short, usually dissonant musical chord used to emphasize some sudden and unexpected event.

Stock footage. Preshot material that can be used when called for in various productions.

Stop motion. A technique of animation in which objects are shot one frame at a time and moved slightly between shots.

Stripe. The magnetic track on the edge of mag stripe film.

Super. One picture superimposed over another. Sometimes used for titles.

Tag. A brief sequence at the end of a show.

Take. A single shot.

Tally light. Light on video camera that shows that camera is the one taking the shot.

Tape-to-film transfer. System for recording a videotaped production onto film.

TC. Title card.

TCU. Tight close-up. Chin to forehead.

TD. Technical director.

Teaser. A short "preview" of a program at the start to interest the audience.

Telco. The telephone company.

Teleprompter. A device that projects an image of the script over one-way glass in front of the camera lens, allowing newscasters or performers to look directly at the lens while reading the material. Older models put the scripted material just above or below the lens.

Telop. See *Balop*.

Telecine. A device for projecting motion pictures on television.

Thirty-threes or 33s. Discs recorded at 33 rpm, the standard speed for most broadcast use today. Sometimes called LPs (for long-playing recordings).

Tilt. Camera is tilted up or down as specified from a fixed position. Effect is similar to looking up or down at something from where you are standing.

Time-lapse photography. Pictures shot with long intervals between the exposure of each frame, resulting in highly speeded up action when the film is projected at normal speed.

Timed print. A film print in which exposure errors have been compensated for in printing.

Treatment. The basic theme of a script.

Truck. Camera physically moves sideways in specified direction. Effect is similar to looking out the side window of a moving car.

Two shot. A reasonably tight shot with just two persons.

UHF. Ultra high frequency; TV channels 14 through 82.

Under. Music or some other continuing sound is heard softly along with the main dialog or narrative.

Up. A sound that has been heard UNDER is raised to normal level.

VCU. Very close up; see XCU.

VF. Videfont; a commercial system of keying letters and numbers onto screen from a keyboard. Specify content of written material and location on screen.

VHF. Very high frequency; TV channels 2 through 13.

Videodisc. One of several systems for recording television on rotating discs. One form is used for recording "instant replay" shots in sports coverage.

Videotape. A recording medium for television. The standard for commercial television has been the 2-inch tape, recorded on a transverse-quad head recorder. Helical scan recorders use tapes in widths of ¼, ½, ¾, 1, and 2 inches, with varying head configurations and tape speeds. The 1-inch helical scan format is now coming into wide use in commercial television. Various cassette and cartridge systems are used with many forms of videotape.

Vidicon. An inexpensive, relatively low quality television camera tube.

Vignette. Fading out the picture around the edges.

VIZ. Vizmo; a commercial system for rear projecting television pictures on a large screen.

VTR. Videotape with sound.

VU. Volume units; a measure of audio amplitude.

Wipe. Picture begins at one edge (usually left) of the screen and moves across it, replacing the picture on the screen. There are both *horizontal wipes* and *vertical wipes*.

Woodshed. To rehearse new material.

Wow. Audio distortion caused by inconstant speed in the recording or playback device.

Wrap-up. Closing of a news program.

Wild track. Sound recorded nonsynchronously.

Work print. Film used for editing purposes to protect the original.

XCU. Extreme close-up. Focus on a very small area—lips, hands, eyes. Must be spelled out in script.

X-dissolve. Cross-dissolve.

X/S. Over-the-shoulder shot.

Zip pan. A rapid moving blur used to indicate a

transition in time, location, or both. Also called *swish pan.*

Zoom. Camera angle is progressively made smaller (IN) or wider (OUT). Effect is similar to *dolly,* but camera does not move physically, and movement can be much faster than a dolly.

Ace, Goodman. *Ladies and Gentlemen—Easy Aces.* New York: Doubleday, 1970.

The Associated Press. *Broadcast News Style Book.* New York: The Associated Press, 1972.

Baker, Sheridan. *The Practical Stylist.* 2nd ed. New York: Thomas Y. Crowell Company, 1969.

Bernstein, Theodore M. *The Careful Writer.* New York: Atheneum, 1966.

Bittner, John R., and Bittner, Denise A. *Radio Journalism.* Englewood Cliffs, N. J.: Prentice-Hall, 1977.

Bliss, Edward Jr., and Patterson, John M. *Writing News for Broadcast.* New York: Columbia University Press, 1971.

Blum, Richard A. *Television Writing From Concept to Contract.* New York: Hastings House, 1980.

Brady, Ben. *The Keys to Writing for Television and Film.* 3rd ed. Dubuque, Iowa: Kendall/Hunt, 1978.

Coe, Michelle. *How to Write for Television.* New York: Crown, 1980.

Columbia Broadcasting System. *CBS News Standards.* New York: CBS News, 1976.

Cousins, Michelle. *Writing a Television Play.* New York: The Writer, Inc., 1975.

Fang, Irving E. *Television News,* 3rd ed. St. Paul, Minnesota: Rada Press, 1981.

Field, Stanley. *The Professional Broadcast Writer's Handbook.* Blue Ridge Summit, Pa.: Tab Books, 1974.

Field, Syd. *Screenplay: The Foundations of Screenwriting.* New York: Dell, 1979.

Follett, Wilson. *Modern American Usage.* Edited and completed by Jacques Barzun in collaboration with Carlos Baker, Frederick W. Dupee, Dudley Fitts, James D. Hart, Phyllis McGinley, and Lionel Trilling. New York: Hill & Wang, 1966.

Fowler, H. W. *A Dictionary of Modern English Usage.* New York: Oxford University Press, 1960.

Gerold, David. *The Trouble With Tribbles.* New York: Ballantine Books, 1973.

Hall, Mark W. *Broadcast Journalism: An Introduction to News Writing.* 3rd ed. New York: Hastings House, 1978.

Hilliard, Robert L. *Writing for Television and Radio.* 3rd ed. New York: Hastings House, 1976.

Hunter, Julius K., and Gross, Lynne S. *Broadcast News, the Inside Out.* St. Louis: C. V. Mosby Company, 1980.

Maloney, Martin, and Rubenstein, Paul Max. *Writing for the Media.* Englewood Cliffs, N. J.: Prentice-Hall, 1980.

Nash, Constance, and Oakey, Virginia. *The Television Writer's Handbook.* New York: Barnes and Noble, 1978.

Newman, Edwin. *Strictly Speaking.* New York: Warner Books, 1974.

Nicholson, Margaret. *A Dictionary of American-English Usage Based on Fowler's Modern English Usage.* New York: Oxford University Press, 1957.

Root, Wells. *Writing the Script.* New York: Holt, Rinehart and Winston, 1980.

Strunk, William Jr., and White, E. B. *The Elements of Style.* 3rd ed. New York: Macmillan, 1979.

Wainwright, Charles Anthony. *Television Commercials.* 1st ed. rev. New York: Hastings House, 1970.

White, Paul W. *News on the Air.* New York: Harcourt, Brace and Company, 1947.

Willis, Edgar E., and D'Arienzo, Camille. *Writing Scripts for Television, Radio, and Film.* New York: Holt, Rinehart and Winston, 1981.

Wimer, Arthur, and Brix, Dale. *Workbook for Radio and TV News Editing and Writing.* 5th ed. Dubuque, Iowa: Wm. C. Brown Company, Publishers, 1981.

Zeigler, Sherilyn, and Howard, Herbert H. *Broadcast Advertising: A Comprehensive Working Textbook.* Columbus, Ohio: Grid Publishing, 1978.

Index

Ace, Goodman, 108
Advertising: on children's programs, 234–35; copywriter, 248–49; political, 120–25. *See also* Radio commercials, Television commercials
American Radio Theater, 149
Appeals, commercial, 113–18, 140–41, 164
Audience: children as, 230–31; fooling the, 97; medium and, 240–41; PSA, 141–42; soap opera, 86–87; studio, 60; writing news for, 208–9

Balliett, Whitney, 13*n*
Bandura, Paul, 233
Barbera, Joseph, 232
Berdis, Bert, 164, 165
Black(s): programs, 239, 241; writing dialect for, 103
Blind, programs for, 236–37
Blume, Mary, 105*n*
Broughton, Philip, 7
Brown, James, 108*n*
Burditt, George, 91
Buzz words, 7–8, 103

Call-in shows, 225–27
Capitalization, 41–42, 185–86
Carlin, George, 161
Cart stories, 45–46
Character(s): adding new, 56; development, 71–77, 81–82; docudrama, 81–82; radio commercial, 156–57; radio drama, 154; soap opera, 84; TV comedy, 89; TV drama, 54–56; traits, 55–56, 98; word distortion to illustrate, 105
Children's television, 229–35;

audience for, 230–31; commercials on, 234–35; repetition in, 231; techniques, 231; violence in, 232–34
Clichés, 7–9
Comedy. *See* Humor, Radio comedy, Television comedy
Commentary, news, 202–4
Commercials. *See* Children's television, Radio commercials, Television commercials
Cook, David, 83*n*
Copyright law, 179, 221
Cues: radio drama, 150–52; TV news, 48–50, 207–10

Dialect, writing, 102–5
Disc jockey shows, 217–23; format, 221–23; music, 218–19, 221; restrictions on, 220–21; script, 219–20; writing, 250
Docudrama(s), 79–82, 210–11; characters, 81–82; flashbacks in, 82; structure, 81
Documentaries, TV news, 210–16; researching, 213–14; script, 215–16
Down style, 39, 41–42
Drama. *See* Radio drama, Television drama

Editing, on- and off-line, 95*n*
Ethnic programs, 239

Fairness Doctrine, 226
Federal Communications Commission, 138–39, 161, 180
Flashbacks, 82
Formats, script, 21–52; disc jockey show, 221–23; PSAs, 173–77; radio drama, 39–41; radio news,

41−46, 182−86; rules, 22−23, 25−36, 37; television, film, 23−36; television, live, 36−38; television news, 46−51
Fox, Fred S., 107

Gallery, Michele, 67−68, 75
Gerrold, David, 57*n*
Glossary of Special Terms, 256−74
Glover, John, 149
Green, Larry, 149*n*
Grierson, John, 79, 80, 211

Hanna, William, 232
Harvey, Paul, 202
Humor: in commercials, 117−18, 167, 168; defining, 159−60; dialog, 101−6; limitations on, 161−62; in PSAs, 142; radio comedy, 158−60; situation, 97−101; TV comedy, 97−109

Instructional programs, 238
Interviews, 213−16, 225−27

Jacobs, Seaman, 107
Jargon, 7, 10−11
Jobs, broadcasting, 243−55; agents for, 251−52; in advertising, 248−49; disc jockey, 250; freelance, 249; news writing, 246−48; on talk shows, 249−50; TV series, 244−46; unions and, 252−54; volunteer, 250−51
Jorry, Tom, 230*n*, 231*n*

Kinoy, Ernest, 80

Larkin, Bill, 115
Lesser, Gerald, 234
Lindsey, Robert, 148*n*
Live television: production techniques, 58−59; script format, 36−38
Local programs, 149−50, 156
Location shooting: of commercials, 132−34; costs, 57−58

McMahan, Harry, 120
Margin settings: radio news, 42, 185; TV news, 47, 206
Margulies, Lee, 232*n*
May, Elaine, 165
Meara, Anne, 165, 167
Meliès, Georges, 79
Messages, commercial, 118−20
Meyer, Karl, 80
Milligan, Terrance (Spike), 158*n*
Miniseries, 77−79
Morgan, Henry, 108
Motion picture script format, 23−25
Music programs, 223−25. *See also* Disc jockey shows

Nash, Constance, 25
National Association of Broadcast Employees and Technicians (NABET), 254
National Public Radio, 147−48
National Radio Theater, 149
Needs, human, appeals to, 113−18, 121−23, 140−41
Newman, Edwin, 14
News. *See* Radio news, Television news
New Yorker, 8, 112
Nichols, Mike, 165

Oakey, Virginia, 25
Orkin, Dick, 164, 165

Pacifica Foundation, 149
Paging radio news, 42−43, 184−86
Parody, 13, 107−9
Plots: loose, 94−96; multiplots, 70−71; radio comedy, 160−61; radio drama, 154; soap opera, 83−86; subplots, 69−70; TV comedy, 89−96; TV drama, 61−65; tight, 90−94
Political advertising, 120−25; human needs and, 121−23
Production techniques: for commercials, 127−38; PSA, 173; TV drama, 58−60

Public service announcements (PSAs): appeal of, 140–41, 172; audience, 141–42; budget, 142–45; formats, 173–77; production techniques, 173; radio, 170–77; researching, 139–40; stations for, 172–73; TV, 138–45; voices for, 171–72

Radio comedy, 155–62; characters, 156–57, 159, 162; length, 156; plots, 160–61; sound effects, 157–58
Radio commercials, 163–78; appeal of, 164; distribution, 165; length, 164; prerecorded, 166–70; public service, 170–77; script, 165–70; voices for, 165, 171–72
Radio drama, 147–55, 162; cast, 154; cues, 150–52; market, 155; narration, 155; plots, 154; scope of, 147–50; scripts, 152–55; script format, 39–41
Radio news, 179–205; commentary, 202–4; length, 181; rules for writing, 187–88; script format, 41–46, 182–86; specials, 201–2; stylebook, 189–201; versus print, 179–80; writer's role in, 180–81, 246–48
Rasovsky, Yuri, 149
Redundancy, 17–18
Repetition, 4, 17–18; on children's programs, 231–32
Researching: documentaries, 213–14; interview programs, 226–27; PSAs, 139–40; talk shows, 226–27, 249–50
Rintels, David, 80, 81
Rosten, Leo, 104
Rules: broadcast news, 187–88; broadcast writing, 3–20; script format, 22–23, 25–36, 37; TV news writing, 207–10
Ryan, Cornelius, 16–17

Satire, 107–9
Script(s): disc jockey show, 219–20; documentary, 215–16; formats, 21–52; music program, 223–25; planning, 65–66; radio commercial, 165–70; radio drama, 152–55; semiscripted program, 217–27; talk show, 226–27; TV drama, 65–77; TV news, 206–7; word hazards with, 154–55
Service programs, 227
Sets, 56–58
Sevareid, Eric, 11
Sex: commercial appeal to, 115–16; roles, 98
Shayon, Robert Louis, 79
Siegel, Barry, 84*n*
Simple writing, 6–19; detail, 16–17; redundancy, 17–18; word usage, 6–16
Situation comedy, 97–101
Slugs: radio news, 43–44, 185; TV news, 47–48
Smith, Cecil, 80
Smith, Thorne, 97
Soap operas, 82–87; audience, 86–87; characters, 84; plots, 83–86; production, 86–87
Sound effects, 157–58
Sources, quoting, 19–20
Special interest programs, 228–42; role of radio in, 239–40; writing, 250
Spooner, William A., 105–6
Spoonerisms, 105–6
Stereotyping, 74–75, 102–3
Stiller, Jerry, 165, 167
Storyboards, 125–26
Story treatments, TV, 60–65
Stylebook, radio-TV news, 189–201
Sullivan, Frank, 8–9

Talk shows, 225–27; writing, 249–50
Television comedy, 88–109;

characters, 89; humor, 97−109; plots, 89−96; themes, 88−89

Television commercials, 110−46; appeal of, 113−18; getting message across, 118−20; image, product, 112−13; kinds of, 111−12; political advertisements, 120−25; production techniques, 127−38; public service, 130−45; storyboards, 125−26

Television drama, 53−87; characters, 54−56; docudramas, 79−82; miniseries, 77−79; production techniques, 58−60; scripts, 65−77; script formats, 23−36, 36−38; sets, 56−58; soap operas, 82−87: story treatments, 60−65; themes, 53−54

Television news, 206−16; cues, 207−10; documentaries, 210−16; rules for, 207−10; scripts, 206−7; script format, 46−51; stylebook, 189−201; writing, 246−48

Themes: TV comedy, 88−89; TV drama, 53−54

Thurber, James, 99

Unions, broadcasting, 252−54

U.S. Supreme Court, 161, 221

Verbal comedy, 101−6, 159

Violence on children's television, 232−34

Voegeli, Tom, 148

Wayne, Paul, 91

White, Paul, 12*n*, 203

Wolfe, Thomas, 11

Women's programs, 237−38, 240−41

Word usage, 6−16; hazards in, 154−55; to illustrate character, 105; in radio news, 44; suited to action, 209−10

Writers Guild, 244, 254

Writing, *passim*: agents, 251−52; advertising copy, 248−49; jobs, 243−55; news, 246−48; rules for broadcast, 3−20; special interest programs, 249−50; TV series, 244−46